Communications in Computer and Information Science 2832

Series Editors

Gang Li, *School of Information Technology, Deakin University, Burwood, VIC, Australia*

Joaquim Filipe, *Polytechnic Institute of Setúbal, Setúbal, Portugal*

Zhiwei Xu, *Chinese Academy of Sciences, Beijing, China*

Rationale

The CCIS series is devoted to the publication of proceedings of computer science conferences. Its aim is to efficiently disseminate original research results in informatics in printed and electronic form. While the focus is on publication of peer-reviewed full papers presenting mature work, inclusion of reviewed short papers reporting on work in progress is welcome, too. Besides globally relevant meetings with internationally representative program committees guaranteeing a strict peer-reviewing and paper selection process, conferences run by societies or of high regional or national relevance are also considered for publication.

Topics

The topical scope of CCIS spans the entire spectrum of informatics ranging from foundational topics in the theory of computing to information and communications science and technology and a broad variety of interdisciplinary application fields.

Information for Volume Editors and Authors

Publication in CCIS is free of charge. No royalties are paid, however, we offer registered conference participants temporary free access to the online version of the conference proceedings on SpringerLink (http://link.springer.com) by means of an http referrer from the conference website and/or a number of complimentary printed copies, as specified in the official acceptance email of the event.

CCIS proceedings can be published in time for distribution at conferences or as post-proceedings, and delivered in the form of printed books and/or electronically as USBs and/or e-content licenses for accessing proceedings at SpringerLink. Furthermore, CCIS proceedings are included in the CCIS electronic book series hosted in the SpringerLink digital library at http://link.springer.com/bookseries/7899. Conferences publishing in CCIS are allowed to use Online Conference Service (OCS) for managing the whole proceedings lifecycle (from submission and reviewing to preparing for publication) free of charge.

Publication process

The language of publication is exclusively English. Authors publishing in CCIS have to sign the Springer CCIS copyright transfer form, however, they are free to use their material published in CCIS for substantially changed, more elaborate subsequent publications elsewhere. For the preparation of the camera-ready papers/files, authors have to strictly adhere to the Springer CCIS Authors' Instructions and are strongly encouraged to use the CCIS LaTeX style files or templates.

Abstracting/Indexing

CCIS is abstracted/indexed in DBLP, Google Scholar, EI-Compendex, Mathematical Reviews, SCImago, Scopus. CCIS volumes are also submitted for the inclusion in ISI Proceedings.

How to start

To start the evaluation of your proposal for inclusion in the CCIS series, please send an e-mail to ccis@springer.com.

Divna Petković · Olena Saint-Joanis ·
Max Silberztein
Editors

Formalizing Natural Languages: Applications to Natural Language Processing and Digital Humanities

19th International Conference, NooJ 2025
Paris, France, June 11–13, 2025
Revised Selected Papers

Editors
Divna Petković
Télécom Paris
Palaiseau, France

Olena Saint-Joanis
INALCO
Paris, France

Max Silberztein
Université de Franche-Comté
Besançon, France

ISSN 1865-0929   ISSN 1865-0937 (electronic)
Communications in Computer and Information Science
ISBN 978-3-032-17102-3   ISBN 978-3-032-17103-0 (eBook)
https://doi.org/10.1007/978-3-032-17103-0

This Springer imprint is published by the registered company Springer Nature Switzerland AG
The registered company address is: Gewerbestrasse 11, 6330 Cham, Switzerland

If disposing of this product, please recycle the paper.

Preface

With the success of software that employs empirical approaches to process texts written in natural languages, such as LLM-based chatbots, many researchers in Natural Language Processing are now convinced that the linguistic approach to analyzing texts has become irrelevant. We firmly disagree. Beyond the intrinsic problems related to empirical methods—ethical issues linked to the collection of training data, absence of control of the "black box" approach, and unreliability of the results produced—we are convinced that linguists must keep studying languages and describing them formally to accumulate exhaustive and precise linguistic resources, and keep the domain of linguistics "in control" by accumulating handcrafted descriptions that are accurate, testable, and therefore falsifiable.

NooJ is a linguistic development environment that provides a platform for linguists to develop handcrafted linguistic resources that formalize a wide range of linguistic phenomena: typography, orthography, lexicons for simple words, multiword units, discontinuous expressions, inflectional, derivational, and agglutinative morphology, local, phrase-structure, and dependency grammars, as well as transformational and semantic grammars.

To describe each type of linguistic phenomenon, NooJ offers formalisms that cover the extent of Chomsky-Schützenberger's hierarchy: regular grammars, context-free grammars, context-sensitive grammars, and unrestricted grammars. Grammars can then be applied to texts automatically by NooJ's parsers, which range from very efficient finite-state automata and transducers to very powerful Turing Machines. This variety of tools makes NooJ's approach different from most other computational linguistic tools that offer a unique formalism to their users and are incompatible. NooJ contains a rich toolbox that allows linguists to construct, test, debug, maintain, accumulate, and share extensive linguistic resources for any natural language.

NooJ can apply sets of linguistic resources to corpora of texts automatically, for example, to extract or annotate occurrences of lexical, syntactic, or semantic patterns and perform statistical analyses, and thus can be used in corpus linguistics and discourse analysis. Because NooJ's linguistic resources are neutral, NooJ can also use them to generate texts automatically. Combining NooJ's parsers and generators, one can construct sophisticated software applications, such as automatic machine translation, semantic analysis, and paraphrasing software.

Since its first release in 2002, several private companies and institutions have used NooJ's linguistic engine to construct applications in several domains, from Business Intelligence to Opinion Analysis. Linguistic resources ("NooJ modules") are available for over 30 languages. In 2013, a free and open-source version of NooJ was released, based on Java technology, and it is supported and distributed by the European Metashare platform. The NooJ platform is in constant evolution:

– NooJ has recently been enhanced with new features to respond to the needs of researchers who analyze texts in various domains of Human and Social Sciences (history, literature, political studies, psychology, sociology, etc.) and, more generally, of all professionals who need to explore their corpus of texts and perform discourse analyses. An interface specifically designed for the Digital Humanities has been implemented in the ATISHS software; see: https://atishs.univ-fcomte.fr. A new Web application has been developed for teaching Corpus Linguistics, Formal Grammars, and Textual Statistics and is available at http://webnooj.univ-fcomte.fr.

This volume contains 17 full papers, carefully reviewed and selected from 47 submissions received for the 19th NooJ International Conference, held at the Institut National des Langues et Civilisations Orientales (INALCO) in Paris, France from June 11th to 13th, 2025. Each paper was reviewed by at least 3 members of the scientific committee in a single-blind process.

We have organized these articles into three parts: "Lexical and Morphological Resources," "Syntactic Resources," and "Corpus Linguistics and Natural Language Processing Applications."

The five articles in the first part address the construction of electronic dictionaries and morphological grammars to formalize the vocabulary and morphological system of Mwotlap, Ukrainian, Croatian, Belarusian, and Rioplatense Spanish:

- In "Introducing Mwotlap Language Resources for NooJ," Fabio Meroni presents the new set of linguistic resources for the Mwotlap language, an endangered Oceanic language. The methodological decisions underlying the construction of these resources were informed by both theoretical considerations and practical challenges, to accurately reflect Mwotlap's morphology and syntax. As for many other languages, Mwotlap's specific morphological phenomena required the design of new morphological operators.
- In "Formalizing Relative Adjectives and Participles with NooJ for Ukrainian," Olena Saint-Joanis shows that modern tools for exploring Ukrainian corpora have several limitations, the most important being that derived words such as derived adjectives are treated as independent entries, instead of being linked. Olena Saint-Joanis then presents a set of morphological grammars that connect all derived forms of adjectives to a single lexical entry, which enhances linguistic tools used in Corpus Linguistics.
- In "Affixoids in Action: a NooJ Journey through Croatian Neoclassical Compounds," Krešimir Šojat and Kristina Kocijan present two morphological grammars capable of recognizing and annotating Croatian wordforms that contain prefixoids and suffixoids derived from Latin and Greek. They then apply these grammars to various corpora of texts (from children's literature to medical texts): the result highlights how these complex wordforms are recognized in relation to the different corpora. This study results in a robust linguistic resource that formalizes the behavior of 75 suffixoids and 224 prefixoids.
- In "Updating the Belarusian NooJ module: Integrating new lexical and grammatical resources," Yuras Hetsevich, Valery Varanovich, and Mikita Suprunchuk describe updates and improvements of the Belarusian NooJ dictionary that was created in 2012, using a corpus that contains 1.5 million word forms. Beside the dictionary extension, they have developed new morphological grammars to take derived forms into account, as well as syntactic grammars to disambiguate words according to their contexts.

– In "Formalization Proposal of Verbal Idioms with Psychological Predicates in Rioplatense Spanish," Walter Koza and Sol Schmidt study verbal idiomatic psychological predicates (VIPP) in Rioplatense Spanish. They show that the syntax of these idioms occupies an intermediate position between phrase-level and sentence-level structures, which makes them particularly challenging to formalize. For this task, they have developed a dictionary of VIPP paired with a set of syntactic grammars, designed to recognize and annotate these idioms in their context.

The seven articles in the second part present various syntactic resources for Belarusian, French, Medieval Latin, Quechua, Rioplatense Spanish, and Rromani, as well as a comparison between representations in Croatian and German of semantic roles attributed to workers, and a comparison between Ukrainian and Serbian temporal expressions:

– In "Describing French Simple Declarative Sentences," Max Silberztein aims to describe French simple declarative sentences by constructing a set of formalized linguistic resources in the form of electronic dictionaries and local syntactic grammars. The sentence grammar describes sentences with structures N_0 V, N_0 V (àldelε) N_1, and N_0 V (àldelε) N_1 (àldelε) N_2. It consists of local grammars that describe pre-determiners and determiners, simple noun phrases, and sentences. Max Silberztein tested these resources by applying them to the text *La femme de trente ans* [Balzac, 1881].
– In "Disambiguation in Medieval Latin," Linda Mijić and Anita Bartulović address the identification and resolution of specific ambiguities in MedText, a historical corpus of medieval Latin last wills and testaments from the city of Zadar (13th–15th centuries). Within the corpus of approximately 500,000 tokens, around 5,800 ambiguities were identified. The article distinguishes three types of ambiguity: morphological, syntactic, and lexical. Here, special attention was given to morphosyntactic ambiguities, including overlaps between adjectives and nouns, verbs and pronouns, as well as prepositions and conjunctions. A substantial portion of ambiguous cases was resolved through syntactic grammars.
– In "Transformations and Paraphrases of Quechua Interrogative Sentences," Maximiliano Duran presents a formalized classification of Quechua interrogative sentences. The study covers various types of interrogative sentences. Maximiliano Duran has gathered texts from ancient chronicles, contemporary publications, and transcriptions of oral recordings of native speakers. The analysis of this corpus allowed him to identify morphosyntactic and semantic patterns and forms of interrogations. Then, he formalized the grammatically valid transformations by developing grammars that can be used to generate paraphrases of a given Quechua interrogative sentence automatically.
– In "Formalizing the Language of Young University Students," Andrea Fernanda Rodrigo, Silvia Susana Reyes, and Mariana González constructed a corpus to identify salient features of Rioplatense Spanish within a specific community: young university students over eighteen years of age, for the goal of expanding the dictionaries and grammars available in their Spanish/Argentinian module. This has allowed them to examine the linguistic diversity of the corpus, and introduce a new category of expressions, labeled as [+GRJOV] for "*gramática de jóvenes*" [youth grammar].
– In "Disambiguation of Rromani Adjective-Noun Phrases," Masako Watabe studies reports on Rromani morphosyntactic studies, and presents two syntactic grammars

that describe Adjective-Noun phrases and thus can be used to disambiguate most Rromani word forms that can correspond either to adjectives or to nouns.

- In "Foreign Workers in the Spotlight: Linguistic and Sociocultural Insights from German and Croatian web portals," Anja Brnjaković, Mirela Landsman Vinković, and Kristina Kocijan analyze the discursive representation of foreign workers in Croatian and German online media. Using a corpus of 223 articles collected from ideologically diverse news portals, they annotated mentions of foreign workers according to four semantic roles: victim, perpetrator, user, and contributor. Results reveal contrasting national patterns: Croatian media predominantly frame foreign workers as victims, emphasizing vulnerability and marginalization, whereas German media highlight the contributor role, focusing on economic integration and labor market participation. A source-level analysis indicates that sensationalist outlets favor victim narratives, while conservative media emphasize perpetrator portrayals and downplay contributions. The findings demonstrate that media framing of foreign workers is shaped by national migration histories and editorial ideologies. This study contributes a replicable semantic role framework for cross-cultural discourse analysis and lays the groundwork for future sentiment and emotional mapping using the NRC Word–Emotion Association Lexicon.

- In "Creation and Comparison of NooJ Grammars for Temporal Expressions in Ukrainian and Serbian," Divna Petković and Victor Rabiet describe temporal expressions in Serbian and in Ukrainian. This allowed them to compare temporal expressions in both languages and identify patterns of concordance, as well as points of divergence. This study highlights under-explored similarities, such as paucal numeral phrases with numbers 2, 3, and 4, as well as numbers greater than 20 that end in these digits. These paucal forms determine the case and the number of the nouns and adjectives that follow them, exhibiting inflectional features distinct from both the singular and the plural.

The last section, dedicated to the presentation of various Natural Language Processing Applications, contains five articles:

- In "Empirical and Linguistic Approaches to NLP: LLMs & NLP: Might resistance be futile from now on?," Christian Boitet shows that, contrary to some popular views, the performance of general empirical approaches (statistical, neural) to many NLP tasks remains inferior to that of linguistic (expert) approaches, at least when specific sublanguages are concerned. Christian Boitet shows that Large Language Models (LLMs)-based automatic translators do not surpass the performance level of expert human translators in all tasks. However, a synergy between LLMs and expert resources (such as NooJ-based dictionaries and grammars) might be used to "inflate" the data (corpora) fed to the LLM and thus improve performance.

- In "Use of LLMs for Semantic Relation Extraction and Development of NooJ Lingware Applied to Drug Trafficking Language," Nicolas Boffo, Mathieu Lafourcarde, and Christian Boitet investigate the possibility of using LLMs to extract semantic relations from specialized corpora, particularly drug trafficking language, not directly, but in conjunction with the NooJ platform for local execution. In that hybrid approach, LLMs construct NooJ grammars and dictionaries automatically, later compiled into deterministic NooJ transducers, which run on regular PCs. Experiments on a corpus of 75 text files (164,000 tokens, 27,000 distinct words) highlight challenges in alias recognition and structured evaluation importance. Results show that while direct LLM extraction produces noisy outputs, automatic FST induction through LLMs significantly accelerates grammar development for specialized domains.

- In "Personalizing Learning Paths: Analyzing Student Interactions on Moodle Using the NooJ platform," Amira Abbes, Héla Fehri, Leila Ghorbel, Corinne Amel Zayani, and Ronan Champagnat propose a method for classifying learning paths on Moodle using syntactic transducers built with the NooJ platform. The proposed method consists of three main steps: (1) Data Extraction from Moodle event logs, (2) Data Classification through NooJ grammars that model activity sequences, and (3) Interactive Dashboard Development to visualize student progress and provide personalized recommendations. To evaluate and validate the method, they have applied it to a Moodle course titled "Semantic technology". The results were highly satisfactory and demonstrate the method's effectiveness in analyzing learning behaviors and supporting personalized education.

- In "The Annotation of Indonesian Clitics by Nooj and Other Computational Tools," Prihantoro qualitatively compares three corpus annotation tools that can be used to analyse Indonesian clitics: MorphInd, TreeTagger, and NooJ. TreeTagger requires a separate tool to delineate a clitic from its host before annotation. Conversely, NooJ and MorphInd integrate the clitic delineation and clitic annotation process, as shown in SANTI-POS. In terms of resources, MorphInd resource development seems to be restricted to its developers. Unlike MorphInd, TreeTagger and NooJ resources can easily be developed as they are available to the public. He presents a survey that confirmed that NooJ has a better user-friendly interface and visual and transparent representation of its analyses. Going beyond annotation, he then demonstrates how NooJ allows users to represent and identify a clitic's surface form as well as its free form.

- In "Formalization of Numerical Expressions in Rioplatense Spanish," Carmen González, Celina Colussi, and Iván Oliva present a pedagogical application that aims to teach Rioplatense Spanish as a second language. More specifically, the authors have focused on the formalization of numerical expressions. First, this set of new resources is intended to complete the dictionaries and inflectional grammars for Argentinian Spanish. Second, they have designed grammars that can analyze, or generate, numerical expressions automatically.

This volume should interest all users of the NooJ software because it presents the latest development of lexical, morphological, and syntactic resources, and a new set of Natural Language Processing applications. Linguists and Computational Linguists who work on Belarusian, Croatian, French, Indonesian, Medieval Latin, Mwotlap, Rromani, Rioplatense Spanish, Persian, Quechua, Serbian, or Ukrainian will find advanced, up-to-the-minute linguistic studies for these languages.

The reader will appreciate the importance of this volume, both for the intrinsic scientific value of each linguistic formalization and its underlying methodology, and for the potential for developing linguistic-based NLP applications.

Divna Petković
Olena Saint-Joanis
Max Silberztein

Organization

Organization Committee

Olena Saint-Joanis (Chair)	INALCO, France
Max Silberztein (Co-chair)	Université de Franche-Comté, France
Vincent Bénet	INALCO, France
Snejana Gadjeva	INALCO, France
Svetlana Krylosova	INALCO, France
Divna Petković	INALCO, France
Marzieh Rabiei	Université de Franche-Comté, France
Victor Rabiet	INALCO, France
Jeanna Vassilioutchek	INALCO, France
Masako Watabe	Université de Franche-Comté, France

Scientific Committee

Max Silberztein (Chair)	Université de Franche-Comté, France
Divna Petković (Co-chair)	INALCO, France
Olena Saint-Joanis (Co-chair)	INALCO, France
Marco Angster	University of Zadar, Croatia
Anita Bartulović	University of Zadar, Croatia
Vincent Bénet	INALCO, France
Magali Bigey	Université de Franche-Comté, France
Xavier Blanco	Autonomous University of Barcelona, Spain
Christian Boitet	Université Grenoble Alpes, France
Christine Bonnot	INALCO, France
Antoine Chalvin	INALCO, France
Outi Duvallon	INALCO, France
Héla Fehri	University of Sfax, Tunisia
Zoe Gavriilidou	Democritus University of Thrace, Greece
Yuras Hetsevich	National Academy of Sciences, Belarus
Kristina Kocijan	University of Zagreb, Croatia
Walter Koza	National University of General Sarmiento, Argentina
Svetlana Krylosova	INALCO, France
Laetitia Leonarduzzi	Université d'Aix-Marseille, France
Stefania Maci	Università di Bergamo, Italy

Contents

Lexical and Morphological Resources

Introducing Mwotlap Language Resources for NooJ 3
Fabio Meroni

Formalizing Relative Adjectives and Participles with NooJ for Ukrainian 16
Olena Saint-Joanis

Affixoids in Action: A NooJ Journey Through Croatian Neoclassical
Compounds 27
Krešimir Šojat and Kristina Kocijan

Formalization Proposal of Verbal Idioms with Psychological Predicates
in Rioplatense Spanish 39
Walter Koza and Sol Schmidt

Syntactic and Semantic Resources

Updating the Belarusian NooJ Module: Integrating New Lexical
and Grammatical Resources 53
Yuras Hetsevich, Valery Varanovich, and Mikita Suprunchuk

Describing French Simple Declarative Sentences 65
Max Silberztein

Disambiguation in Medieval Latin 77
Linda Mijić and Anita Bartulović

Transformations and Paraphrases of Quechua Interrogative Sentences 89
Maximiliano Duran

Formalizing the Language of Young University Students 101
Andrea Fernanda Rodrigo, Silvia Susana Reyes, and Mariana González

Formalization of Numerical Expressions in Rioplatense Spanish:
A Pedagogical Application 112
Carmen González, Celina Colussi, and Iván Oliva

Disambiguation of Rromani Adjective-Noun Phrases 124
Masako Watabe

Foreign Workers in the Spotlight: Linguistic and Sociocultural Insights
from German and Croatian Web Portals   137
   Anja Brnjaković, Mirela Landsman Vinković, and Kristina Kocijan

Creation and Comparison of NooJ Grammars for Temporal Expressions
in Ukrainian and Serbian   150
   Divna Petković and Victor Rabiet

Natural Language Processing Applications

Empirical and Linguistic Approaches to NLP: LLMs & NLP: Might
Resistance Be Futile from Now on?   165
   Christian Boitet

Use of LLMs for Semantic Relation Extraction and Development of NooJ
Lingware Applied to Drug Trafficking Language   177
   Nicolas Boffo, Mathieu Lafourcade, and Christian Boitet

Personalizing Learning Paths: Analyzing Student Interactions on Moodle
Using the NooJ Platform   189
   *Amira Abbes, Héla Fehri, Leila Ghorbel, Corinne Amel Zayani,
   and Ronan Champagnat*

The Annotation of Indonesian Clitics by Nooj and Other Computational
Tools   201
   Prihantoro

Author Index   211

Lexical and Morphological Resources

Introducing Mwotlap Language Resources
for NooJ

Fabio Meroni$^{(\boxtimes)}$ (iD)

Università Degli Studi Di Bergamo, Bergamo, Italy
`f.meroni2@studenti.unibg.it`

Abstract. This chapter introduces Mwotlap language resources for the software NooJ. The present contribution explores the module's design choices and methodology, detailing how the digital resources for the NooJ Mwotlap module were developed starting from Alexandre François's online dictionary of the language and integrating the various accounts of research he produced in the scientific literature, to provide a solid foundation for the encoding of formalized rules and processes, along with a sound theoretical background for their description and annotation. Since key characteristics of Mwotlap led to updates in NooJ itself, such new features are explored and their utility explained. All basic morphological and syntactic parsing tools needed for processing texts and corpora in Mwotlap are covered in this overview, though additional features are present in the module.

Keywords: NooJ · Mwotlap · Natural Language Formalization · Computational Morphology · Computational Syntax · Finite-State Language Processing

1 Introduction

Mwotlap (endonym *na-vap to-M̄otlap*, ISO 639–3: `mlv`[1]; Glottocode: `mot11237`), spoken by an estimated 2,100 people primarily on Mota Lava and Vanua Lava (Vanuatu), is the most widely spoken language within the Torres–Banks linkage of Oceanic languages, a subgroup of the Austronesian family [1]. Beyond its sociolinguistic vitality, Mwotlap has also been the focus of extensive scholarly attention through the descriptive and analytical work of Alexandre François, most notably his 1,000-page doctoral dissertation, which serves as the only long grammar of the language ever written [2]. His research has provided the language with a solid documentary foundation, enriched by resources available online, such as a comprehensive dictionary [3] and a partially transcribed corpus hosted in the Pangloss Collection [4]. These materials serve as critical support for the development of computational resources and, in particular, formed the base for the creation of the computational linguistic resources specifically tailored to Mwotlap [5] presented in this chapter.

---

[1] Since NooJ only accepts two-letter codes for naming language modules, and Mwotlap does not have an official ISO 639-1 code (since it does not meet the thresholds for widespread international use required for inclusion in such standard), the unofficial two-letter code mw to represent it within the NooJ framework was assigned.

D. Petković et al. (Eds.): NooJ 2025, CCIS 2832, pp. 3–15, 2026.
https://doi.org/10.1007/978-3-032-17103-0_1

The development of Mwotlap language resources for the NooJ platform [6] builds upon a framework that prioritizes a linguistic approach to NLP, in which formal models of language are constructed directly from descriptive and theoretical analyses rather than from large-scale statistical data [6]. In line with this approach, the digital resources developed for NooJ originate from François's online dictionary [3], complemented by his extensive published research. Throughout the project, François was regularly consulted to ensure the accuracy and appropriateness of all resources developed.

For languages like Mwotlap, which are richly described and documented but computationally under-resourced, this approach enables a new level of linguistic inquiry: once formalized within NooJ, these resources can be applied to corpus data, now drawn from François's fieldwork archives and susceptible of expansion in the future; by enabling the annotation and analysis of such material, the Mwotlap module shifts the focus from static documentation towards dynamic exploration of the language in use. This approach makes it possible to identify recurring patterns, to query specific constructions across a large body of texts, and to gain insights into the distribution of linguistic phenomena in context.

The choice of NooJ is reinforced by its successful application to other low-resource languages. Previous projects have demonstrated how the platform can support the computational modeling of Quechua [7], Rromani [8], Kabyle [9], and other languages that were once similarly limited in digital representation. By drawing on these precedents, the Mwotlap module aims not only to expand the digital resources available for an Oceanic language but also to contribute to the broader field of NLP for under-documented languages.

2 Encoding

The Mwotlap alphabet introduced by Alexandre François [2, 10] makes use of the 24 letters shown in Table 1, obeying a simplicity principle enunciated as "one grapheme, one phoneme", plus ⟨p⟩ for [p], which is only encountered as an allophone of /v/ (see Sect. 4.2).

Table 1. The Mwotlap alphabet.

a	b	d	e	ē	g	h	i	k	l	m	m̄
/a/	/ᵐb/	/ⁿd/	/ɛ/	/ɪ/	/ɣ/	/h/	/i/	/k/	/l/	/m/	/ŋ͡mʷ/
[a]	[ᵐb]	[ⁿd]	[ɛ]	[ɪ]	[ɣ]	[h]	[i]	[k]	[l]	[m]	[ŋ͡mʷ]

n	ñ	o	ō	p	q	s	t	u	v	w	y
/n/	/ŋ/	/ɔ/	/ʊ/	/v/	/k͡pʷ/	/s/	/t/	/u/	/v/	/w/	/j/
[n]	[ŋ]	[ɔ]	[ʊ]	[p]	[k͡pʷ]	[s]	[t]	[u]	[β]	[w]	[j]

The macron diacritic (ō̄) is added to some graphemes for different reasons. Regarding vowels, the macron is used to mark a raising in height from the unmarked correspondent. Hence, from low-mid ⟨e⟩ /ɛ/ and ⟨o⟩ /ɔ/, we respectively obtain the near-high vowels ⟨ē⟩ /ɪ/ and ⟨ō⟩ /ʊ/. Regarding consonants, the macron is used to mark extension in the case of ⟨m̄⟩ /ŋ͡mʷ/, while it is used just to oppose the regular alveolar nasal ⟨n⟩ /n/ to the velar nasal ⟨n̄⟩ /ŋ/.

NooJ handles the "combining macron" (ō̄, -), preserving it as a separate combining diacritic in ⟨m̄⟩ and ⟨n̄⟩, not integrating it into a precomposed character (e.g., m⁻ is how ⟨m̄⟩ appears in NooJ dictionaries and grammars' rule editor, since NooJ can be said to be Unicode-aware, but it lacks any focus on rendering). Although it lacks this merely aesthetic requirement, NooJ can perfectly process ⟨m̄⟩ and ⟨n̄⟩ along with all other characters of the Mwotlap alphabet. The most important point in this regard is that, when processing encoded rules of inflectional and derivational morphology, NooJ considers ⟨m̄⟩ and ⟨n̄⟩ as if they were single characters, thanks to a slight modification of <L>, <R>, <D>, <W>, <P> and <N> operators of.nof grammars introduced with a special update; in dictionaries, +UNAMB is used in entries containing ⟨m̄⟩ and ⟨n̄⟩ to prevent NooJ from seeing a word boundary just after the macron (see Sect. 4 and Table 3).

3 Bringing Mwotlap Vocabulary in NooJ Dictionaries

The Mwotlap online dictionary by Alexandre François [3] was put online as an XML file augmented for User Experience (UX) with HTML, CSS, and JavaScript to make it readable, well-formatted, and interactive. Morphemes that function as lexical words were automatically extracted from that source XML file and put in LWOTLAP.nod, while morphemes that serve a structural and grammatical function in Mwotlap are all listed in GWOTLAP.nod. Each Part-of-Speech (PoS) was assigned a tag, as per Table 2. The latter were extracted manually due to their limited number and their need for localized attention (since much of the necessary information that concerns them is not automatically extractable in such an easy way).

Table 2. PoS tags in NooJ Mwotlap language resources.

Lexical morphemes		Grammatical morphemes	
Adjectives	ADJ	Coordinators	COORD
Adverbs	ADV	Deictics	DEI
Locatives	LOC	Determiners	DET
Nouns	N	Directionals	DIR
Numerals	NUM	Intensifiers	INTENS
Postverbs	POSTV	Interjections	INTERJ
Predicatives	PRED	Linkers	LINK
Verbs	V	Particles	PART

(continued)

Table 2. (continued)

Lexical morphemes		Grammatical morphemes	
		Possessive classifiers	POSS
		Prepositions	PREP
		Pronouns	PRO
		Quantifiers	QTF
		Relativizers	REL
		Subordinators	SUB
		Tense, Aspect, Mood markers	TAM
		Clause topicalizers	TOP

4 Formalization of Morphology and Morphophonology

With the adopted orthography explained and the lexical inventory established, the following phase in developing the NooJ module involved formalizing the language's morphological system, a crucial step for enabling the software to analyze the full range of word forms found in the language.

Morphological peculiarities of the Mwotlap language have also informed the development of NooJ, with Max Silberztein himself taking on the challenge to expand the capabilities of the software, introducing new features, as exposed in Table 3. It is hoped, if not believed, that this will be valuable not only for the representation of Mwotlap, but also for other languages that exhibit similar phenomena, thereby contributing more broadly to the computational modeling of morphology.

Table 3. Major updates to NooJ (December 2024–April 2025) that enabled the creation of the Mwotlap module.

Update	Introduced Feature	NooJ file extension
v7.3 b20241212	<C> (**C**onsonants) and <V> (**V**owels)	.nom
v7.3 b20250406	<W> (**SW**ap) Operator	.nom
v7.3 b20250410	Operators <L>, <R>, <D>, <W>, <P> and <N> read the macron (ō̄, -) as part of the previous letter	.nof

4.1 Inflection and Derivation

It is necessary to distinguish between "copiable" and "invariable" prefixes, a central concept for understanding the language's morphophonology, and particularly how vowels behave at the boundary between a prefix and a radical [2, 10]. Table 4 below shows the eight productive copiable prefixes of Mwotlap. Both tables show the property linked to each prefix, together with its encoding in the NooJ properties' definition file (.def) and the PoS with which it can be combined.

The convention *nA-*, *mE-*, etc. does not refer to a true archiphoneme that would group together a subset of vowels. Rather, it marks the position of a variable phoneme that can potentially be any vowel or zero (Ø), but which, by default, will be realized as /a/ in *nA-*, /ɛ/ in *mE-* etc. The use of a capital letter is meant to highlight the special phonological status of these "floating vowels" [11]. Table 5 illustrates the five processes these floating vowels cause in prefixation: vowel elision, vowel copy, vowel insertion, vowel transfer, and vowel blockage.

Table 4. Copiable prefixes of Mwotlap.

Prefix	Property	Property in NooJ	Prefixed to
nA-	Article	+ART	Nouns
bE-	Adverbializer	N → ADV	
lE-	Locativizer	N → LOC	
mE-	Perfect	+PFT	Verbs, nouns, adjectives
nE	Stative	+STA	
tE-	Future	+FUT	
tE-	Adjectivizer	LOC → ADJ	Locatives
vĒ-	Enumerator	PREF	Numerals

Table 5. The five processes tied to copiable prefixes illustrated with five radicals.

Process	Rule	Word (Radical)	Prefixation with *nA-*
Vowel elision	$C_0V_0\text{-} + \#V_1C_1\text{-} \rightarrow$ $\#C_0\text{-}V_1C_1\text{-}$	*apol* (APOL)	*apol* → <u>n</u>-*apol* 'apple'
Vowel copy	$C_0V_0\text{-} + \#C_1V_1C_2\text{-} \rightarrow$ $\#C_0V_1\text{-}C_1V_1C_2\text{-}$	*bem* (BEM)	*bem* → *n<u>e</u>-b<u>e</u>m* 'butterfly'
Vowel insertion	$\#C_1C_2V_1\text{-} \rightarrow$ $\#C_1V_1C_2V_1\text{-}$	*mitig* (MTIG)	*m[i]tig* → *na-mtig* 'coconut'
Vowel transfer	$C_0V_0\text{-} + \#C_1V_1C_2V_2\text{-} \rightarrow$ $\#C_0V_1\text{-}C_1C_2V_2\text{-}$	*wumet* (WUMET)	*w⟨u⟩met* → *n<u>u</u>-wmet* 'bowl'
Vowel blockage	$C_0V_0\text{-} + \#C_1V_1C_2\text{-} \rightarrow$ $\#C_0V_0\text{-}C_1V_1C_2\text{-}$	*lo* (LO)	°*lo* → <u>na</u>-*lo* 'sun'

Before update v7.3 b20250406, the approach to inflectional paradigms in the NooJ Mwotlap module was designed to follow a grapheme-per-grapheme ruling when handling the copiable prefixes shown in Table 4, failing to distinguish between #CCV-

radicals, that undergo vowel insertion to become #C[V]CV-, and #C⟨V⟩C- radicals[2], which, when prefixed, follow a rule of vowel transfer. It also did not account for the default forms of the prefixes, generalizing to *nV-*, *mV-*, etc., what was, in reality, *nA-*, *mE-*, etc. Moreover, and more importantly, it reduced vowel copy, vowel insertion, and vowel transfer to what seemed to be a case-by-case application of rules, which proves to be very distant from the actual processes underlying vowel copy, vowel insertion, and vowel transfer.

Since productive rules like these should find a way to be productively applied, with a general formal definition that is then applicable to the range of particular cases it pertains to, the <W> operator was introduced to swap characters in the right position when performing vowel copy, vowel insertion, and vowel transfer. Table 6 presents how the new operator, together with the old ones [12], effectively achieves the description of the correct standalone or prefixed words, using the same radicals from Table 5 as an example.

Table 6. Integration of the newly introduced swap operator.

Process	.nof rule pattern (*nA-* or standalone)	Word (Radical)	Rule applied
Vowel copy	<LW><R2><D><L><W><LW>n	*bem* (BEM)	*bem* → *ne-bem* 'butterfly'
Vowel insertion	<LW><R3><D><L><W>	*mitig* (MTIG)	*m[i]tig* → *na-mtig* 'coconut'
Vowel transfer	<LW><R2><D><L><W><R><LW>n	*wumet* (WUMET)	*w⟨u⟩met* → *nu-wmet* 'bowl'

In all processes that use it, the <D> operator duplicates the vowel of interest (V_1), giving <W> the task to move it to the desired position (V_0, in the prefix). Such a process is, all in all, equivalent to a copy-paste operation, without the need for a clipboard.

4.2   Non-concatenative Morphology

Allophonic Alternation. In Mwotlap, the surface forms of certain consonants are shaped not only by their phonological environment but also by their position in the syllable (see Sect. 4.1). These interactions lead to systematic alternations that are both phonetically regular and orthographically reflected.

The most obvious example is that [p] is a complementary allophonic realization of /v/, encountered just syllable-finally:

$$/v/ \rightarrow [p]/\_\_\sigma$$

---

[2] [V] and ⟨V⟩ are conventions found in the online Mwotlap dictionary [3], for distinguishing radicals that respectively undergo vowel insertion and vowel transfer. Lexical entries marked with °, also used conventionally, block vowel copy operations. All of these conventions are respected in this chapter for ease of consultation.

For instance, a word like *ep* 'fire' is phonologically /ɛv/ but phonetically [ɛp] as reflected in orthography. When morphological operations such as prefixation cause /v/ to become the coda of a syllable, the orthography reflects this as ⟨v⟩ → ⟨p⟩.

Additionally, the prenasalized stops /ᵐb/ and /ⁿd/, are realized as the corresponding nasal syllable-finally, with a complete loss of their plosive phase.

$$\begin{bmatrix} +\text{prenasalized} \\ -\text{nasal} \\ -\text{sonorant} \end{bmatrix} \rightarrow \begin{bmatrix} -\text{prenasalized} \\ +\text{nasal} \\ +\text{sonorant} \end{bmatrix} / \_\_\sigma$$

This is phonologically reflected when morphological operations such as prefixation are enacted, in /ᵐb/ → [m] and /ⁿd/ → [n], which again orthographically surface to ⟨b⟩ → ⟨m⟩ and ⟨d⟩ → ⟨n⟩. The examples in Table 7 show instances of these morphophonological changes. The respective phonetic, phonological, and orthographical consequences are also included for clarity. Prefixation is exemplified with the prefix *mE-* (forming perfect past), while reduplication is exemplified with its unprefixed form.

Table 7. Bound consonantic allophony in Mwotlap, illustrated in three examples.

Radical	Operation	//	[]	⟨⟩
b[i]yiŋ 'help'	Prefixation	/meᵐbjiŋ/	[memjiŋ]	*me-myiñ*
	Reduplication	/ᵐbijiᵐbjiŋ/	[ᵐbijimjiŋ]	*biyimyiñ*
d[e]ñeg 'startle'	Prefixation	/mɛⁿdŋɛɣ/	[mɛnŋɛɣ]	*me-nñeg*
	Reduplication	/ⁿdɛŋɛⁿdŋɛɣ/	[ⁿdɛŋɛnŋɛɣ]	*denenñeg*
v[a]lag 'run'	Prefixation	/mɛβlaɣ/	[mɛplaɣ]	*me-plag*
	Reduplication	/βalaβlaɣ/	[βalaplaɣ]	*valaplag*

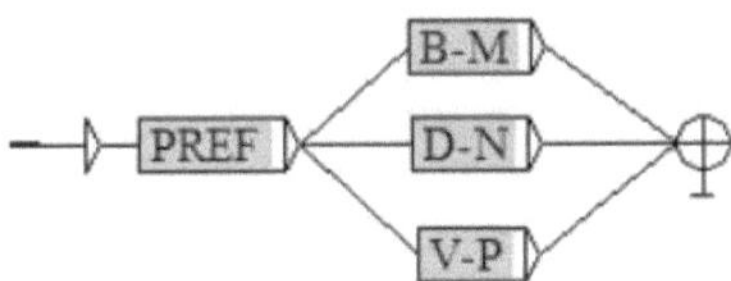

Fig. 1. Main graph of VT_VI_MORPHOPHONOLOGY.nom, the ERTN that handles consonantal morphophonology.

The NooJ Mwotlap module formalizes these morphophonological processes with VT_VI_MORPHOPHONOLOGY.nom. This morphological grammar is an Enhanced Recursive Transition Network (ERTN) with four networks (see Fig. 1 and Fig. 2), corresponding to the three processes and the prefix.

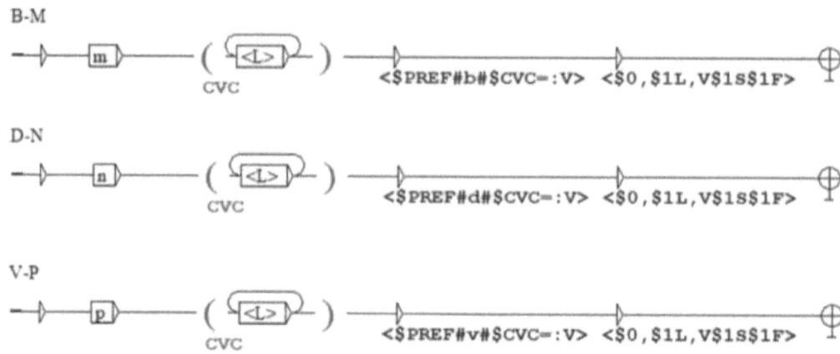

Fig. 2. The three subgraphs (FSTs) of VT_VI_MORPHOPHONOLOGY.nom, :B-M, :D-N and :V-P.

A two-level approach [13] maps m:b, n:d, and p:v, so that the word can be looked up in the dictionary as its lemmatized, unprefixed form, and be associated with the entry in a constraint that outputs the prefixed form with the correct orthography.

Vowel Harmony. In languages that show it, vowel harmony is a set of restrictions that determine the possible and impossible sequences of vowels within a word, usually dividing the vowels of the language into two sets [14]. Mwotlap is one of these languages, and its criterion of distinction is the [±ATR] trait (François, 2001a, pp. 93–95).

In Mwotlap, inalienable nouns with radicals ending in a [+ATR] vowel (/i/ or /u/) undergo vowel harmony when they are suffixed as possessed by first inclusive and third person possessors, lowering their height by one step and becoming their [−ATR] counterparts (/i/ > /ɪ/; /u/ > /ʊ/) [2]. If the penultimate syllable has a [+ATR] vowel as its core, such a vowel is also affected by the harmonization process:

$$V[+ATR] \rightarrow [-ATR] \: / \: \_(V[+ATR]) \: C \ldots \# \: \textit{(iteratively leftwards)}$$

In NooJ, VOWEL_HARMONY.nom was designed to formalize this phenomenon. Depending on the content assigned to each variable, the output is mapped by lexicon constraints that check whether the parsed string is an inalienable noun, to then annotate it with the inflectional properties that are encoded by the optional prefix plus a necessary first inclusive and third person suffixes (Fig. 3 and Fig. 4). The NooJ-powered formalization of vowel harmony in Turkish [15] was a great source of inspiration for the development of this morphological grammar.

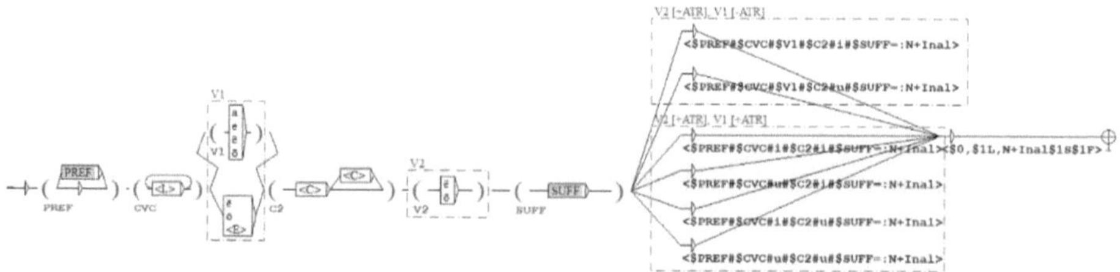

Fig. 3. Main graph of VOWEL_HARMONY.nom, the ERTN {XE "Enhanced Recursive Transition Network (ERTN)"} that handles vowel harmony.

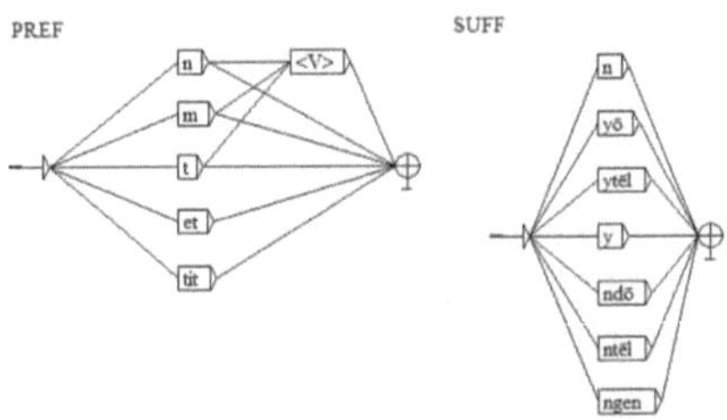

Fig. 4. : PREF and : SUFF FSTs in VOWEL_HARMONY.nom.

Reduplication. As is very common in Austronesian languages [16], Mwotlap is found to share among its characteristics the morphophonological process known as reduplication, in which the repetition of a word, or of segments of a word, not only causes the modification of the word's internal structure, but also affects its various functional and semantic properties.

Table 8. Functioning of REDUPLICATION.nom.

Graph	Rules followed	Radical → Reduplicated
I	a, e, f	\$W → \$W\$W
II	b, k	\$CV#\$C#\$V#\$REST → \$CV#\$CV#\$C#\$V#\$REST
III	c, i	\$CV#h\$REST → \$CV#\$CV#h\$REST
IV	d, j	\$C1#\$V#\$C1#\$REST → \$C1#\$V#\$C1#\$V#\$C1#\$REST
V	g, n	\$V#\$REST → \$V#\$V#\$REST
VI	h, l, m	\$CVC#\$REST → \$CVC#\$CVC#\$REST
VII	o, p, q, r with C_1 $\neq \langle b\rangle \vee \langle d\rangle \vee \langle v\rangle$	\$C1#\$V1#\$C2#\$V2#\$REST → \$C1#\$V1#\$C2#\$V2#\$C1#\$C2#\$V1#\$REST
VIII	o, p, q, r with C_1 $= \langle b\rangle \vee \langle d\rangle \vee \langle v\rangle$	v#\$C2#\$V2#\$REST→ v#\$V1#\$C2#\$V2#p#\$C2#\$V2#\$REST or \$PREF#p#\$C2#\$V2#p#\$C2#\$V2#\$REST

The rules that govern such processes have already been meticulously described by François [2, 17], who also provided the basis for their formalization in more abstract representations that effectively encompass the regular and schematic nature of such rules. Monosyllabic and polysyllabic equivalents of the same morphophonological constraints were incorporated into the same graphs of the REDUPLICATION.nom grammar, which reduced François's 18 formal rules to just 8 FSTs.

5   Formalization of Syntax and Morphosyntax

The approach to syntax in the NooJ Mwotlap module followed the model of Construction Grammar (CxG), a family of usage-based theories of language that treat constructions, defined as conventionalized pairings of form and meaning, as the basic units of grammar [18]. This brings CxG closer to lexicon-grammar, the theoretical foundation of NooJ [9,

19], and encourages the integration of such an approach into formalisms developed with this tool, particularly given the possibility to use the properties associated with dictionary entries as defining the increasing "degrees of schematicity" required in CxG [20]. The objective is not to provide an exhaustive model of the language's entire syntactic system, but rather one that is deliberately more modest and precise: the focus will be confined to the essentials of linguistic analysis through structures that lend themselves to formalization and systematic treatment, Verb Phrases (VP) in particular.

Mwotlap frequently employs complex predicates, where multiple predicatives and their adjuncts combine in a single VP. Among complex predicates, Mwotlap's Serial Verb Constructions (SVCs) are characterized as chains of predicatives that refer to a single, unified action under a single VP, rather than multiple distinct actions occurring in sequence. While the head slot (V_1) of an SVC must be obligatorily filled by a verb, adjuncts (V_2) can also be adjectives[3].

SVCs *lato sensu* are distinguished from resultative serial verbs, which are a specific type of SVC with a causative meaning of the kind $x\ V_1$-$V_2\ y$: 'x performs the action V_1 so as to cause y to undergo the action V_2'. Both constructional patterns are handled by the syntactic grammar SERIALV.nog (see Fig. 5).

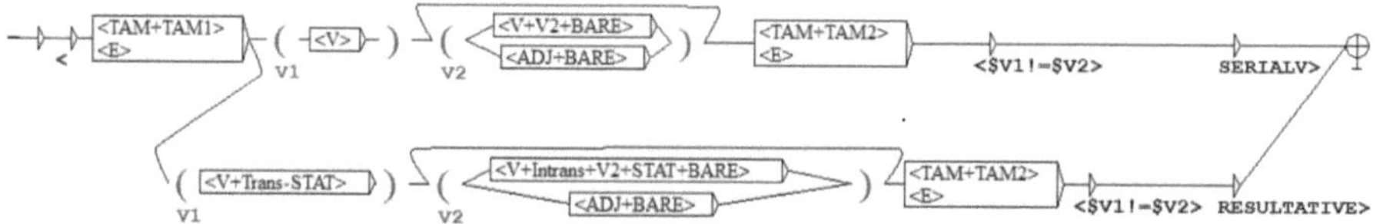

Fig. 5. Main graph of SERIALV.nog, describing and annotating serial verbs

Moreover, the Mwotlap language employs a rich system of 26 distinct TAM categories, comprising 19 affirmative and 7 negative markers. Preclitic TAM markers and/or TAM-marking prefixes appear before the first lexical element of the Verb Complex (VC), and postclitic TAM markers (if any) appear after the last lexical element, leaving the lexical elements in the middle unmarked while framing the entire predicative syntagm in that category. All TAM categories were formalized with syntactic grammars and assigned a complex annotation that allows for their querying, as shown in Table 9.

---

[3] In dictionaries, only verbs with the property +V2 can fill such a slot, while all adjectives can, making it superfluous for them to have a +V2 property.

Table 9. The 26 TAM categories of Mwotlap.

Affirmative	Negative
Iamitive <IAM> **mal {VC}**	Nondumitive <NONDUM> **et-{VC} qete**
Remote Iamitive <REMIAM> **mal {VC} tō**	
Permansive <PERMANSIVE> **{VC} laptō**	Discontinuative <DISCONTINUATIVE> **et-{VC} site**
Stative <STA> **ne-{VC}**	
Perfect <PFT> **me-{VC}**	Realis Negative <REALISNEG> **et-{VC} te**
Preterite <PRET> **me-{VC} tō**	
Aorist <AO> **(ni-){VC}**	
Hortative <HOR> **(ni-){VC} tō**	Prohibitive <PROH> **nitog {VC}**
Prospective <PRO> **so (ni-){VC}**	
Hodiernal Future <HOD> **te-{VC} qiyig**	Negative Future <NEGFUT> **tit-{VC} te**
Future <FUT> **te-{VC}**	Neg. Potential <NEGPOT> **tit-{VC} vēste**
Potential <POT> **te-{VC} vēh**	
Counterfactual <CF> **te-{VC} tō**	
Apprehensive <APPREH> **tiple {VC}**	Neg. Apprehensive <NEGAPPREH> **tiple tit-{VC} te**
Static Presentative <PRSVSTA> **{VC} tō**	Ø
Kinetic Presentative <PRSVKIN> **{VC} vatag**	
Dilatory <DILATFUT> **qoyo {VC}**	
Recent Past <RECPST> **qoyo {VC} (ēwē) tō**	
Prioritive <PRIORITIVE> **(ni-){VC} bah en**	

6   Concluding Remarks

This chapter has presented the design and implementation of Mwotlap language resources for NooJ, highlighting how the integration of Alexandre François's dictionary [3] and related research provided a solid foundation for formal rule encoding and annotation. The methodological decisions underlying the construction of these tools were informed by both theoretical considerations and practical challenges, leading to the development of parsing modules that accurately reflect Mwotlap's morphology and syntax.

A central contribution of this work lies in how the morphological specificities of Mwotlap necessitated updates to NooJ. These enhancements to the platform, developed in response to the challenges of modeling Mwotlap, have significantly extended its functionality, providing a set of tools that can be leveraged in the computational treatment of other languages whose features require similar formalization devices.

In conclusion, it is hoped that this chapter has highlighted both the scientific contributions of this work to the study of Mwotlap and its practical implications for the digital documentation and revitalization of endangered languages.

Acknowledgments. I wish to thank Professor Max Silberztein, who supported the development of Mwotlap resources for NooJ by providing the software itself with the new features I asked for, and Professor Alexandre François, whose teaching was a continual source of inspiration, and who kindly read a first version of this chapter, along with my supervisors Valentina Piunno and Ada Valentini. I extend my deepest respect to the Mwotlap-speaking community. All errors are my own.

References

1. François, A.: The dynamics of linguistic diversity: Egalitarian multilingualism and power imbalance among northern Vanuatu languages. Int. J. Sociol. Lang. **38**(214), 85–110 (2012)
2. François, A.: Contraintes de structures et liberté dans l'organisation du discours. Une description du Mwotlap, langue océanienne du Vanuatu. Doctoral thesis in Linguistics, Université Paris-IV Sorbonne (2001)
3. A Mwotlap – French – English cultural dictionary. http://tiny.cc/Mwotlap-dict. Accessed 9 Sept 2025
4. Mwotlap corpus. https://pangloss.cnrs.fr/corpus/Mwotlap. Accessed 2 Sept 2025
5. NooJ Linguistic Resources. https://nooj.univ-fcomte.fr/resources.html. Accessed 2 Sept 2025
6. Silberztein, M.: Formalizing Natural Languages: The NooJ approach. Wiley (2016)
7. Duran, M.: Quechua module for NooJ multilingual linguistic resources for MT. In: Barone, L., Monteleone, M., Silberztein, M. (eds.) Automatic Processing of Natural Language Electronic Texts with NooJ: Selected Papers from the International Conference NooJ 2016, pp. 48–63. Springer, Cham (2017)
8. Watabe, M.: NooJ Dictionary for the Rromani Language. Toward a NooJ-relevant Sorting of Morphosyntactic Tags. Presentation given at the 11th International NooJ Conference, Kenitra, Morocco, 18–20 May 2017
9. Annouz, H., Kaci, F., Naït Zerrad, K.: Le logiciel Nooj appliqué au kabyle. Iles d'Imesli **5**(1), 341–349 (2013)
10. François, A.: Mouvements et clonages de voyelles en motlav: entre phonologie et morphologie. Bulletin de la Société de Linguistique **94**(1), 437–486 (1999)
11. François, A.: Vowel shifting and cloning in Motlav: historical explanation vs. formal description. In: Klamer, M. (ed.) Proceedings of the Seventh Meeting of Austronesian Formal Linguistics Association, pp. 49–68. Vrije Universiteit Amsterdam, Amsterdam (2000)
12. Silberztein, M.: NooJ Manual. https://nooj.univ-fcomte.fr/files/NooJManual.pdf. Accessed 06 Sept 2025
13. Koskenniemi, K.: Two-Level Morphology: A General Computational Model for Word-Form Recognition and Production. University of Helsinki, Helsinki (1983)
14. Nevins, A.: Locality in Vowel Harmony. MIT Press, Cambridge (2010)
15. Bisazza, A.: Designing a NooJ module for Turkish inflectional analysis: an example of highly productive morphology. In: Hamadou, A.B., Mesfar, S., Silberztein, M. (eds.) Finite-State Language Engineering with NooJ : Selected Papers from the NooJ 2009 International Conference, pp. 19–30. Centre de publication Universitaire, La Manouba (2010)

16. Blust, R.: The Austronesian Languages. Australian National University, Canberra (2013)
17. François, A.: La réduplication en Mwotlap: Les paradoxes du fractionnement. Faits de Langues **24**(1), 17–194 (2004)
18. Fillmore, C.J.: The mechanisms of construction grammar. In: Axmaker, S., Jaisser, A., Singmaster, H. (eds.) Proceedings of the Fourteenth Annual Meeting of the Berkeley Linguistics Society, pp. 35–55. Berkeley Linguistics Society, Berkeley (1988)
19. Gross, M.: Méthodes en syntaxe: régime des constructions complétives. Université de Paris-Vincennes, Paris (1975)
20. Fried, M.: Construction grammar. In: Alexiadou, A., Kiss, T. (eds.) Syntax. Theory and Analysis. An International Handbook, II, pp. 974–1003. De Gruyter-Mouton, Berlin (2015)

Formalizing Relative Adjectives and Participles with NooJ for Ukrainian

Olena Saint-Joanis[✉]

CREE, INALCO, 65 rue Des Grands Moulins, Paris, France
olena.saint-joanis@inalco.fr

Abstract. Modern linguistic tools for Ukrainian, such as GRAC [7], rely on extensive lexical resources like VESUM [5], the largest online dictionary containing over 418,000 lemmas. However, these tools face notable limitations when encountering forms derived from autonomous lexical units (ALUs) (We adopt the term "ALU" (Autonomous Lexical Unit) as proposed by Max Silberztein [8]).) that are not included in existing dictionaries, requiring constant updates to maintain coverage. Moreover, current systems treat derived forms and their base forms as separate entries, without establishing explicit links between them. Ukrainian poses particular challenges in this respect, especially with derived adjectives. Relative adjectives can be formed from proper names, such as place names or personal names. While major toponyms (e.g., *kyjivs'kyj* (Ukrainian is written in the Cyrillic alphabet, however, for the sake of readability, we will use the traditional scholarly transliteration for Ukrainian examples and references. When it is necessary to provide the word in Cyrillic to explain an image, we will include the transliteration alongside it, as in *нськ /ns'k/.*) [from Kyiv]) are covered, derivatives from smaller towns or personal names are usually omitted. Other productive adjective types—diminutive, excessive, and short forms—are also underrepresented, even though they appear frequently in written language. Participles present an additional difficulty due to their hybrid verbal–adjectival nature. Existing tools fail to link participles to their source verbs, resulting in incomplete morphological and semantic analysis. To address these limitations, we have developed several morphological grammars that accurately annotate derived forms—including relative, diminutive, excessive, and short adjectives, as well as participles. These grammars systematically connect derived forms to their base forms, improving both dictionary completeness and linguistic tool performance. This work strengthens Ukrainian NLP resources and contributes to more reliable applications for linguistic research and automatic text processing.

Keywords: NooJ · Ukrainian · Morphological Grammars · Adjectives · Participles

1 Introduction

The formal description of certain grammatical categories, particularly adjectives and participles, remains a challenge in Ukrainian due to the diversity of derivational processes and the dense inflectional system. Both categories are of significant relevance to

D. Petković et al. (Eds.): NooJ 2025, CCIS 2832, pp. 16–26, 2026.
https://doi.org/10.1007/978-3-032-17103-0_2

computational linguistics, since numerous forms are either insufficiently described or not yet included in existing lexical databases.

Among these, derived adjectives present a particular difficulty. Relative adjectives can be formed from proper names, such as place names or personal names, yet most dictionaries include only derivatives from large cities while excluding those from smaller toponyms or anthroponyms.

Participles pose an additional challenge due to their dual verbal–adjectival nature. Current NLP tools often fail to link participles to their base verbs, which limits both morphological and semantic analysis.

To address these issues, this study proposes a formalization of relative adjectives and participles using the NooJ platform. Our approach combines linguistic analysis with the development of morphological grammars capable of generating, recognizing, and annotating derived forms in Ukrainian corpora. This work builds upon previous efforts to expand Ukrainian lexical resources and to strengthen the integration between grammatical description and computational modeling.

2 Formalizing Relative Adjectives

2.1 Description of Adjectives

In Ukrainian, adjectives express the properties of the nouns they modify. In a sentence, they agree in gender, number, and case with the corresponding noun, whether explicit or implied. These grammatical categories are realized both syntactically (agreement with the head noun) and morphologically (through specific inflectional endings).

Ukrainian adjectives have three gender values (masculine, feminine, and neuter), two numbers (singular, plural), and six cases (nominative, accusative, genitive, dative, instrumental, and locative).

In Ukrainian, three main types of adjectives can be distinguished:

- **qualitative adjectives**, which express inherent or descriptive qualities of a noun, e.g., *velykyj* [big],
- **relative adjectives**, which indicate a relation to an object, process, or place, e.g., *universytets'kyj* [university-related], *čytac'kyj* [reading-related], *kyjivs'kyj* [of Kyiv],
- **adjectives of belonging**[1], which denote ownership or association, e.g., *mamyn* [belonging to the mother].

Relative adjectives derived from geographical names are formed by adding suffixes to the noun stem[2], such as.

- -*s'k*-, -*ivs'k*-, -*ans'k*-, -*ens'k*-, or -*yns'k*, e.g., *Poltava* → *poltavs'kyj* [of Poltava], *Rivne* → *rivnens'kyj* [of Rivne], *Jalta* → *jaltyns'kyj* [of Yalta].

Several consonant alternations occur depending on the final consonant of the stem:

- *h, z, ž* + -*s'k*- → -*z'k*-, e.g., *Praha* → *praz'kyj*, *Paryž* → *paryz'kyj*,

---

[1] The formalization of these adjectives within the NooJ platform was previously described in [6].
[2] We use the examples provided in the grammar by Jušuk [3, p. 171].

- *k, c, č* + *-s'k-* → *-c'k-*, e.g., *Vinnycja* → *vinnyc'kyj,*
- *x, s, š* + *-s'k-* → *-s'k-*, e.g., *Odesa* → *odes'kyj.*

Other phonological changes can also be observed, including:

- deletion of *-k-*, e.g., *Žmerynka* → *žmeryns'kyj,*
- loss of the final soft sign, e.g., *Irpin'* → *irpins'kyj,*
- vowel alternation *-o- / -i-*, e.g., *Lozove* → *lozivs'kyj,*
- insertion of a mobile vowel in stems ending in two consonants, e.g., *Moskva* → *moskovs'kyj.*

Additional morphological adjustments are also found in compound place names. For example, *Bila Cerkva* [Bila Tserkva] yields a single derived adjective written as one word: *bilocerkivs'kyj.*

These derivational patterns underscore the importance of developing NLP tools capable of automatically identifying such adjectives—whether through dictionary expansion or the implementation of morphological grammars that formalize these productive word-formation processes.

2.2 Formalization of Relative Adjectives Derived from Proper Nouns

Primarily toponyms, but occasionally first names or family names, can also be used to derive relative adjectives. While adjectives from major cities like *kyjivs'kyj* [of Kyiv] are usually found in dictionaries, those formed from smaller towns, first names, or family names are not.

To handle these forms, we designed the morphological grammar "Adjectives_Relatives_V.1.3.nom" (see Fig. 1).

It consists of 56 embedded graphs. The main graph detects proper nouns, written with an uppercase letter (: $_N$ (<U> <L>), which must first be converted to lowercase (**Step 2:** NLOW). Then, endings of proper nouns are replaced by suffixes (**Step 3:** < NLOW#**o** =:NOUN + Proper + Nominative > such as нськ/*ns'k*/, followed by adjectival endings which assign labels to adjectives (**Step 4:** < NLOW#нський[3], ADJECTIVE + Relative + Nominative + Masculine + Singular).

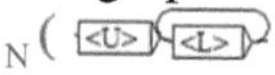

---

[3] *нський /nskyj/.*

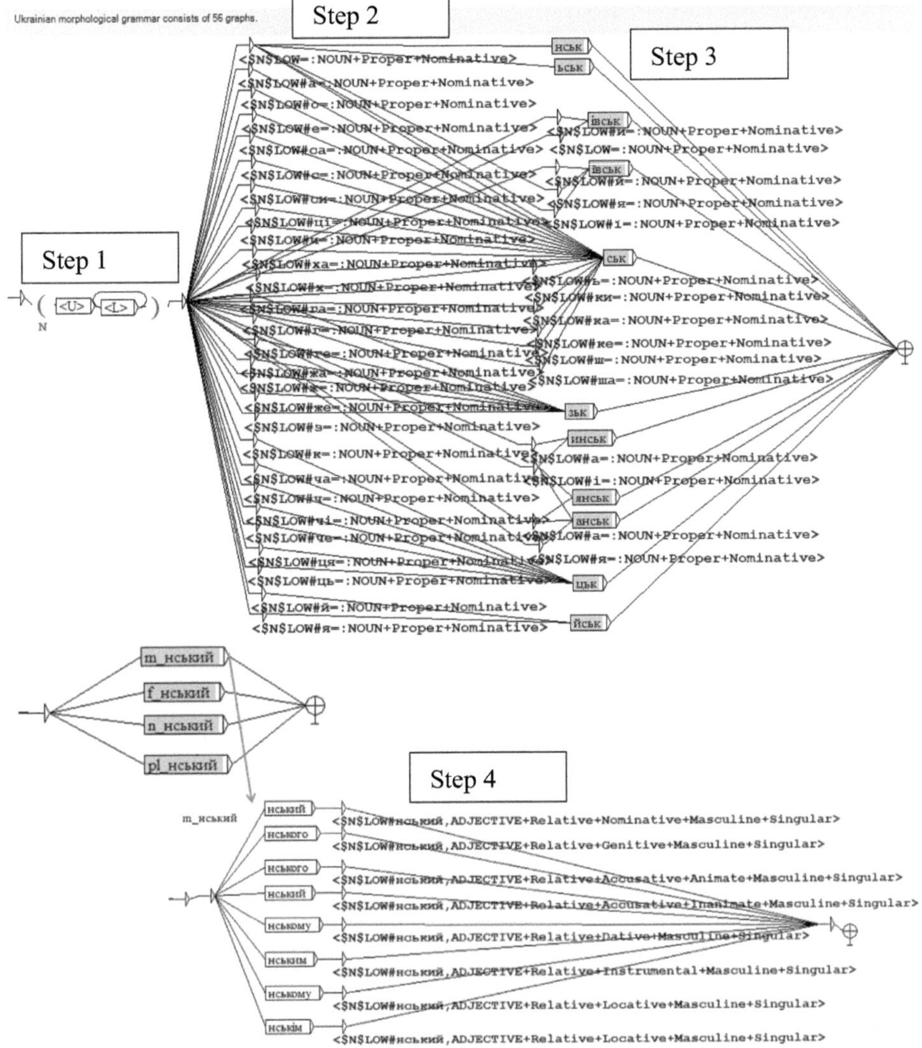

Fig. 1. Grammar formalizing relative adjectives.

With this grammar, relative adjectives formed from proper nouns are now annotated as shown in the example in Fig. 2.

алтайський ліс

0

алтайський,ADJECTIVE+Type=Relative+Case=Accusative+Animation=Inanimate+Gender=Masculine+Number=Singular

Fig. 2. Annotation of the adjective *алтайський* /altajs'kyj/ [from Altai].

3 Formalizing Participles

3.1 Description of Participles

Participles fulfill both verbal functions (action, process, state) and adjectival functions (characterization of an object). They are formed by adding a suffix and adjectival inflection to the infinitive stem or to the present stem of the verb, with which they maintain a semantic relationship. In Ukrainian, three main types are distinguished:

- **past passive participles**, derived from imperfective (IPF) or perfective (PF) verbs by adding the suffixes *-n-*, *-en-*, or *-t-* to the infinitive stem, e.g., *čytanyj* [read], *pryvezenyj* [brought], *probytyj* [pierced],
- **past active participles**[4], derived from perfective verbs by adding the suffix *-l-* to the infinitive stem, e.g., *zhaslyj* [extinguished],
- **present active participles**, derived from imperfective verbs by adding the suffixes *-ač- (-jač)*, or *-uč- (-juč)*[5] to the present stem, e.g., *vyjučyj* [howling].

It should be noted that in Ukrainian, active participles are not productive, meaning that they are not formed from all verbs; therefore, they are excluded from the verbal paradigm. In contemporary Ukrainian, they are used only to a very limited extent.

Participles express verbal categories such as aspect and tense, as well as adjectival categories such as gender, number, and case. They inflect according to the same declensional patterns as adjectives.

Some Ukrainian linguists, such as Vyxovanec', Ševel'ov, and Hrycenko, argue that the participle expresses a property resulting from a process, and therefore consider it closer to an adjective. Other linguists, such as Žovtobrjux and Roussanivs'kyy, emphasize its verbal features and treat it as a form of the verb. Moreover, some participles have become fully lexicalized as adjectives and no longer maintain a direct connection to their base verbs.[6]

As with gerunds, participles are not included in the verbal paradigm in the tools currently available to the general public. We verified this in VESUM [5] (cf., vesum.nlp.net.ua/?w = читаний), Goroh [1] (cf., goroh.pp.ua/Словозміна/читаний), and Sketch Engine [4] (see Table 1).

Table 1. The participle *čytanyj* [read] in existing tools.

Tools	Full description	Category	Lemma
VESUM	adj:m:v_naz:etadjp:pasv:imperf:compb	adjective and participle	čytanyj
Goroh	verbe, passif, participe, passé, non réflexif	verb	čytanyj
Sketch Engine	A-pmsnf-pp-/	adjective	čytanyj

---

[4] Moreover, this is an older form, and additional changes can be observed in the verbal stem, such as the disappearance of verbal suffixes.

[5] T. Shevchenko also used participles with the suffix -jašč- in his poetry [2, p. 217].

[6] We borrow this argument from Horpynyč [2, p. 216].

In these tools, the base verb is not indicated, and in Goroh [1] and Sketch Engine [4], the aspect is not specified either.

Furthermore, participles also appear as independent entries in the academic dictionary SUM-20 [9], where the corresponding base verb is explicitly provided. For example:

PRYVÉZENYJ [brought], *a* [fem.], *e* [neut.], passive participle of the verb *pryveztý* [to bring].

This illustrates that a proper formalization of participles must account not only for their inflectional paradigms, but also for their semantic link to the verb from which they are derived.

3.2 Formalizing Participles with a Dictionary

The list of lemmas we used to prepare the NooJ dictionary also included participles. As mentioned in the previous section, Ukrainian grammarians do not agree on the linguistic status of participles. In existing NLP tools, these ALUs are described either as adjectives or as participles, without any reference to the corresponding base verb, or, in some cases, as verbs, but with the masculine participle form used as the lemma.

We decided to build a morphological grammar capable of generating participles from their base verbs. In addition, we considered it useful to annotate the participles found in our source and to include them in a secondary dictionary. By assigning this dictionary a lower priority than the morphological grammar, NooJ is able to analyze these participle forms whenever they are not recognized by our grammar[7].

In NooJ, every dictionary entry must be associated with a grammatical category. After careful consideration, we introduced a new category, PARTICIPLE, because labeling these ALUs as VERB + Participle seemed inappropriate: verbs are listed in dictionaries only in their infinitive form. Furthermore, some participles are used almost exclusively as adjectives in contemporary Ukrainian, but labeling them only as ADJECTIVE would ignore their semantic link to the verb. Since NooJ allows assigning multiple categories to a single entry, those ALUs functioning as adjectives can therefore be tagged as ADJECTIVE + PARTICIPLE.

Thus, after adding the PARTICIPLE category in the _properties.def file, we prepared an additional set of tags, which is shown in Fig. 3.

In accordance with these tags, we compiled the secondary dictionary "Ukr_dictionary_PARTICIPLES_V.1.3", which includes 13,070 lemmas such as:

dobytyj, PARTICIPLE + Perfective + Passive + Past + FLX = VELYKYJ.

It should be noted that this solution is provisional, and we plan to refine it in future work.

---

[7] NooJ allows each linguistic resource to be assigned a priority level; thus, when annotating the text, the system uses the resources according to these priorities.

```
###########################
###### PARTICIPLE #####
###########################
# Count of categories = 6

PARTICIPLE_Aspect = Imperfective | Perfective; # 2
PARTICIPLE_Case = Accusative | Dative | Genitive | Instrumental | Nominative | Locative; # 6
PARTICIPLE_Gender = Feminine | Masculine | Neuter; # 3
PARTICIPLE_Number = Singular | Plural; # 2
PARTICIPLE_Tense = Past | Present; # 2
PARTICIPLE_Voice = Active | Passive; # 2
```

Fig. 3. Description of participles as a grammatical category.

3.3 Formalizating Participles Using a Morphological Grammar

However, NooJ provides a more suitable solution through the use of morphological grammars. In order to link participles to the verbs from which they are derived, we constructed the morphological grammar "Participles_V.1.3.nom", shown in Fig. 4.

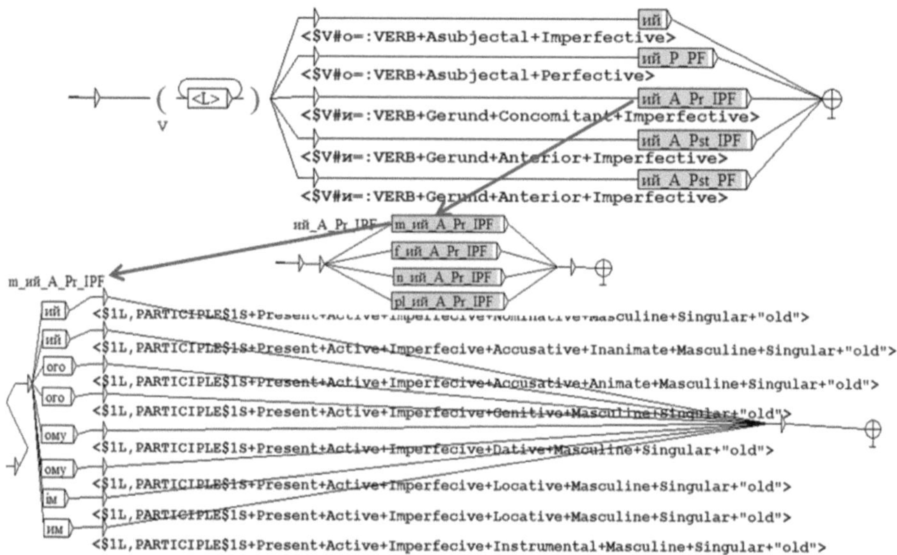

Fig. 4. Morphological grammar for formalizing participles.

This is a contextual grammar consisting of 26 graphs. In the main graph, five nodes represent different constraints:

- The first node contains the schemata describing **imperfective past passive participles**, created from the asubjectal form of imperfective verbs
- (constraint: < $V#o=:VERB+ Asubjectal+ Imperfective>[8]),
- The second node includes the schemata describing **perfective past passive participles**, created from the asubjectal form of perfective verbs

---

[8] This means that the base lemma must be recognized as VERB + Asubjectal + Imperfective, from which the system must remove the final *-o* before generating the new inflected form.

- (constraint: < $V#o=:VERB+ Asubjectal+ Perfective>),
- The third node describes **imperfective present active participles**, created from the concomitant gerund form of imperfective verbs
- (constraint: <$V#и=:VERB+ Gerund+ Concomitant+ Imperfective>),
- The fourth node contains the schemata for **imperfective past active participles**, created from the anterior gerund of imperfective verbs
- (constraint: <$V#и=:VERB+ Gerund+ Anterior+ Imperfective>),
- The fifth node includes the schemata describing **perfective past active participles**, created from the anterior gerund of perfective verbs
- (constraint: <$V#и=:VERB+ Gerund+ Anterior+ Perfective>).

Each embedded graph describes the full paradigm of the participle, that is, its declension, taking into account gender (masculine, feminine, and neuter), number, represented by four nodes in the first embedded graph, and then case and animacy, which are nested within these four nodes.

The inflected forms recognized in this way are annotated as participles. They receive tags specifying the base verb (lemma), tense, voice, aspect, case, gender, and number. In addition, active participles include the extra annotation "old", since, as mentioned earlier, this form is no longer productive in contemporary Ukrainian.

We can see how the imperfective present active participle *vyjučyj* [howling] is annotated in the example shown in Fig. 5.

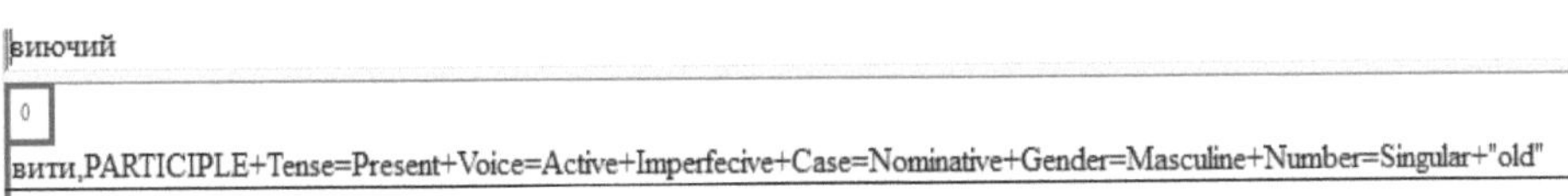

Fig. 5. Annotation of the participle *виючий* /*vyjučyj*/ [howling] with lemma *вити* /*vyty*/ [to howl].

4 Evaluation of the Grammars

To evaluate our grammars, we used a corpus consisting of seven texts representing different varieties and usage contexts of the Ukrainian language. The corpus includes:

1. An excerpt from the novella *Bez puttja* [The Useless Ones] by Ivan Netchuy-Levytskyi; 2012 edition (first written and published in 1900 in *želexivka*[9] spelling). Although updated to current orthographic standards, it still contains left-bank vocabulary considered non-normative (7,737 tokens).
2. An excerpt from the novella *V nedilju rano zillja kopala* [She Gathered Herbs Early on Sunday] by Olha Kobylianska; 1963 edition (first published in 1909 in *želexivka* spelling). The text is rich in Bukovinian vocabulary and expressions, today considered dialectal (18,534 tokens).
3. The novella *Začarovana Desna* [The Enchanted Desna] by Oleksandr Dovzhenko, written in 1954. The text contains colloquial expressions and Russicisms (16,035 tokens).

---

[9] This spelling was introduced by Jevhnn Želexivs′kyj in the Little Russyn–German Dictionary, published in Lviv in 1886.

4. The novella *Kazka pro kalynovu sopilku* [A Tale of the Viburnum Flute] by Oksana Zabuzhko, written in 1999. Zabuzhko's language is known for its lexical richness, including neologisms, *suržyk*[10], and right-bank dialectisms (19,124 tokens).
5. An excerpt from the Ukrainian translation of *Le Père Goriot* [Old Goriot] by Honoré de Balzac (1834), translated by Yelyzaveta Starynkievych (2016 edition). Translated works are often examples of well-structured, standard language (21,512 tokens).
6. A set of beginner-level texts from the reader *Čytajemo ukrajins'koju* [Reading in Ukrainian] (2005), prepared by Oksana Maliarenko and Alina Shevtsova from Sumy University. The language is very simple, intended for learners of Ukrainian (13,339 tokens).
7. An excerpt from articles published on the Ukrainian news site *Tyžden'.ua* [The Week]. This provides a sample of contemporary journalistic language (12,158 tokens).

To build our corpus, we used open-access resources from the Ukrlib website (the Ukrainian literature digital library) [12] for texts 1–5, from the institutional repository of Sumy State University [10] for text 6, and from the official website of the journal *Ukrajins'kyj tyžden'* [Ukrainian Week] [11] for text 7.

4.1 Evaluation of the "Adjectives_Relatives_V.1.3.Nom" Grammar

Applying this grammar to our test corpus produced the results shown in Table 2. In the column "Number of unrecognized occurrences", value 1 corresponds to the statistics before applying the grammar, and value 2 corresponds to those after applying the grammar.

Table 2. Evaluation of the "Adjectives_Relatives_V.1.3.nom" grammar.

Resources used	Number of occurrences in the corpus	Number of unrecognized occurrences	Number of recognized occurrences
Grammar (1)	108,137	6,072 → 6,013	59

Legend: (1) "Adjectives_Relatives_V.1.3.nom".

Thanks to this grammar, 59 relational adjectives derived from proper nouns were successfully recognized.

Furthermore, in Ukrainian, some proper nouns may produce two relational adjectives. For example, *Sofija* [Sofiia] can form both *sofijs'kyj* and *sofijivs'kyj*, while *Efiopija* [Ethiopia], which also ends in *-ija*, produces only *efiops'kyj* according to current orthographic standards.

This means that the grammar may also recognize non-standard forms, such as *efiopijs'kyj*, formed by analogy with *sofijs'kyj*.

---

[10] The use of Russian loanwords and Russian grammatical norms in Ukrainian has led to the emergence of a hybrid of the two languages known as suržyk. It is a spontaneous, non-standardized variety that developed in a context of bilingualism. In general, suržyk is described as a sociolect, often associated with speakers of limited formal education who do not fully command either standard Ukrainian or standard Russian.

4.2 Evaluation of the "Participles_V.1.3.Nom" Grammar

This grammar also models the productive participle-formation patterns but does not yet cover non-productive or low-frequency patterns, such as perfective past active participles in *-l-* (e.g., *zahaslyj* [extinguished]).

It therefore needs to be complemented with the secondary dictionary. The results are presented in Table 3.

Table 3. Evaluation of the "Participles_V.1.3.nom" grammar.

Resources used	Number of occurrences in the corpus	Number of unrecognized occurrences	Number of recognized occurrences
Grammar (1)	108,137	6,072 → 5,496	576
Grammar (1) + Dictionary (2)	108,137	6,072 → 5,259	813

Legend: (1) "Participles_V.1.3.nom".
(2) "Ukr_dictionary_Participles_V.1.3".

Using only the grammar allows us to recognize 576 additional occurrences. By adding the secondary dictionary, a further 237 participles are recognized. In future work, we plan to revise the grammar to better capture non-productive patterns.

5 Conclusion and Perspectives

This study has presented a formalization of relative adjectives and participles in Ukrainian through the development of morphological grammars implemented in the NooJ platform. Our approach enabled a systematic description of the derivational and inflectional mechanisms that characterize these two categories, which are often insufficiently represented in existing resources.

The results contribute to the enrichment of Ukrainian lexical databases and demonstrate the benefits of explicit modeling for improving the automatic recognition and annotation of derived forms in corpora. This work thus supports ongoing efforts to strengthen the link between grammatical description and natural language processing, particularly for languages with rich morphological systems.

Looking ahead, progressively extending the grammars—especially by integrating additional derivational patterns and less frequent forms—will allow us to enhance coverage and improve the robustness of the system. Ultimately, the goal is to provide reliable and scalable morphological tools capable of supporting the development of computational resources tailored to the specific linguistic properties of Ukrainian.

References

1. Goroh (Linguistic portal) Homepage. http://goroh.pp.ua/. Accessed 10 Sept 2025

2. Horpynyč, V.: Morfolohija ukrajins′koji movy. Akademija, Kyjiv (2004)
3. Jušuk, I.P.: Ukrajins′ka mova. Lybid′, Kyjiv (2000)
4. Kilgarriff, A., Rychly, P., Smrz, P., Tugwell, D.: Sketch Engine Homepage, https://auth.ske tchengine.eu/. Accessed 12 May 2025
5. Rysin, A., Starko, V.: VESUM (The Comprehensive Electronic Dictionary of Ukrainian) Homepage. https://vesum.nlp.net.ua/. Accessed 10 Sept 2025
6. Saint-Joanis, O.: A new set of linguistic resources for Ukrainian. In: Silberztein, M. (ed.) Linguistic Resources for Natural Language Processing - On the Necessity of Using Linguistic Methods to Develop NLP Software, pp. 85–102. Springer, Cham (2024)
7. Shvedova, M., et al.: GRAC (General Regionally Annotated Corpus of Ukrainian) Homepage. https://uacorpus.org/en/informaciya-pro-grak/versiyi-korpusu. Accessed 10 Sept 2025
8. Silberztein, M.: Formalisation des langues. L'approche de NooJ. Université de Franche-Comté, ISTE Edition (2015)
9. SUM-20 (The major online Ukrainian dictionary of Institute of Linguistics, National Academy of Sciences of Ukraine) Homepage. https://sum20ua.com/. Accessed 10 Sept 2025
10. Sumy State University Homepage. https://essuir.sumdu.edu.ua/. Accessed 10 Sept 2025
11. Ukrajins′kyj tyžden′ [Ukrainian Week] Homepage. https://tyzhden.ua/. Accessed 10 Sept 2025
12. Ukrlib website (The Ukrainian literature digital library) Homepage. https://www.ukrlib.com. ua/books/. Accessed 10 Sept 2025

Affixoids in Action: A NooJ Journey Through Croatian Neoclassical Compounds

Krešimir Šojat[1(✉)] and Kristina Kocijan[2]

[1] Department of Linguistics, Faculty of Humanities and Social Sciences, University of Zagreb,
10 000 Zagreb, Croatia
ksojat@ffzg.unizg.hr
[2] Department of Information and Communication Sciences, Faculty of Humanities and Social
Sciences, University of Zagreb, 10 000 Zagreb, Croatia
krkocijan@ffzg.unizg.hr

Abstract. This study explores the application of the NooJ tool in detecting and analyzing Croatian words that contain affixoids, namely, prefixoids and suffixoids, primarily derived from Latin and Greek. Known as neoclassical compounds, these words significantly influence modern Croatian, notably in scientific, technical, and cultural registers. Although previous studies have addressed classical word-formation processes, comprehensive lists and consistent classifications of these affixoids remain scarce. To address this gap, two morphological grammars were developed to recognize prefixoids and suffixoids, respectively, and were tested across six diverse corpora: children's literature, adult literature, parliamentary speeches, medical texts, and web content. The grammars were refined through manual verification and further analyzed using visualization tools such as Tableau and Voyant. The results reveal clear domain-based variation in affixoid use and segmentation accuracy, highlight challenges in suffixoid detection, and lead to an expanded dataset comprising 75 suffixoids and 224 prefixoids. By integrating linguistic theory with computational implementation, this study offers a robust framework for affixoid recognition and contributes to the development of scalable tools for morphological analysis in Croatian and other morphologically rich languages.

Keywords: affixoids · neoclassical compounds · prefixoids · suffixoids · morphology · word-formation · Croatian · NooJ

1 Introduction

In today's dynamic linguistic landscape, where morphological innovation increasingly reflects the demands of specialized communication, the study of affixoids offers valuable insights into the structural mechanisms of word formation. In Croatian, neoclassical compounds, formed through the combination of affixoids and lexical elements, play a prominent role in expanding vocabularies across scientific, technical, and cultural domains. For the purposes of this study, **affixoids** are defined as elements that resemble

© The Author(s), under exclusive license to Springer Nature Switzerland AG 2026
D. Petković et al. (Eds.): NooJ 2025, CCIS 2832, pp. 27–38, 2026.
https://doi.org/10.1007/978-3-032-17103-0_3

traditional affixes in position and form, yet retain a degree of independent lexical meaning. We distinguish between **prefixoids** (which appear at the beginning of a compound) and **suffixoids** (which appear at the end). In describing compound structure, we refer to the base element, the segment of the word that the affixoid attaches to, as either the first element (in suffixoid compounds) or the second element (in prefixoid compounds).

While previous scholarship has acknowledged the relevance of affixoids in Croatian word formation (e.g., Babić, 2002; Silić & Pranjković, 2005; Tafra & Košutar, 2009), the existing literature remains fragmented, lacking both comprehensive inventories and a unified approach to classification. This gap is especially relevant given the growing importance of computational linguistics and the development of advanced language processing tools, which require scalable and linguistically informed models.

The increasing complexity of language use in contemporary digital, scientific, and institutional communication has only heightened the need for robust morphological modelling. In languages with rich inflectional systems, such as Croatian, compound formation involving affixoids often introduces additional layers of ambiguity, especially since affixoids resemble free morphemes, or when orthographic variation and inflectional endings obscure clear segmentation. These challenges are further exacerbated by the absence of consistent annotation standards and the limited availability of computational resources tailored specifically to Croatian.

Affixoids also play a key role in the diachronic and typological perspectives. Their presence across European languages, and particularly their Latin and Greek origins, positions them as valuable units for tracing lexical borrowing, semantic shift, and morphological productivity over time. Understanding how affixoids behave in Croatian not only sheds light on the structure of neologisms and terminological innovation but also provides comparative insights relevant to broader Slavic and European linguistics.

From an applied perspective, the ability to detect and annotate affixoids with precision holds significant potential for improving downstream natural language processing tasks, including automatic term extraction, information retrieval, and machine translation. As such, the framework presented here addresses both theoretical questions in morphology and practical concerns in language technology, particularly for under-resourced and morphologically rich languages.

To address these challenges, this study leverages NooJ, a linguistic development environment well-suited for integrating lexical resources with detailed and formalized morphological rules. Two dedicated morphological grammars were designed: one for recognizing prefixoids and one for suffixoids. These grammars were applied to six domain-specific Croatian corpora, encompassing children's and adult literature, parliamentary debates (with gender distinction), medical texts, and web-based content. Outputs were subsequently verified manually and further analyzed using visualization tools such as Tableau and Voyant.

The paper is organized as follows: Sect. 2 reviews the state of the art and the underlying theoretical frameworks of neoclassical word formation; Sect. 3 details the methodology and corpus selection, emphasizing the development of the morphological grammars; Sect. 4 presents the results and analytical findings, including the expansion of the initial affixoids dataset; and Sect. 5 discusses the implications and prospects for future research. By bridging linguistic theory with computational implementation, this study contributes to a more systematic understanding of Croatian affixoids and offers a foundation for scalable language processing applications.

2 Theoretical Framework

This chapter establishes the conceptual underpinnings of our study by situating it within the broader field of morphological analysis and word formation. It outlines the key linguistic concepts and theoretical models that inform our understanding of neoclassical compounds and affixoids, thereby setting the stage for a detailed exploration of the mechanisms behind the formation of new lexical items in Croatian, particularly those derived from Latin and Greek elements.

Word formation in Croatian primarily involves derivation and compounding, alongside processes such as conversion, blending, acronym formation and others. Derivation typically employs a single base, while compounding combines two or more. Unlike inflection, which relies solely on suffixation, word formation utilizes both suffixes and prefixes, their combinations, as well as systematic vowel variation (ablaut) within lexical morphemes. Comprehensive overviews of Croatian derivational patterns and their typology can be found in Babić (2002), Filko et al. (2020) and Šojat and Filko (2023). When it comes to compounding, bases are often connected via a linking vowel or interfix. Recent research (Šojat, 2025) has further explored compound formation through the development of a computational lexicon for Croatian, highlighting patterns relevant for formal modelling.

Within this broader typological and morphological landscape, the present study narrows its focus to the category of neoclassical compounds, complex lexical items constructed using elements primarily of Latin and Greek origin that resemble affixes in form and position but retain a degree of lexical meaning. These elements, commonly referred to as affixoids, include both prefixoids (e.g. *bio-, tele-, mikro-*) and suffixoids (e.g. *-logija, -grafija, -patija*), and are typically found in scientific, technical, and specialized vocabularies. Compounds such as microscope, television or archeology (*mikroskop, televizija, arheologija*) are typical examples. They consist of classical components such as *micro-, tele-* and *-logy,* which are functionally bound, yet semantically transparent.

Affixoids resemble traditional affixes (prefixes or suffixes) but differ in important ways: they retain independent semantic content and exhibit regular productivity across domains.These borderline cases between compounding and affixation have long been noted in Slavic word-formation theory (Klajn2002), which offers a framework for interpreting affixoids as semi-bound, semantically stable formative elements.In Croatian linguistic literature, they are often referred to as *bound stems* or *bound lexical morphemes* (Barić et al., 1995; Babić, 2002). However, affixoids are not lexical morphemes or stems derived from lexical morphemes, as they cannot function as independent stems for affixation. Marković (2012:53) highlights their semantic stability and repeatability, as well as their productive role in new word formation. This distinguishes them from other derivational bases and traditional affixes, both of which may show more variation in meaning and use.

Affixoids of Latin and Greek origin are widely used across European languages, typically maintaining consistent meanings and contributing significantly to the formation of new words. Babić (2002) as well as Silić and Pranjković (2005) provide extensive overviews of word-formation processes relevant to understanding such lexical phenomena.

In Croatian, neoclassical affixoids can combine with native or borrowed base elements to form new words. Examples of prefixoid formations include *bioznanost* 'bioscience', *mikroprocesor* 'microprocessor', and *supermodel* 'supermodel'. Similarly, suffixoids are found in formations such as *filmofil* 'filmophile', *kartografija* 'cartography', and *papirologija* 'paperwork'. This dual capacity reflects both the adaptability of the affixoids and their compatibility with native morphological patterns.

A representative case is the prefixoid *filo-*, derived from Ancient Greek and meaning 'love' or 'affinity'. As a prefixoid, it forms compounds that express a positive orientation toward the meaning of the base element. Unlike standard affixes, which typically modify words in a grammatical sense, *filo-* retains a degree of independent lexical meaning. In both Italian and Croatian, for example, it combines with various stems in words such as *filosofo/filozof* 'philosopher' (literally 'lover of wisdom'), *filarmonico/filharmonija* (relating to a love of harmony), and *filantropo/filantrop* (denoting affinity for humanity). This productive morphological process plays a significant role in the evolution of contemporary vocabulary, particularly in languages with a strong neoclassical heritage, underscoring the dynamic interplay between historical linguistic elements and modern word formation practices.

Compounds composed exclusively of neoclassical affixoids are frequent across European languages, including Croatian. This word-formation strategy is particularly productive in specialized and scientific registers. Despite their frequency and continued productivity, existing inventories of neoclassical affixoids in Croatian remain both incomplete and inconsistent. Furthermore, there is ongoing debate regarding the status of certain elements, specifically whether they should be classified as affixoids of affixes.

Recognizing the need for greater clarity and formalization, the present study pursues the following goals: (1) to identify a core set of neoclassical affixoids in Croatian, (2) to analyze their distribution across a range of textual domains, and (3) to develop morphological grammars for their automatic recognition. To this end, an initial list of 30 suffixoids and 125 prefixoids was compiled based on established sources (Barić et al., 1995; Silić and Pranjković, 2005). These elements were tested across multiple Croatian corpora, and the results were manually analyzed and evaluated. Based on the observed patterns and iterative refinement, the inventory was subsequently expanded to include 75 suffixoids and 224 prefixoids, reflecting both previously undocumented forms and domain-specific variations. The following chapter provides a detailed account of the methodology employed in this study, including corpus design, grammar development, and validation strategies.

3 Methodology

Emphasizing a systematic blend of computational and manual approaches, the methodology outlines how custom morphological grammars were devised to identify affixoids, specifically prefixoids and suffixoids, across multiple Croatian corpora. This approach builds on earlier rule-based methods that combine automatic processing with manual validation, as demonstrated in NooJ-based studies on aspectual derivation and diminutive and pejorative verb forms in Croatian (Kocijan et al., 2018; Kocijan & Šojat, 2024). However, our focus on affixoids introduces a more nuanced morphological layer, requiring elaborate segmentation and classification procedures.

The first step involved selecting six domain-specific corpora: children's literature, adult literature, parliamentary speeches (segmented by gender), medical texts, and web content. Each corpus was chosen to capture varied stylistic and functional registers of Croatian, thereby providing a diversified linguistic landscape that underpins robust analysis of neoclassical word formation.

The next phase involved the systematic creation of two morphological grammars tailored for detecting prefixoids and suffixoids. Initial affixoid lists were extracted from seminal works and refined based on formal linguistic criteria. The rules were designed to account for word boundaries, inflectional paradigms, and contextual constraints, in order to accurately capture neoclassical compounds in Croatian.

The NooJ platform served as the computational environment for designing and implementing the morphological grammars. These grammars were assigned a lower priority than standard dictionary resources to minimize false positives, particularly in the case of homographs.

The prefixoid grammar (Fig. 1) identifies words beginning with one of the prefixoids listed in variable $P. To manage the high number of prefixoids, each is grouped into sub-graphs by initial letter. For example, Fig. 1 presents a visual representation of the sub-graph for the letter F, which lists prefixoids such as *femto, fero, fito, fizio, fono, foto, franko, farmako, filo*, and *freno*, thereby illustrating how these prefixoids are structured within the sub-graph. When a match is found, the remainder of the word is placed into variable $R, and three annotations are added: + Root = $R to capture the base element, + Affixoid = $P to record the specific prefixoid, and an additional attribute that indicates whether the affixoid is functioning as a prefixoid (Fig. 1) or suffixoid (Fig. 2).

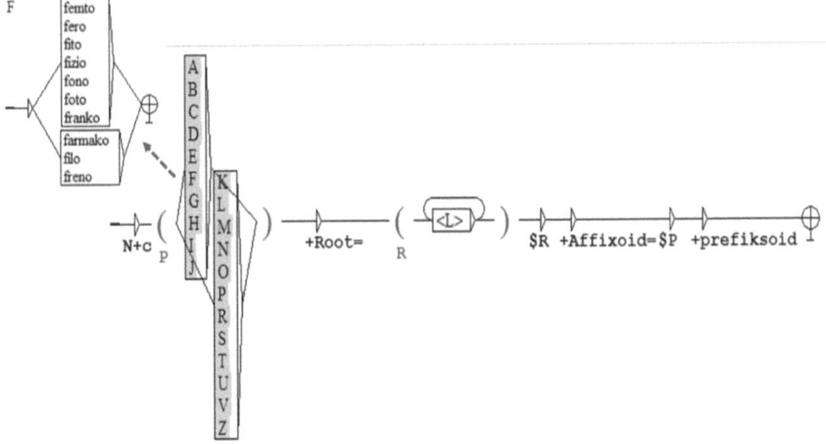

Fig. 1. Morphological Grammar for Prefixoid Detection.

The suffixoid grammar (Fig. 2) identifies words ending in suffixoids taking into account Croatian case morphology which makes it more complex in design. The grammar uses two variables: $R captures the base, and $S isolates the suffixoid. For paths where a single suffixoid is associated with a specific case paradigm the transducer output is inserted directly at the corresponding node. However, for paths associated with multiple potential suffixoids, the variable $S is used to compute and adjust the transducer output to the specific suffixoid. For example, within the branch recognizing words that use the ALAT paradigm for case endings, a dedicated sub-grammar (S_ALAT) stored in the variable $S processes a list of potential suffixoids (including *bus, cid, cit, drom, fon, gen, gram, id, itis, man, oid, om, onim, pat, stat, tom,* and *top*).

Special cases are handled by adapting the suffixoid form depending on the inflectional ending. For instance, the suffixoid *"plazma"* is shortened to *"plazm"* in the variable $S when followed by the case ending *"-ama"*, while *"logija"* is stored as *"log"* with the final *"ija"* subsequently added through the transducer output (if the characters *"ij"* appear before the case ending). These steps ensure the extraction of both the base element and the affixoid, along with full syntactic metadata for further processing.

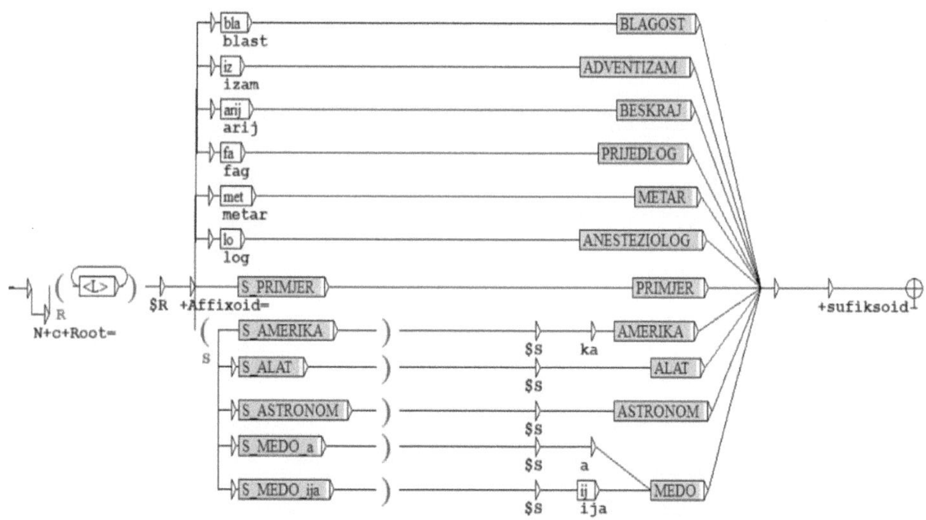

Fig. 2. Morphological Grammar for Suffixoid Detection.

An additional syntactic grammar (Fig. 3) integrates with the output of the morphological analysis. It targets nouns annotated as <N+ prefiksoid> or <N+ afiksoid>, adds a semantic label <AF>, and preserves the original syntactic properties originally assigned to each noun through the dictionary. Metadata about the corpus and the specific text source are also retained to enable further visualization and analysis in Tableau.

Following automatic extraction, manual verification was conducted to ensure the accuracy and validity of the identified affixoids. Two evaluation cycles have been completed so far. The first, based on affixoids listed in the literature, led to the identification

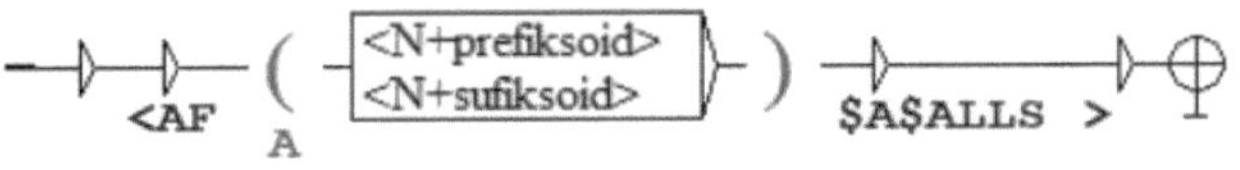

Fig. 3. Syntactic Grammar for Affixoids: the rule identifies nouns annotated as <N+prefiksoid> or <N+akiksoid>, augmenting their annotation with an additional <AF> label while preserving syntactic properties for subsequent data extraction and visualization in Tableau.

of new affixoids, which were then incorporated into the grammars. These updates and results are presented in the next chapter. The list remains open to expansion based on future analyses. In this way, the methodological framework presented here directly supports the overarching goals of the study: identifying a core set of neoclassical affixoids, analyzing their distribution, and implementing formal grammars for their detection.

4 Results

This section presents an overview of the main findings obtained through the application of the custom-developed morphological grammars for the detection of Croatian neoclassical compounds. The results include both quantitative measures (detailing frequency distributions, statistical measures, and comparative analyses across different domains) and qualitative insights (e.g., morphological patterns, contextual variations, and morphological intricacies). Taken together, they demonstrate the effectiveness of the computational approach in capturing the interplay between base elements and affixoids and lay the groundwork for further in-depth linguistic analysis. As part of this process, the original inventory of affixoids was significantly expanded. Through empirical testing and manual verification, the list was extended from 30 to 75 suffixoids and from 125 to 224 prefixoids, reflecting both domain-specific variation and previously unrecorded formations.

Table 1 displays the distribution and density of affixoids across different corpora, revealing notable variation depending on genre and register. A lower token-to-affixoid ratio indicates higher affixoid density, i.e., greater frequency of affixoids in a given corpus. In parliamentary corpora, affixoid density is nearly identical across gendered subcorpora: while the male-speaker corpus contains more absolute affixoid occurrences (14,941 affixoids in 7,586,232 tokens) than the female-speaker corpus (3,521 affixoids in 1,763,655 tokens), their token-to-affixoid ratios (508 and 501, respectively) suggest only minimal variation. This implies a comparable reliance on complex word-formation strategies among both groups. Nevertheless, compared to specialized medical corpora, the density remains relatively modest, reflecting the broader lexical range and less terminologically fixed nature of political speech.

By contrast, the Medical corpus exhibits the highest affixoid density (159,604 affixoids in 9,528,770 tokens), reflecting its highly specialized and technical vocabulary where affixoids are commonly employed to create precise definitions, which often incorporate numerous neoclassical compounds. The MaCoCu web corpus also shows a relatively high frequency (55,036 affixoids in 9,918,816 tokens), although somewhat lower due to the informal and conversational nature of online discourse. Literary corpora, particularly children's (2,958 affixoids in 3,312,531 tokens) and adult literature (2,763 affixoids in 3,128,150 tokens), show the lowest affixoid frequency, highlighting the stylistic and functional differences between narrative writing and technical or informational texts.

Table 1. Corpus size vs. number of correct affixoids detected.

Corpus	Total token count	Detected affixoids	Token-to-affixoid ratio
Children's lit	3 312 531	2 958	1 120
Adult lit	3 128 150	2 763	1 132
Parliament speech-F	1 763 655	3 521	501
Parliament speech-M	7 586 232	14 941	508
Medical texts	9 528 770	159 604	60
web content	9 918 816	55 036	180

The analysis of affixoid classification accuracy (Fig. 4) reveals a marked disparity between prefixoids and suffixoids. While 51.76% of prefixoids were correctly identified, the corresponding accuracy for suffixoids was significantly lower, at just 19.90%. Consequently, nearly half of the prefixoids and over 80% of the suffixoids were incorrectly annotated. These results point to the relative ease of detecting prefixoids, which exhibit more stable forms, compared to suffixoids, which are subject to greater phonological variation, broader semantic scope, and syntactic ambiguity.

These findings suggest that existing annotation strategies may not fully capture the variability of suffixoidal formations. Enhancing suffixoid recognition should involve deeper error analysis to better differentiate productive suffixoids from lexicalized formations. Targeted error analysis and strict formal criteria should be central to future grammar refinements.

Overall, these findings highlight clear domain-specific variations in the use of neo-classical affixoids. The data suggest that technical and online registers feature a higher frequency of specialized compound forms, whereas literary texts exhibit a much more restrained use of such linguistic elements.

An in-depth examination of suffixoid accuracy (Fig. 5) confirms domain-dependent performance. In the Medical corpus, several suffixoids such as *-logija*, *-grafija*, *-cit*, *-oza*, *-emija*, and *-drom* were identified with 100% accuracy, highlighting the structured nature of medical terminology. In contrast, in more heterogeneous or creative domains such as parliamentary speech and literary texts, suffixoid detection proves far less reliable. Misclassification rates of 80–90% were not uncommon, particularly for items used in less conventional or stylistically varied ways.

Prefixoid analysis (Table 6) shows greater consistency overall. Again, technical corpora such as the Medical corpus yield higher accuracy in identifying prefixoids like

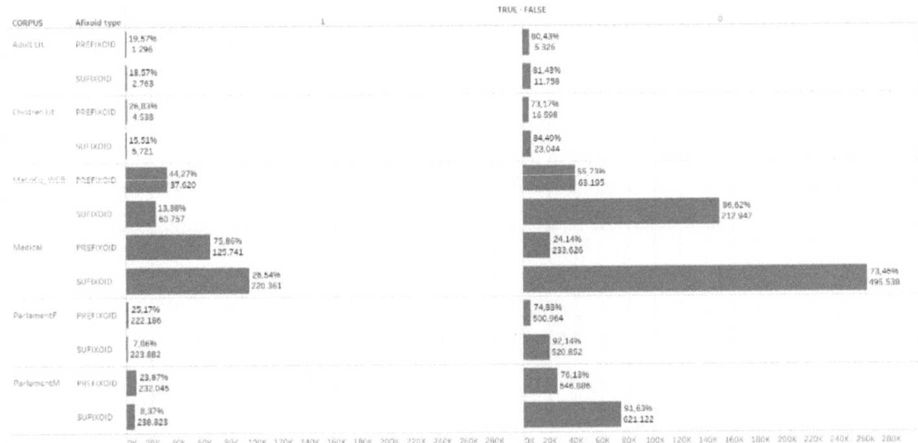

Fig. 4. Percentage and count of correctly (left) and incorrectly (right) identified affixoids across all six sub-corpora.

PREFIKSOID	Adult Lit.	Children Lit.	MaCoCu_WEB	Medical 〒	ParlamentF	ParlamentM
			CORPUS			
hipo	41	29	2 183	21.307	6	11 63
tera	65	86	1.287 1	12.415	79	122
hidro	4	7	4 211	5.398	24	84
mikro	14	32	897	3.067	30	141
bio	8 17	1 13	404 1.574	508 2.468	5 38	24 119
poli	507 14	494 74	3.953 921	22 2.297	1.459 15	6.904 37
mono	62	25	23 440	1 2.251	16	116
proto	12 10	9	376 219	991 955	115 1	605 7
euro	15	40	2.318 193	1.627 1	452 61	1.799 248
neo	162 11	123	531 66	942 246	134 4	496 10
auto	150 71	102 262	3.248 2.965	18 814	32 217	170 1.324
repro	5	5	108 6	695	13 3	45 10
radio	20 1	50 12	4.788 3.112	573	43 31	56 183

Fig. 5. Prefixoids with the highest frequency across all corpora. Green numbers indicate correctly recognized prefixoids, while red numbers indicate incorrectly recognized ones.

hipo-, *mikro-*, and *poli-*. Meanwhile, political and web sources demonstrate more fluctuation, likely reflecting innovative and less conventional word-formation strategies in these genres. Overall, these findings emphasize that the precision of automated morphological analysis is strongly influenced by domain-specific language practices, and they highlight the need for tailored approaches when parsing texts from creative versus technical registers.

The analysis also identified structural and orthographic challenges that hinder affixoid recognition. In the MaCoCu corpus, orthographic irregularities, such as missing diacritics (e.g., *nožom* rendered as *nozom*), frequently interfere with segmentation. Ambiguous compound structures further complicate detection. For instance, the term *arteriopatija* may be segmented as *arterio* + *patija* or *arteri* + *opatija*, both plausible, but only one contextually accurate. Similarly, the prefixoid *filo-* introduces polysemy-related ambiguity, as forms such as *phyllo-* (meaning 'leaf'), *phylo-* ('race') and *philo-* (affinity) are morphologically identical in Croatian. Moreover, the suffixoid *-om* often coincides with the instrumental singular case ending, obscuring its status as an affixoid.

These challenges explain the higher recognition accuracy in regulated domains like medicine, where lexical patterns are clearer and terminological consistency supports rule-based parsing.

Despite these limitations, several prefixoids, such as *micro-*, were reliably identified across all domains. However, their collocational patterns varied. In children's and adult literature, *mikro-* combined with a limited and often creative set of base forms (e.g., *fon, fončić, kozmos*, and *skop*), whereas in medical and web corpora, a broader and more specialized vocabulary was observed (e.g., *abrazija* 'abrasion', *alga* 'alga', *biocid* 'biocide', *endoskopija* ' endoscopy', and *lokacija* 'location'). Parliamentary texts showed subtle gender variations: female speakers tended to use base elements linked to biology, film, or finance (e.g., *biolog* 'biologist', *film* 'film', *fon* ' phone', *kredit* ' credit'), while male speakers more often used terms from technology and economics (e.g., *čip* ' chip' and injekcija ' injection').

This register-specific variation is further illustrated in Fig. 6, which visualizes the distribution of the prefixoid *mikro-* and its associated base elements across all six corpora using Voyant Tools. The largest graph (leftmost) displays the full network of *mikro-* combinations based on all corpora combined, while the six smaller graphs (arranged in two rows: children's literature, female parliamentary discourse, medical texts; adult literature, male parliamentary discourse, web content) represent corpus-specific distributions of base elements. These smaller visualizations clearly demonstrate that, although the potential for combinations is extensive, actual usage is constrained by domain-specific preferences and vocabulary. For instance, the medical corpus shows a concentration of technical terms, while literary and parliamentary corpora reflect more limited or stylistically marked usage.

In summary, the consistent detection of *micro-* across all corpora is accompanied by notable variation in the selection of base elements, reflecting underlying register-specific differences in lexical repertoire, discourse function, and stylistic conventions.

These findings collectively underscore the importance of domain-specific modeling in the accurate identification and interpretation of neoclassical affixoids. They also highlight the potential of computational tools, when carefully designed and evaluated, to uncover nuanced patterns of word formation.

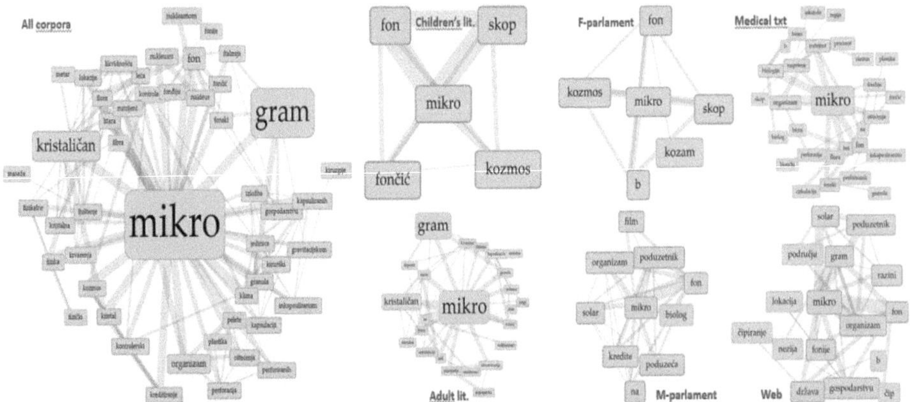

Fig. 6. Distribution of *mikro-* across text types and associated base elements.

5   Conclusion and Future Research

This study set out to explore the identification and morphological behavior of affixoids, specifically prefixoids and suffixoids, and their role in shaping Croatian compound word formation. Building on foundational theoretical work in neoclassical word-formation, we designed and implemented custom morphological and syntactic grammars to detect these elements across multiple corpora. Through a combination of automated extraction and manual validation, supported by both quantitative analysis and qualitative insights, our findings revealed distinct patterns in affixoid distribution and usage across various domains. In doing so, we also substantially expanded the initial set of affixoids derived from existing literature, ultimately identifying 75 suffixoids and 224 prefixoids. This enhanced inventory offers a more comprehensive foundation for future morphological research and resource development.

The results confirm that the proposed approach can reliably detect Croatian affixoids, though performance varies depending on corpus type and linguistic context. Prefixoids, which tend to appear in more semantically transparent positions, were more accurately recognized than suffixoids, which often undergo morphological variations. Moreover, the frequency and composition of neoclassical compounds proved to be highly domain-specific. These findings not only enhance our understanding of affixoid behavior in Croatian but also demonstrate the potential of rule-based approaches for analyzing morphologically complex structures. At the same time, the study revealed several challenges, such as ambiguous segmentation, orthographic variation, and context-sensitive usage, that future research must address. Improving recognition accuracy, particularly for suffixoids, will require more refined grammatical modeling and expanded lexicon resources. Such advancements will be essential for improving computational models of Croatian language processing and for facilitating broader comparative studies in morphologically rich languages.

In sum, this study contributes to a deeper theoretical and practical understanding of Croatian word formation by providing a structured framework for the detection and analysis of affixoids. It opens new avenues for exploring morphological productivity across genres and registers, and provides a groundwork for improving computational tools in language technology, thus supporting future advances in both applied and theoretical linguistics.

References

1. Babić, S.: Tvorba riječi u hrvatskome književnome jeziku. Hrvatska akademija znanosti i umjetnosti : Globus, Zagreb (2002)
2. Barić, E., et al.: Hrvatska gramatika. Školska knjiga, Zagreb (1995)
3. Filko, M., Šojat, K., Štefanec, V.: The design of croderiv 2.0. Prague Bull. Math. Linguist. **115**, 83–104 (2020)
4. Klajn, I.: Tvorba reči u savremenom srpskom jeziku: prvi deo: slaganje i prefiksacija. Zavod za udžbenike i nastavna sredstva : Institut za srpski jezik SANU ; Matica srpska, Novi Sad, Beograd (2002)
5. Kocijan, K., Šojat, K.: Exposing diminutive and pejorative verbs in Croatian. In: Bartulović, A., Mijić, L., Silberztein, M. (eds.) Formalizing Natural Languages: Applications to Natural Language Processing and Digital Humanities, Springer Cham, Switzerland, pp. 39–51 (2024). https://doi.org/10.1007/978-3-031-89810-5_4
6. Kocijan, K., Šojat, K., Poljak, D.: Designing croatian aspectual derivatives dictionary: preliminary stages. In: Proceedings of the First Workshop on Linguistic Resources for Natural Language Processing (LR4NLP-2018). Stroudsburg (PA): Association for Computational Linguistics (ACL), pp. 28–37 (2018)
7. Marković, I.: Uvod u jezičnu morfologiju. Disput, Zagreb (2012)
8. Silić, J., Pranjković, I.: Gramatika hrvatskoga jezika: za gimnazije i visoka učilišta. Školska knjiga, Zagreb (2005)
9. Šojat, K.: CroComp – lexicon of croatian compounds. In: Huyghe, R., Prudent, M., Salvadori, J.F. (eds.) Proceedings of the Fifth International Workshop on Resources and Tools for Derivational Morphology. Switzerland, pp. 141–150 (2025)
10. Tafra, B., Košutar, P.: Rječotvorni modeli u hrvatskom jeziku. Suvremena lingvistika **35**(67) (2009)
11. Šojat, K., Filko, M.: Processing Croatian Morphology: Roots, Segmentation and Derivational Families. In: Filko, M.; Šojat, K. (eds.) Proceedings of the Fourth International Workshop on Resources and Tools for Derivational Morphology (DeriMo2023), Hrvatsko društvo za jezicne tehnologije, Zagreb, pp. 61-70 (2023)

Formalization Proposal of Verbal Idioms with Psychological Predicates in Rioplatense Spanish

Walter Koza[1]([✉]) and Sol Schmidt[2]

[1] Facultad de Filosofía y Humanidades, Departamento de Lingüística, Universidad de Chile, Of. 316, Ignacio Carrera Pinto, 1025, 7800284 Santiago, Chile
`walter.koza@uchile.cl`
[2] Facultad de Filosofía y Letras, Universidad de Buenos Aires, Puan 480, C14120 Caba, Argentina

Abstract. Psychological predicates (PPs), referring to psychological, mental, or emotional states, pose challenges for both grammatical theory and natural language processing (NLP) tasks. While previous research has mostly addressed PPs expressed by a single word (typically verbs, but also nouns and adjectives), idioms such as *ahogarse en un vaso de agua* ("to worry excessively about something unimportant") have received little attention. This study, situated within computational linguistics, focuses on verbal idiomatic psychological predicates (VIPP) in Rioplatense Spanish. We argue that the syntax of idioms occupies an intermediate position between phrase-level and sentence-level syntax, which makes them particularly challenging to model computationally. To explore this, we use NooJ, a linguistic development environment that enables the construction of linguistic resources that can be used by automatic text alorithms. Our methodology combines two components: (i) the formal description of a representative set of VIPP, and (ii) the implementation of syntactic grammars designed to recognize these idioms and their participants. The resulting algorithm was tested on a collection of sentences extracted from publicly available corpora. The evaluation demonstrates that the system successfully identifies VIPP along with their associated arguments, showing the feasibility of capturing this type of predicate in a computational framework. These findings contribute both to the grammatical characterization of idioms and to their automatic treatment in NLP applications.

Keywords: Psychological Predicates · Verbal Idioms · NooJ

1   Introduction

Psychological predicates (PPs) [1–3], understood as those that denote an emotion or mental state experienced by an individual, have long been recognized as a relevant phenomenon both for grammatical studies and for certain natural language processing (NLP) tasks [4]. From a grammatical perspective, interest in these expressions arises from the fact that they often fail to conform to certain morphosyntactic generalizations [3, 5]. From the perspective of NLP, their automatic identification is useful for tasks such as sentiment detection and emotion analysis (cf. [6], among others).

D. Petković et al. (Eds.): NooJ 2025, CCIS 2832, pp. 39–50, 2026.
https://doi.org/10.1007/978-3-032-17103-0_4

Although several studies have addressed this phenomenon from both linguistic and computational angles, most research has focused on single-word predicates (mainly verbs, and to a lesser extent, nouns and adjectives). By contrast, idiomatic expressions such as *sacar de quicio* ("to drive someone crazy"), *ahogarse en un vaso de agua* ("to worry excessively about something trivial"), or *sacarle canas verdes* ("to cause someone a great deal of stress") have received relatively little attention (Dąbrowska, 2018 [7]; Islas & Solís [8]). An idiom is defined as a multiword structure whose meaning is not derived from the sum of its parts (Corpas [9]; Penadés [10]). Such expressions can be classified into grammatical categories according to their syntactic function in the sentence (Corpas [9]; Penadés [10]). Thus, one can identify nominal idioms (*ojo de buey* "bull's eye"), adjectival idioms (*de rechupete* "delicious"), verbal idioms (*tener en cuenta* "to take into account"), adverbial idioms (*al pie de la letra* "literally"), and prepositional idioms (*de cara a* "facing / towards").

The present study, framed within computational linguistics, aims to provide a formal description of the syntactic behavior of verbal idioms that denote psychological predicates (VIPP), in order to develop a computational model for automatic analysis. This model consists of an algorithm designed to perform a syntactic-semantic analysis of VIPP in natural language texts and, in turn, to generate sentences that include this type of predicate.

For the computational implementation, we rely on NooJ (Silberztein [11]), a linguistic development environment for automatic analysis based on the Chomsky–Schützenberger hierarchy (1963). NooJ provides various resources, such as electronic dictionaries and computational grammars, which facilitate the modeling of complex linguistic phenomena.

Our methodology combines the formal description of a selected set of VIPP with the design of computational grammars capable of recognizing these idioms together with their participants. The algorithm was tested on a corpus of River Plate Spanish texts, yielding results that support the feasibility of further research along this line.

The remainder of this article is structured as follows. The next section presents the theoretical background of the study. We then describe the methodology and discuss the results obtained. Finally, we outline the main conclusions of the research.

2 Theoretical Framework

This section provides a brief overview of studies dealing with the complexities of psychological predicates (PPs). We then turn to the problem of verbal idioms of this type of predicate, reviewing the proposals of Dąbrowska [7] for English and of Islas and Solís [8] for Mexican Spanish. Finally, we describe the work addressing this phenomenon in the field of computational natural language processing.

2.1 On Psychological Predicates

The literature includes numerous attempts to define what counts as a PP [3]. As noted in the introduction, a PP is a predicate in which an individual experiences a mental state. Landau [2] offers the following formalization:

1. Let P be an n-place predicate. P is psychological iff:
   $P(<x1\ldots ,xi, \ldots,xn>)=1 \Rightarrow \exists xi\ \exists s\ (xi\ is\ in\ s)$ [s = some mental state]

   In other words, a predicate is psychological only if, given the truth of the minimal proposition in which it occurs, one of its arguments is an experiencer of a mental state. Espejel [12] further emphasizes the need to distinguish conceptual from grammatical notions: although conceptually plausible, a verb is not necessarily psychological in the grammatical sense.

   Another relevant property of PPs is that they may appear in verbal (2a), nominal (2b), or adjectival form (2c):

2. *a. Juan adora a María.*
      b. Juan le tiene miedo a María.
      c. María le es indiferente a Juan.

   What has especially drawn attention is the variation in how arguments are encoded: the experiencer (an animate, typically human entity who feels an emotion) and the stimulus (the entity, person, thing, or situation provoking the emotion) (Mellis [13]). Following Belletti & Rizzi's [1] classic work, three classes can be distinguished: those where the experiencer surfaces as subject (VPE-S / Class I) (3a), as object (VPE-O / Class II) (3b), or as dative object (VPE-D / Class III) (3c).

3. *a. Juan ama a María.*
      b. El ruido molesta a Juan.
      c. A Clemente le gustan las aceitunas.

   According to Rozwadowska [5], theoretical approaches to PPs fall into two broad categories: (i) those focusing exclusively on syntax (e.g., [1]) and (ii) those linking psychological effects to different types of lexical-semantic decomposition, often correlated with aspectual or event structure properties. In line with the goals of this study, attention will be given to research addressing the syntactic positions of experiencers, alternations across the three classes, and interpretive possibilities.

2.2 On Idioms

In addition to free word combinations (phrases, clauses, etc.), languages also contain fixed structures with greater stability. According to Corpas [9], such units are characterized by: (i) consisting of two or more orthographic words; (ii) exhibiting some degree of lexicalization; and (iii) displaying a high frequency of co-occurrence. Corpas designates them as *phraseological units*. Within this category, *idioms* are defined as fixed word combinations that function as a sentence element whose meaning cannot be derived compositionally [10]. Idioms correspond to a grammatical category derived from their syntactic function in the sentence. Thus, they can be nominal (*ojo de buey* "bull's eye"), adjectival (*de rechupete* "delicious"), adverbial (*a lo bestia* "wildly"), prepositional (*por entre* "through"), or verbal (*llorar la carta* "to plead desperately"). Among these, certain verbal idioms correspond to PPs.

Studies addressing the complexities of verbal idiomatic psychological predicates (VIPP) include Dąbrowska [7] for English and Islas & Solís [8] for Spanish. Dąbrowska analyzes English idioms denoting psychological states from a syntactic perspective, focusing on argument structure realization and the constraints imposed by the verb. The author distinguishes between *idiomatically combining expressions* (ICE) and *idiomatic phrases* (IdP). The key diagnostic is compositionality [14]: ICEs are decomposable and maintain a closer link to their literal meaning (e.g., *spill the beans* "divulge the secret"), whereas IdPs are opaque and non-decomposable (e.g., *kick the bucket* "die"). ICEs can undergo syntactic operations such as quantification, topicalization, ellipsis, or anaphora, and may be replaced by synonyms. IdPs, by contrast, resist such manipulations. From a theoretical standpoint, Dąbrowska aligns with approaches where the syntactic realization of predicates and the functions assumed by their arguments correlate with their semantic representations, i.e., the syntax-semantics interface [15].

For Spanish, Islas & Solís [8] analyze over one hundred idioms in Mexican Spanish denoting emotional predicates, classifying them on both syntactic and semantic grounds. Like Dąbrowska, they sought to identify recurrent syntactic-semantic patterns. They propose six main structures, including: (a) verb + resulting state of the experiencer (*estar hecho un mar de lágrimas* "be in floods of tears"); (b) verb + out of control (*estar loco por alguien* "be crazy about someone"); (c) verb + to the point of exhaustion (*estar hasta la coronilla* "be fed up"); (d) X carries away the experiencer (*llevarse la tristeza a alguien* "carry away someone's sadness"); (e) break + body part of the experiencer (*partirle el alma a alguien* "break someone's heart"); and (f) have + NP (*tener un nudo en el estómago* "have a knot in one's stomach"). They also highlight semantic resources such as metaphor, temperature, or spatial imagery.

2.3 Treatment of Psychological Predicates in Automatic Analysis

Most studies addressing PPs in computational contexts have been conducted within NLP, usually as a subtopic of broader work on emotions. This is closely related to tasks such as automatic sentiment and emotion detection [16]. For this purpose, various emotion lexicons have been developed, mainly for English. ANEW (Affective Norms for English Words) [17], based on the three dimensions of valence, arousal, and dominance, was later adapted to Spanish [18].

Several emotion recognition tools have been developed specifically for Spanish. The *Spanish Emotion Lexicon* [19] contains 2,036 words based on Ekman's categories. *EmoFinder* [20] is a web-based resource covering 16,375 words with assigned affective properties. It offers two functions: searching for words that match specific affective criteria, or retrieving the properties of a given word set. Its output is customizable, available online or exportable, and its architecture is easily scalable to integrate new normative databases for Spanish.

3   Methodology

For the selection of units to be analyzed, we consulted the *Diccionario de habla de los argentinos* [21], the *Diccionario de la lengua de la Argentina* [22], and the *Diccionario etimológico del lunfardo* [23]. In addition, we included the expressions analyzed by Islas and Soliz [8] that are not attested in these dictionaries but are nonetheless known to the researcher. In (4), a subset of the analyzed units is presented.

4. *afanarle/robarle el corazón; agarrar la moto; caerle la ficha; cagarse en las patas; calarle hondo; hacerse la cabeza/la película; hincharle/romperle las bolas/pelotas; llegarle al alma/corazón; llevar el apunte; no entrarle en la cabeza; pasar un calor (bárbaro); sacar de quicio; sacarse el sombrero; saltarle la térmica; subírsele la mostaza; tener cola de paja; tener sangre de pato; tocar el cielo con las manos; tomarlo con soda; verle las patas a la sota; volverle el alma al cuerpo.*

Building on the proposals reviewed, this study establishes a classification of VIPP that considers: (i) the syntactic function of the experiencer; (ii) the arguments projected by the argument structure; (iii) the roles of goal and stimulus involved; (iv) the requirement of the pronominal *se*, and (v) other specific particularities of the idioms. This analysis lays the groundwork for the creation of computational resources.

For the computational work, we made use of NooJ's electronic dictionaries for Spanish, *Diccionario RAE.dic* and *Diccionario EF RAE.dic*, developed in previous work [24]. The resource contains a lemma list of 72,997 entries and is linked to inflectional grammars. This dictionary is further associated with the context-dependent grammars developed for the present study. At this stage, only inflected VIPP were considered, leaving for future research those including non-finite verb forms, with the exception of compound tenses (*haber* + participle, as in *le había roto las pelotas durante mucho tiempo* 'he had been a pain in the neck for a long time'). The following section describes the development of the grammars for VIPP.

VIPPs with Subject-Experiencer. For the recognition of the argument structure of subject-experiencer VIPP, two grammars were developed: one for cases where the argument structure contains a single argument (*Juan se ahoga en un vaso de agua* 'Juan makes a mountain out of a molehill'), and another for those requiring two arguments, with the second bearing the thematic role of *theme* (*Juan le da bola a la economía* 'Juan pays attention to the economy'). In addition, we distinguish idioms that require the pronominal *se*. Figure 1 presents the grammar structure for the argument structure of mono-argumental subject-experiencer VIPPs. A figure caption is always placed below the illustration. Short captions are centered, while long ones are justified. The macro button chooses the correct format automatically.

In the structure that does not contain the pronominal *se*, the grammar begins with a bracket indicating the grammatical label to be assigned—in this case, LVPP. It is followed by the subject, which in turn contains an embedded grammar ':Sujeto'. This argument is highlighted as the variable 'Exp', indicated in brackets ($Exp). After the subject, the verb appears, which must be in the indicative or subjunctive mood, since psychological predicates reject the imperative. The verb must also agree in person and number with the head of the noun phrase functioning as the subject; this is ensured by means of a

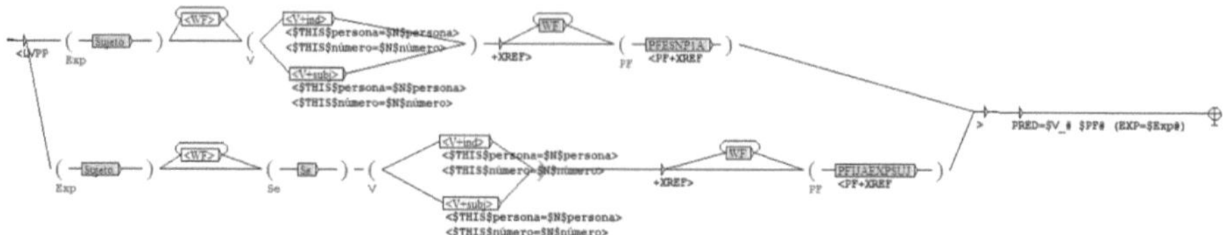

Fig. 1. Grammar for the argument structure of mono-argumental subject-experiencer VIPPs.

context-dependent grammar using the commands ' < \$THIS\$persona = \$N\$persona >' and ' < \$THIS\$número = \$N\$número >'.

The fixed part, ':PFESNP1A' (*Parte Fija Experimentante Sujeto No Pronominal 1 Argumento*), is the final component of the construction. Finally, thematic-role labels are declared: the predicate is defined as the variable \$V plus \$PF ('PRED = \$V_# \$PF'), and the subject is assigned the label of experiencer ('EXP = \$Exp').

The embedded grammar ':Sujeto' is structured as shown in Fig. 2.

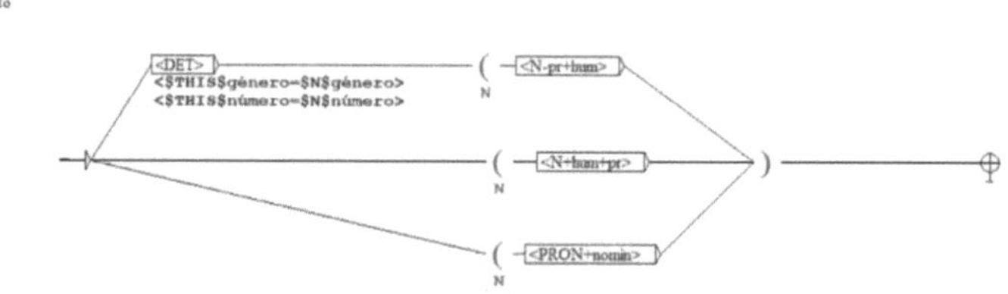

Fig. 2. Embedded grammar ':Sujeto'.

The variable '\$N', which agrees with the verb of the idiom (\$V), can be a human proper noun (' < N + hum + pr >', e.g., *Juan*), a common human noun (' < N-pr + hum >', e.g., *hombre* 'man'), or a nominative pronoun (' < PRON + nomin >'). In the case of ' < N-pr + hum >', a determiner (' < DET >') is assigned, which must agree in gender and number.

Finally, in the fixed part, the remainder of the idioms is included, with their corresponding restrictions (see Fig. 3).

Each fixed part incorporates its respective restriction, linking it exclusively to its verb. For example, *el cielo con las manos* ('the sky with one's hands') will only form a VIPP with the verb *tocar* ('to touch'), which is specified through the command ' < \$V =:tocar,V >'.

In addition to the elements mentioned above, since these expressions can be discontinuous [11], the node:*WF* indicates the possibility of an adverbial phrase appearing between the verb and the fixed part, as shown in Fig. 4.

In order to identify the structure 'V + PF' as a single unit, the commands ' + XREF >' and ' < PF + REF' are used. In this way, it is possible to analyze sentences such as *Él pierde los estribos* ('He loses his temper') (Fig. 5), as well as *Él pierde siempre los estribos* ('He always loses his temper') (Fig. 6).

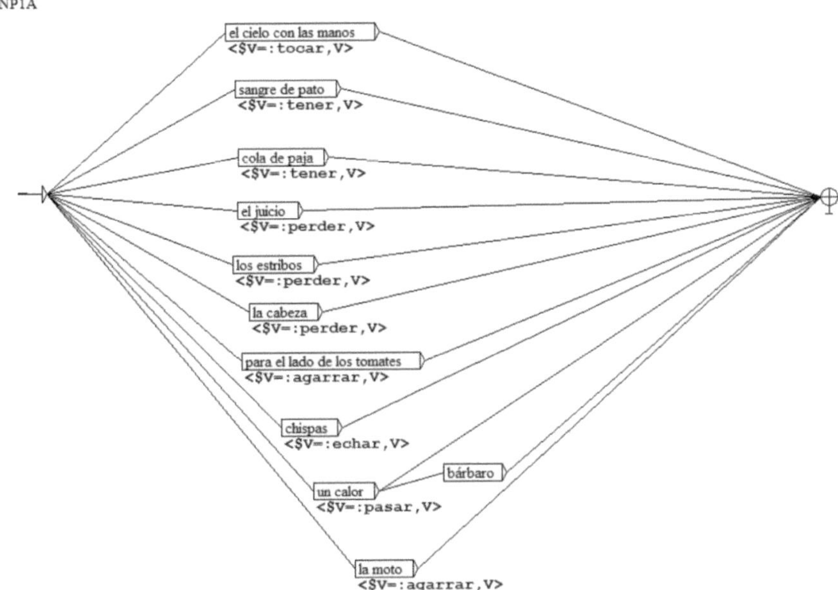

Fig. 3. Embedded grammar:PFESNP1A.

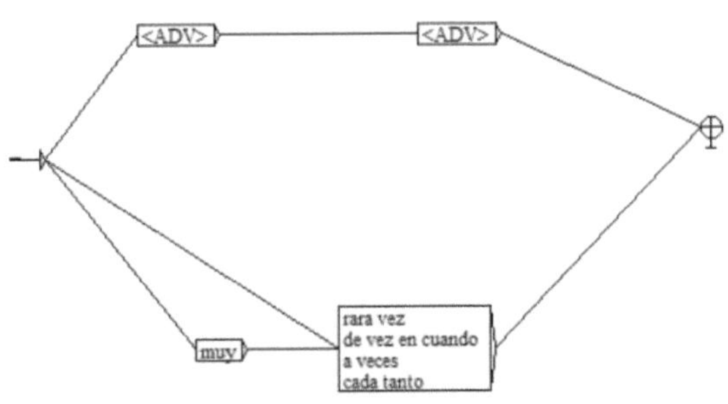

Fig. 4. Embedded grammar:WF.

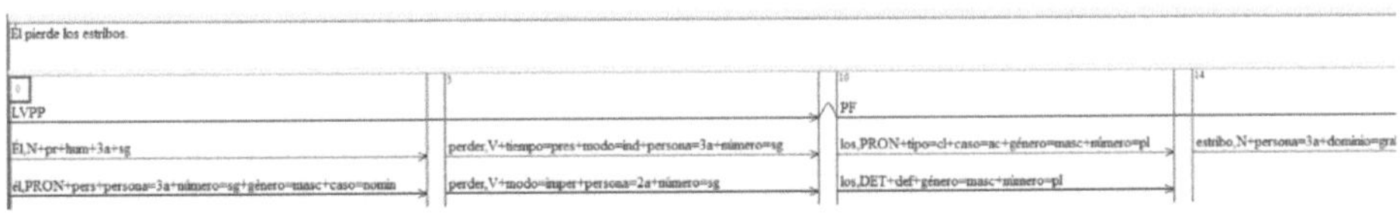

Él pierde los estribos.

0	5	10	14
LVPP		PF	
Él,N+pr+hum+3a+sg	perder,V+tiempo=pres+modo=ind+persona=3a+número=sg	los,PRON+tipo=cl+caso=ac+género=masc+número=pl	estribo,N+persona=3a+dominio=gra
él,PRON+pers+persona=3a+número=sg+género=masc+caso=nomin	perder,V+modo=imper+persona=2a+número=sg	los,DET+def+género=masc+número=pl	

Fig. 5. Syntactic analysis of the sentence: 'Él pierde los estribos' (He loses the stirrups. ['He loses his temper']).

As can be seen in Fig. 6, a jump indicates the link between the different parts of the idiom. In addition, NooJ allows for semantic analysis, which is illustrated in Fig. 7.

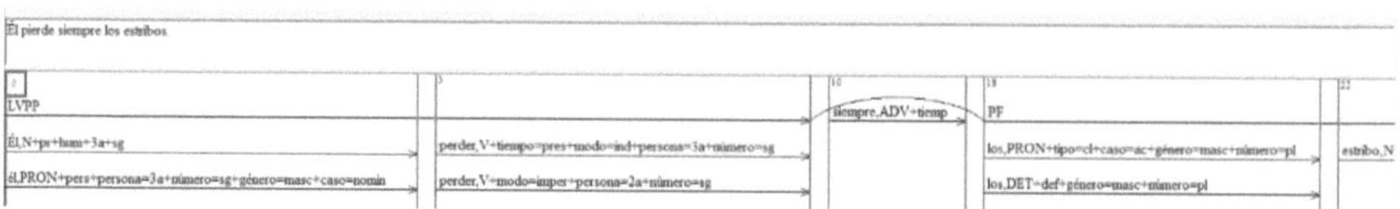

Fig. 6. Syntactic analysis of the sentence: 'Él siempre pierde los estribos' (He—always— loses the stirrups. ['He loses his temper, ever']).

Él pierde los estribos/<LVPP+XREF><PF+XREF>PRED=perder los estribos (EXP=ÉI)
Él pierde siempre los estribos/<LVPP+XREF><PF+XREF>PRED=perder los estribos (EXP=ÉI)

Fig. 7. Semantic analysis of the sentences 'Él pierde los estribos' and 'Él siempre pierde los estribos'.

This is achieved by specifying, after the final state, that the predicate ('PRED') consists of the verb variable plus the fixed part, and that the variable 'Estim' is marked as the stimulus ('ESTIM'): $PRED = \$V\_\# \$PF\# (EXP = \$Exp\#)$. The same procedure is applied for the recognition of the semantic roles *goal* and *stimulus*.

Object-Experiencer VIPP. The grammar for the recognition of object-experiencer VIPP includes two main nodes: one for experiencers expressed as a noun phrase headed by a noun, and another for those expressed by an accusative clitic, as shown in Fig. 8

Fig. 8. Grammar for the recognition of object-experiencer VIPP.

In this case, the subject is assigned the general semantic label of *stimulus* ('Estim'), thereby identifying the entity that provokes the emotion.

Dative-Object Experiencer VIPP. This class presents four variants:

(i) cases where the subject functions as the stimulus, with an alternation in which the experiencer may also appear as part of the head of the noun phrase in the fixed part, introduced by a prepositional phrase (21);

(ii) cases where the head requires only the experiencer, since the subject is already contained in the fixed part (22);

(iii) cases where the subject functions as the stimulus, but, unlike the experiencer, cannot be part of the fixed expression (23), and

(iv) middle voice constructions with the pronoun *se* (19).

(18) a. María le robó el corazón (a Juan). 'María stole Juan's heart.' b. María se robó el corazón de Juan. 'María stole Juan's heart away.'

(19) Juan me rompe los huevos. 'Juan really annoys me / Juan gets on my nerves.'

(20) Me cayó la ficha. 'I finally got it / The penny dropped.'

(21) Se le subió la mostaza. 'He/She got really angry / He/She lost their temper.'

For reasons of space, only variant (i) will be described; its structure is shown in Fig. 9.

Fig. 9. The results obtained are presented above.

4   Results

The developed grammar was tested on a corpus of examples extracted from CORPES XXI, using searches based on combinations of the words that make up the idioms. The procedure allowed for discontinuity between the verb and the words of the fixed part, ranging from 1 to 5 intervening words. The corpus was drawn from texts from Argentina and Uruguay.

The results were exported to a NooJ *.texte* file, yielding a corpus of 48,711 words. The algorithm identified 236 VIPP together with their experiencers, corresponding to cases where the verb of the idiom was conjugated. For subject-experiencer expressions, only those with an explicit subject argument were considered. Fig. 10 shows a fragment of the NooJ output.

Seq.
me da bola/<LV+PP<EXP>+XREF><PF+XREF>>PRED=dar+bola (EXP= , EXP=me)
no me da bola/<LV+PP+Neg<EXP>+XREF><PF+XREF>>PRED=dar+bola (EXP= , EXP=me)
te da bola/<LV+PP<EXP>+XREF><PF+XREF>>PRED=dar+bola (EXP= , EXP=te)
me da bolilla/<LV+PP<EXP>+XREF><PF+XREF>>PRED=dar+bolilla (EXP= , EXP=me)
te da pelota/<LV+PP<EXP>+XREF><PF+XREF>>PRED=dar+pelota (EXP= , EXP=te)
le daba pelota/<LV+PP<EXP>+XREF><PF+XREF>>PRED=dar+pelota (EXP= , EXP=le)
se le cruza por la cabeza/<LV+PP<EXP>+XREF><PF+XREF>>PRED=cruzar+por la cabeza (EXP= , EXP=le)
se nos cruza por la cabeza/<LV+PP<EXP>+XREF><PF+XREF>>PRED=cruzar+por la cabeza (EXP= , EXP=nos)
se me cruza por la cabeza/<LV+PP<EXP>+XREF><PF+XREF>>PRED=cruzar+por la cabeza (EXP= , EXP=me)
se te cruza por la cabeza/<LV+PP<EXP>+XREF><PF+XREF>>PRED=cruzar+por la cabeza (EXP= , EXP=te)
se le cruza por la cabeza/<LV+PP<EXP>+XREF><PF+XREF>>PRED=cruzar+por la cabeza (EXP= , EXP=le)
no se le cruza por la cabeza/<LV+PP+Neg<EXP>+XREF><PF+XREF>>PRED=cruzar+por la cabeza (EXP= , EXP=le)
se le pasa por la cabeza/<LV+PP<EXP>+XREF><PF+XREF>>PRED=pasar+por la cabeza (EXP= , EXP=le)
se me pasa por la cabeza/<LV+PP<EXP>+XREF><PF+XREF>>PRED=pasar+por la cabeza (EXP= , EXP=me)
se les pasa por la cabeza/<LV+PP<EXP>+XREF><PF+XREF>>PRED=pasar+por la cabeza (EXP= , EXP=les)
se me prendió la lamparita/<LV+PP<EXP>+XREF><PF+XREF>>PRED=prender+la lamparita (EXP= , EXP=me)
Se le encogia el corazón/<LV+PP<EXP>+XREF><PF+XREF>>PRED=encoger+el corazón (EXP= , EXP=le)
yo estoy en la gloria/<LV+PP+XREF><XREF>>PRED=estar+en la gloria (EXP=yo , EXP=)
Él estaba loco por ella/<LV+PP+XREF><XREF>>PRED=estar+loco por ella (EXP=Él , EXP=)
Se me rompe el corazón/<LV+PP<EXP>+XREF><PF+XREF>>PRED=romper+el corazón (EXP= , EXP=me)
me pone los pelos de punta/<LV+PP<EXP>+XREF><PF+XREF>>PRED=poner+los pelos de punta (EXP= , EXP=me)
se le ponen los pelos de punta/<LV+PP<EXP>+XREF><PF+XREF>>PRED=poner+los pelos de punta (EXP= , EXP=le)
se me pusieron los pelos de punta/<LV+PP<EXP>+XREF><PF+XREF>>PRED=poner+los pelos de punta (EXP= , EXP=me)
se le pongan los pelos de punta/<LV+PP<EXP>+XREF><PF+XREF>>PRED=poner+los pelos de punta (EXP= , EXP=le)
se me puso la piel de gallina/<LV+PP<EXP>+XREF><PF+XREF>>PRED=poner+la piel de gallina (EXP= , EXP=me)
Se te pone la piel de gallina/<LV+PP<EXP>+XREF><PF+XREF>>PRED=poner+la piel de gallina (EXP= , EXP=te)
se me pone la piel de gallina/<LV+PP<EXP>+XREF><PF+XREF>>PRED=poner+la piel de gallina (EXP= , EXP=me)
Yo tenía un nudo en la garganta/<LV+PP+XREF><XREF>>PRED=tener+un nudo en la garganta (EXP=Yo , EXP=)
Nos volvió el alma al cuerpo/<LV+PP<EXP>+XREF><PF+XREF>>PRED=volver+el alma al cuerpo (EXP= , EXP=Nos)
le volvia el alma al cuerpo/<LV+PP<EXP>+XREF><PF+XREF>>PRED=volver+el alma al cuerpo (EXP= , EXP=le)
les volvió el alma al cuerpo/<LV+PP<EXP>+XREF><PF+XREF>>PRED=volver+el alma al cuerpo (EXP= , EXP=les)
Me volvió el alma al cuerpo/<LV+PP<EXP>+XREF><PF+XREF>>PRED=volver+el alma al cuerpo (EXP= , EXP=Me)
me volvió el alma al cuerpo/<LV+PP<EXP>+XREF><PF+XREF>>PRED=volver+el alma al cuerpo (EXP= , EXP=me)
le volvia el alma al cuerpo/<LV+PP<EXP>+XREF><PF+XREF>>PRED=volver+el alma al cuerpo (EXP= , EXP=le)
me volvió el alma al cuerpo/<LV+PP<EXP>+XREF><PF+XREF>>PRED=volver+el alma al cuerpo (EXP= , EXP=me)
me volvió el alma al cuerpo/<LV+PP<EXP>+XREF><PF+XREF>>PRED=volver+el alma al cuerpo (EXP= , EXP=me)
Me volvió el alma al cuerpo/<LV+PP<EXP>+XREF><PF+XREF>>PRED=volver+el alma al cuerpo (EXP= , EXP=Me)
Me volvió el alma al cuerpo/<LV+PP<EXP>+XREF><PF+XREF>>PRED=volver+el alma al cuerpo (EXP= , EXP=Me)
me chupa un huevo/<LV+PP<EXP>+XREF><PF+XREF>>PRED=chupar+un huevo (EXP= , EXP=me)

Fig. 10. NooJ output for automatic VIPP recognition.

In the review, 17 false positives were observed in the case of *dar bola*, and the results were therefore as follows (Table 1).

Table 1. Results obtained.

Total VIPP	236	Recall	100
TP	236	Precision	93.2806324
FP	17	F1-Score	96.5235174

The following section presents the final considerations of this study.

5   Final Considerations

This study presents a formal proposal for the automatic analysis of verbal idiomatic psychological predicates (VIPP) in River Plate Spanish. To this end, we reviewed previous approaches to the phenomenon and proposed a classification based on Belletti and Rizzi [1]. The results suggest that object-experiencer cases (e.g., *sacar de quicio* 'to drive someone crazy') are not particularly productive, whereas subject-experiencer and dative-object experiencer cases appear in similar numbers. For the latter, some idioms contained a light verb such as *dar* ('to give') or *hacer* ('to make'), combined with a fixed part headed by a non-eventive noun (*bola* 'ball', *cabeza* 'head'). This pattern is consistent with Di Tullio's [25] observation that, in such cases, the syntactic construction itself motivates the psychological interpretation.

As for the algorithm, the grammar developed here offers several advantages over similar proposals, such as that of Machonis [26]. Unlike in this author's proposal, idioms do not need to be listed in the dictionary, thus avoiding the expansion of the lexicon. Moreover, a syntax layer preceding sentence structure appears to be adequate.

However, some ambiguities were observed in expressions such as *dar bola* ('to pay attention' / 'to give the ball'). Since the system allowed for any word group ($<$WF $>$) between the verb and the fixed part, ungrammatical or unintended readings could arise. Introducing constraints here might be useful, although, given that the primary aim of the computational tool was to validate the linguistic description, the current approach can be considered satisfactory.

References

1. Belletti, A., Rizzi, L.: Psych-verbs and o-theory. Nat. Lang. Linguist. Theory **6**, 291–352 (1988)
2. Landau, I.: Psych-adjectives and semantic selection. Linguist. Rev. **16**, 333–358 (1999)
3. Marín, R.: Los Predicados Psicológicos. Visor Libros, Madrid (2015)
4. Amzali, A., Mourchid, M., Mouloudi, A., Mbarki, S.: Arabic psychological verb recognition through NooJ transformational grammars. Commun. Comput. Inf. Sci. **1389**, 74–84 (2021)
5. Rozwadowska, B.: Psychological verbs and psychological adjectives. In: Everaert, M., van Riemsdijk, H. (eds.) The Wiley Blackwell Companion to Syntax, 2nd edn., pp. 24–55. Wiley, Hoboken (2017)
6. Lombardo, V., Osella, B.: A rule-based model of emotion appraisal for narratives. In: Jorge, A., Campos, R., Jatowt, A., Aizawa, A. (eds.) Proceedings of the First AI4 Narratives Workshop (2020)
7. Dąbrowska, A.: A Syntactic Study of Idioms. Cambridge Scholar Publishing, Newcastle (2018)
8. Islas, M., Soliz, M.: ¿Se sacó de onda o se lo llevó la tostada? Locuciones de emoción en el español de México. Estud. Lingüíst. Apl. **64**, 83–111 (2016)
9. Corpas, G.: Manual de Fraseología Española. Gredos, Madrid (1996)
10. Penadés, I.: Gramática y semántica de las locuciones. Servicio de Publicaciones de la Universidad de Alcalá, Alcalá de Henares (2012)
11. Silberztein, M.: Formalizing Natural Languages: The NooJ Approach. ISTE-Wiley, London (2016)
12. Espejel, M.: Diacronía de los verbos psicológicos parasintéticos: estructura argumental y estructura eventiva. Anuari de Filologia. Estudis de Lingüística **13**, 257–279 (2023)

13. Melis, C.: Los causativos emocionales del español. Un estudio aspectual. Anuario de Letras: Lingüística y Filología **VII**, 105–156 (2019)
14. Corver, N., Temmerman, T., Leufkens, S., van Cranenbroeck, J., Hladnik, M.: Idioms: Phasehood and compositionality. Utrecht University (2017)
15. Croft, W.: Verbs: Aspect and Argument Structure. Oxford University Press, Oxford (2012)
16. Barnes, J.: Sentiment and emotions classification in low resource settings. In: Proceedings of the 13th Workshop on Computational Approaches to Subjectivity, Sentiment, & Social Media Analysis, pp. 290–304 (2023)
17. Bradley, M., Lang, P.: Affective norms for English words (ANEW): instruction manual and affective ratings. Technical Report, Center for Research in Psychophysiology, University of Florida, Gainesville (n.d.)
18. Redondo, J., Fraga, I., Padrón, I., Comesaña, M.: The Spanish adaptation of ANEW (Affective Norms for English Words). Behav. Res. Methods **39**, 600–605 (2007)
19. Rangel, I., Sidorov, G., Guerra, S.: Creación y evaluación de un diccionario marcado con emociones y ponderado para el español. Onomázein **29**, 31–46 (2014)
20. Fraga, I., Guasch, M., Haro, J., Padrón, I., Ferrer, P.: EmoFinder: the meeting point for Spanish emotional words. Behav. Res. Methods **50**(1), 84–93 (2018)
21. Academia Argentina de Letras: Diccionario del habla de los argentinos. Emecé, Buenos Aires (2017)
22. Academia Argentina de Letras: Diccionario de la lengua de los argentinos. Colihue, Buenos Aires (2019)
23. Conde, O.: Diccionario etimológico del lunfardo. Taurus, Buenos Aires (2019)
24. Koza, W., Suy, C.: Automatic detection and generation of argument structures within the medical domain. Commun. Comput. Inf. Sci. **1520**, 198–207 (2021)
25. Di Tullio, Á.: Variantes sintéticas y analíticas de los predicados psicológicos. In: Marín, R. (ed.) Los predicados psicológicos, pp. 185–210. Visor Libros, Madrid (2015)
26. Machonis, P.: Sorting NooJ out to take multiword expressions into account. In: Vučković, K., Bekavac, B., Silberztein, M. (eds.) Selected Papers from the NooJ 2011 International Conference, pp. 152–165. Cambridge Scholars Publishing, Newcastle (2012)

Syntactic and Semantic Resources

Updating the Belarusian NooJ Module: Integrating New Lexical and Grammatical Resources

Yuras Hetsevich[1]([✉]), Valery Varanovich[2], and Mikita Suprunchuk[2]

[1] SoftClub-Software Development Center LLC, Niezaliezhnasci Ave. 168/1, Minsk, Belarus
gamrat.vvv@gmail.com
[2] Belarusian State University, Nezavisimosti Ave. 4, Minsk, Belarus

Abstract. This paper describes several key updates and improvements to the NooJ Belarusian module, which was developed in 2012. These recent additions focus on enhancing NooJ's ability to process and analyze the Belarusian language. The following specific actions were taken. Corpus Variation: We have prepared a new representative mini corpus containing 1.5 million word forms. This extensive text collection provides a basis for linguistic and extralinguistic analysis. Dictionary and grammar updates: we have revised the Belarusian basic dictionary, with particular attention to the tagging of gerunds. We have developed new syntactic rules to improve the automatic tagging of homonyms and to enable consistent processing of phraseological units. Vocabulary expansion: we have added approximately 300 new words to the dictionary, and we have supplemented grammatical information for existing entries. These updates aim to increase the accuracy and efficiency of NooJ in the linguistic analysis of Belarusian.

Keywords: Belarusian Language · Corpus Manager · Homonymy · NLP · NooJ · Syntactic Grammar · Text Corpus

1 Creation of the Belarusian NooJ Module

The Belarusian module for NooJ was created during the period 2011–2012. The authors of the first version were Yuras Hetsevich and Sviatlana Hetsevich from the Speech Recognition and Synthesis Laboratory of the United Institute of Informatics Problems, National Academy of Sciences of Belarus (Minsk), and Yauheniya Yakubovich from the Universitat Autònoma de Barcelona (Bellaterra, Spain). It consisted of the following parts: texts, dictionary, grammars, samples, and projects.

Over the following years, several planned tasks were accomplished, for example:

- translation of quantitative expressions from English into Belarusian (2015);
- improvement of the grammar database of the National corpus of Belarusian (2015) [6];
- attempt to add IPA transcription to the Belarusian Module (2016);
- development of a desktop Java NooJ version (2018);

© The Author(s), under exclusive license to Springer Nature Switzerland AG 2026
D. Petković et al. (Eds.): NooJ 2025, CCIS 2832, pp. 53–64, 2026.
https://doi.org/10.1007/978-3-032-17103-0_5

- construction of syntactic grammars to identify frozen expressions (idioms, set expressions, terms, etc.) (2019);
- development of grammars for sentiment analysis of the vitamin D intake (2020);
- creation of a legal-domain and medical-domain corpora (2021–2022) [9, 14];
- development of syntactic grammars for automatic text segmentation to improve synthetic speech (2022);
- creation of a Belarusian – Russian – English dictionary of legal terms (2022) [14];
- identification of words missing from the Belarusian NooJ module (2024, 2025);
- development of syntactic grammars for grammatical and lexical disambiguation (2023, 2024, 2025) [10].

As is often the case, practical use revealed errors, inaccuracies, and opportunities for optimization, while our requirements and expectations for the NooJ program evolved. For changes and additions from previous years, see our earlier articles [10, 14]. The current changes from the year 2025 are presented below.

2 Enlargement of the Basic Dictionary with Paradigms

We selected words for the compilation of relevant thematic dictionaries (legal, medical, social) and commonly used words that should be added to the general dictionary (cf. previous research in [9, 14]). While creating and processing a corpus of legal texts, as well as corpora of the medical and social domains, we discovered a number of unknown lexemes, both common words and terms. They include:

- words and word forms that are not included in the general dictionary general_be.nod: *зносіны* 'relations', *нармаванне* 'standardization';
- English words and symbols: *http, documents*;
- Roman numerals: *IV, XI*;
- simple mistakes and typographical errors: *мажех (межах), сваечасова (своечасова)*;
- words with an apostrophe (the apostrophe divides words into parts): *адаб'ецца* '[it will] reflect', *аб'яднаць* 'unite'.

A special service was developed to automatically assign the appropriate word class (i.e., the paradigm), and it is available on the website corpus.by. The Word Paradigm Generator [12] produces several annotation variants in NooJ format [8] (Fig. 1).

It should be noted that six numerals were included in this list, because Belarusian spelling was officially changed in 2010, and these numerals should be written differently: *дзевяты > дзявяты* 'ninth', *семнаццаць > сямнаццаць* 'seventeen', etc.

A total of 213 words was added to the dictionary, including 106 nouns, 56 adjectives, 6 numerals, 16 verbs, 16 participles, 6 adverbs, 1 pronoun, 1 preposition, and 5 abbreviations, for example:

- каштоўны,UNKNOWN E – > каштоўны,ADJECTIVE + FLX = ААЗІСНЫ
- квартал,UNKNOWN E – > квартал,NOUN + FLX = ВУГАЛ
- ліхтар,UNKNOWN E – > ліхтар,NOUN + FLX = СЕЛЬГАСІНВЕНТАР
- лічыць,UNKNOWN E – > лічыць,VERB + FLX = АБАЗНАЧЫЦЬ

```
інтэрнэт,NOUN+FLX=IЎРЫТ
інтэрнэт/Accusative+Common+Inanimate+Masculine
інтэрнэт/Common+Inanimate+Masculine+Nominative
інтэрнэта/Common+Genitive+Inanimate+Masculine
інтэрнэтам/Common+Inanimate+Instrumental+Masculine
інтэрнэту/Common+Dative+Inanimate+Masculine
інтэрнэце/Common+Inanimate+Masculine+Prepositional;
IЎРЫТ =
<B1>т/Accusative+Common+Inanimate+Masculine
+ <B1>т/Common+Inanimate+Masculine+Nominative
+ <B1>та/Common+Genitive+Inanimate+Masculine
+ <B1>там/Common+Inanimate+Instrumental+Masculine
+ <B1>ту/Common+Dative+Inanimate+Masculine
+ <B1>це/Common+Inanimate+Masculine+Prepositional;
```

Fig. 1. The New Paradigm Generation.

- маёмасць,UNKNOWN E – > маёмасць,NOUN + FLX = АБРОЦЬ
- навучэнец,UNKNOWN E – > навучэнец,NOUN + FLX = АДЗІНЕЦ

Afterward, all previously unknown words were annotated with the appropriate features (cf. the corrected annotation of the token *прастора (prastora)* 'wide space' in Fig. 2).

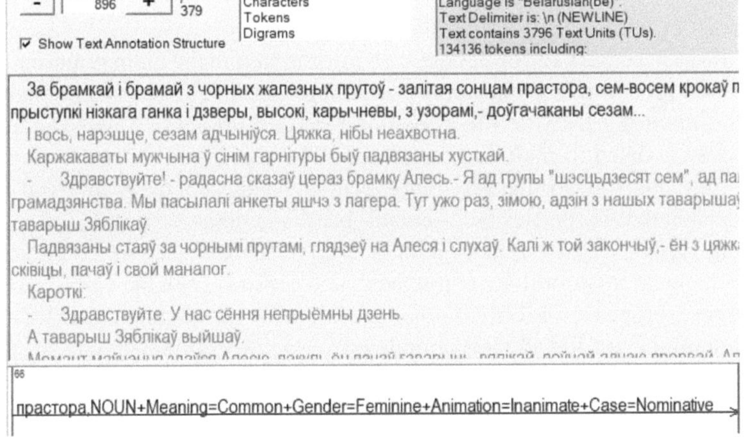

Fig. 2. Annotation of the previously unknown word *прастора (prastora)* 'wide space'.

3   Improving the Grammar Module

3.1   The Problem of Gerunds

We also found that the gerund (the invariable form of the verb, also called the "adverbial participle") was processed incorrectly in Belarusian texts. This form is typically considered part of the verb paradigm in Slavic linguistics. However, during the creation of the NooJ inflectional dictionary, the gerund was treated as a separate part of speech, and this decision led to processing issues.

The first problem was that some finite verb forms were defined as the gerund (Fig. 3), and the second issue was that some gerunds were not annotated properly.

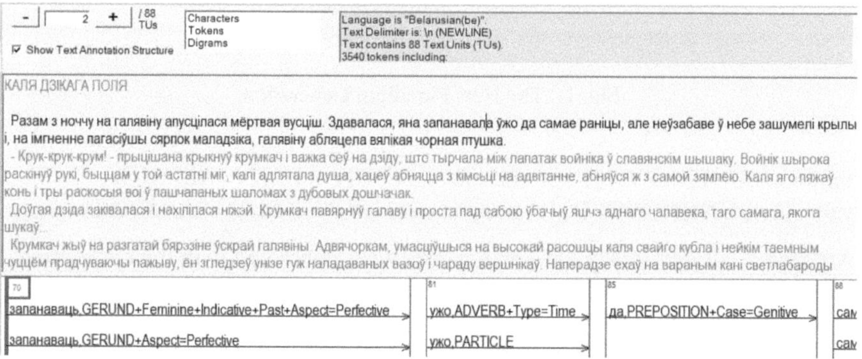

Fig. 3. Incorrect annotation of the word *запанавала* '[it] began to dominate'.

Thus, it was necessary to correct the verb information in the main grammatical tagset spreadsheet and recompile the general_be.dic dictionary. The following changes were made to the main tag list: the file containing gerund tags was deleted, and the verb tagset file was updated to include gerund tags. The algorithm for converting the main dictionary files into NooJ format was then executed. As a result, the main NooJ dictionary files were generated: properties.def, general_be.dic, general_be.nof. Consequently, the verb tagging system was fixed and rebuilt, and all forms were separated into three main groups: unchangeable (infinitive), conjugated, and gerund. Then the verb form tags were updated in the _properties.def file, with a gerund value automatically added. In Fig. 4, the new general_be.nof file shows the updated verbal inflectional classes.

```
АБАНІРАВАЦЬ =
<B5>аваў/Conjugated+Indicative+Masculine+Past+Perfective+Singular
+ <B5>аваўшы/Gerund+Perfective
+ <B5>авалі/Conjugated+Past+Perfective+Plural
+ <B5>авала/Conjugated+Feminine+Indicative+Past+Perfective+Singular
+ <B5>авала/Conjugated+Neuter+Past+Perfective+Singular
+ <B5>аваць/Perfective+infinitive
+ <B5>уе/3+Conjugated+Future+Indicative+Perfective+Singular
+ <B5>уем/1+Conjugated+Future+Indicative+Perfective+Plural
+ <B5>уеце/2+Conjugated+Future+Indicative+Perfective+Plural
+ <B5>уеш/2+Conjugated+Future+Indicative+Perfective+Singular
+ <B5>уй/Conjugated+Imperative+Perfective
+ <B5>уйце/Conjugated+Imperative+Perfective
+ <B5>ую/1+Conjugated+Future+Indicative+Perfective+Singular
+ <B5>уюць/3+Conjugated+Future+Indicative+Perfective+Plural;
```

Fig. 4. Updated general_be.nof.

The gerund problem has been resolved. "Запанавала" ('to dominate', past tense) is now correctly defined as a verb form with the tense marked as Past (Fig. 5).

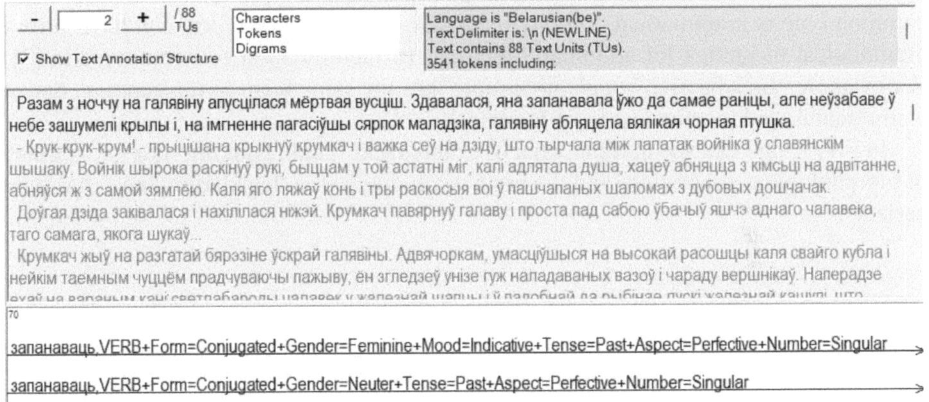

Fig. 5. The gerund problem is solved.

As a result of these updates, the verb tagging system was reorganized, and the verbal forms were distributed into three main categories: invariable (infinitive), conjugated, and gerund. The following changes were made to the main tag list: the file with adverbial tags was deleted, and the verb tag file was updated. Subsequently, an algorithm was launched to convert the main dictionary files into NooJ format (Fig. 6).

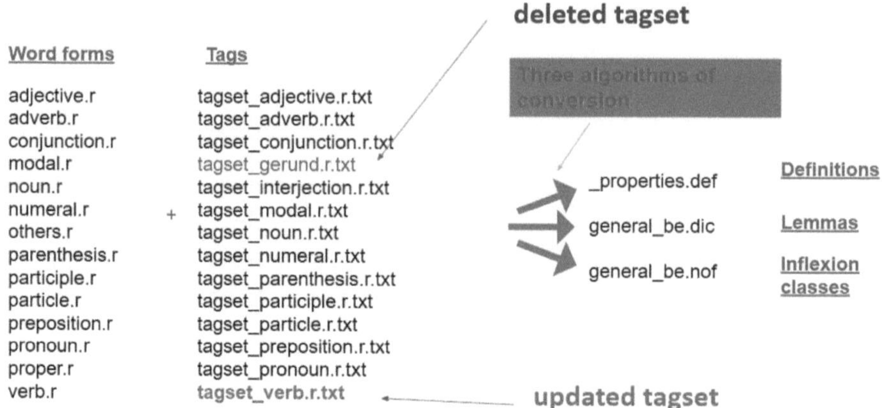

Fig. 6. Correction of tagsets.

3.2 The Problem of Homonymy

Automatic analysis of Belarusian texts frequently encounters the problem of homonymy (for more about homonymy as a general phenomenon, see [5, 7, 13, 15]). The most common type is grammatical homonymy, where the same word form can have several grammatical meanings (cf. automatic methods of identification of homonyms in [3]). For example, the adjective *простай* 'simple' has the same form in the genitive, dative, instrumental, and locative cases (if feminine).

In Fig. 7, one can see that the adjective *банкаўскі* 'bank, banking' has two variants of morphological annotation, and the noun *заканадаўства* 'legislation, laws' has three variants.

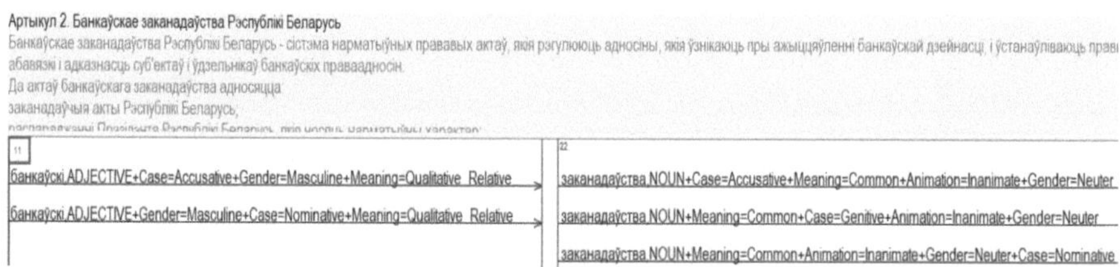

Fig. 7. The problem of homonymy.

As our previous studies have shown, ambiguity in Belarusian texts can reach up to 50% [10]. For the past ten years, the Belarusian NooJ Team has been investigating methods to reduce this ambiguity. Many types of homonymy in Belarusian can be resolved using the NooJ linguistic processor; therefore, we have developed a number of rules to reduce ambiguity. A grammar was considered effective and included in the final set if its coverage exceeded 50%. For the current update of the Belarusian NooJ module, 50 algorithms (rules) were selected and added to the previous version to assist with text tagging (for Ukrainian, cf. [7]). These can be grouped as follows:

– grammars for resolving homonymy (about 30),
– grammars for identifying phraseological units (7),
– grammars for identifying numerical expressions (13),
– grammars for identifying descriptive predicates (2).

To determine whether *калі* is an adverb, a conjunction, or a verb, we examine the left context (Fig. 8). If it is followed by a conjunction or punctuation mark, it is classified as an adverb. If it appears in phrases such as *да таго часу* 'until then' or *з тых пор* 'since then' followed by a comma, it is classified as a conjunction.

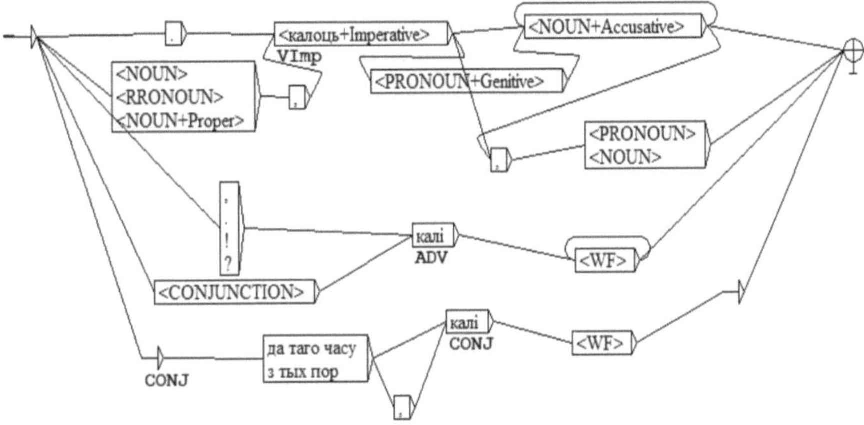

Fig. 8. Disambiguation grammar.

The next grammar allows one to find descriptive predicates in sentences with explicator verbs: *праводзіць (праводзіцца)* 'to conduct', *адбывацца (адбыцца)* 'to happen' (Fig. 9). The basic grammar for defining numerical expressions consists of 39 subgraphs and allows one to highlight numbers in texts in any form and combination (Fig. 10).

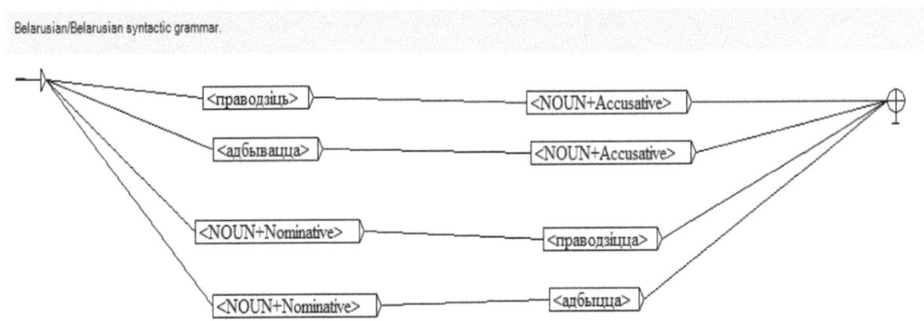

Fig. 9. Grammar for identifying descriptive predicates.

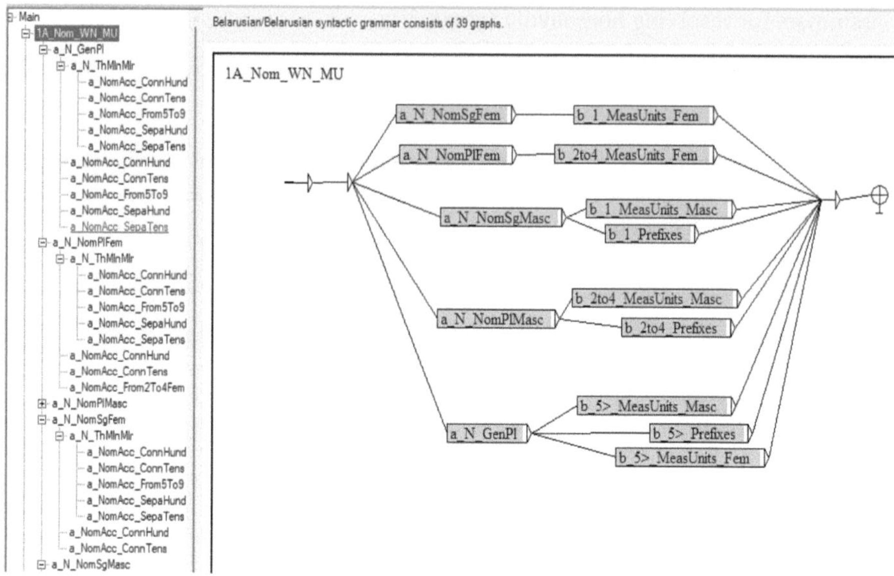

Fig. 10. Numerical grammar.

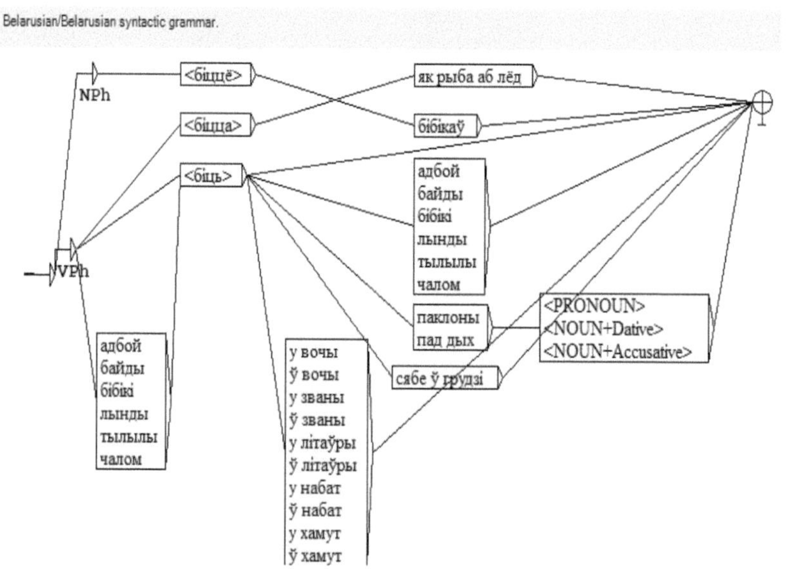

Fig. 11. Phraseological grammar.

Phraseological units are a distinctive component of the language system. According to NooJ terminology, they are treated as Atomic Linguistic Units [8, p. 69], meaning they are considered a unified structure (a single sign), rather than a combination of individual words. The list of Belarusian idioms was compiled on the basis of the "Etymological Dictionary of Phraseological Units" by Ivan Liepieshaw [4]. Twelve syntactic grammars were created to handle 1,000 variable phraseological units. Idioms are characterized by their imagery, stability, and idiomaticity, i. e. they possess a unified meaning. They present significant challenges for syntactic and semantic text annotation, as well as for machine translation. To address these challenges, rules for automatically detecting and annotating idioms have been developed (see Fig. 11 for an example). Such grammars allow the identification of stable expressions in texts containing the word *біць* 'beat; hit; strike'.

3.3 New Texts for the Sample Corpus

To improve the Belarusian NooJ module, it was decided to expand the standard mini-corpus supplied in the kit. The Belarusian module for NooJ was prepared in 2012. At that time, it included a sample fragment from the Belarusian historical novel "Ears of Rye under Thy Sickle" (1965) by Uladzimir Karatkevich, consisting of about 40,000 words. Subsequently, a corpus of Belarusian texts totaling 1 million words was prepared over several years. Unfortunately, it was never completed and remained largely unknown to researchers. Given this, work began on collecting a new corpus. The decision was made to continue expanding the standard collection of texts (see [6]) and increase its size to 1.5 million words. The newly developed corpus includes fiction, historical, medical, scientific, social, journalistic, and legal texts.

Improvements to the corpus included the following:

– correction or removal of texts containing errors;
– elimination of texts in old orthography;
– addition of new texts;
– modification of the corpus composition.

Special attention was paid to the representativeness and balance of the corpus. Requirements for corpus composition vary among researchers. For example, Professor Douglas Biber pointed out: "A corpus with this design might contain roughly 90% conversation and 3% letters and notes, with the remaining 7% divided among registers such as press reportage, popular magazines, academic prose, fiction, lectures, news broadcasts, and unpublished writing" [1, 247]. Apparently, this recommendation has never been fully realized.

Therefore, the organization of the British National Corpus was examined. As its creators stated, "There is a broad consensus among the participants in the project and among corpus linguists that a general-purpose corpus of the English language would ideally contain a high proportion of spoken language in relation to written texts. However, it is significantly more expensive to record and transcribe natural speech than to acquire written text in computer-readable form. Consequently, the spoken component of the BNC constitutes approximately 10 per cent (10 million words) of the total and the written component 90 per cent (90 million words)" [2]. The structure of the written part is presented in Fig. 12.

	texts	w-units	%	s-units	%
Imaginative	476	16496420	18.75	1352150	27.10
Informative: natural & pure science	146	3821902	4.34	183384	3.67
Informative: applied science	370	7174152	8.15	356662	7.15
Informative: social science	526	14025537	15.94	698218	13.99
Informative: world affairs	483	17244534	19.60	798503	16.00
Informative: commerce & finance	295	7341163	8.34	382374	7.66
Informative: arts	261	6574857	7.47	321140	6.43
Informative: belief & thought	146	3037533	3.45	151283	3.03
Informative: leisure	438	12237834	13.91	744490	14.92

Fig. 12. Design of the written component of the British National Corpus.

Several other corpora (Belarusian, Russian, American, Serbian) were also studied, and the Czech corpus was selected as the preliminary model. "The SYN2020 corpus is a synchronous representative and reference corpus of contemporary written Czech, containing 100 million text words, including punctuation (tokens)" [11]. Its creators paid particular attention to text selection to ensure balance and representativeness. As noted in its documentation, "SYN2020 contains a large spectrum of different types of texts in order to cover the vast majority of varieties the corpus aims to represent. This corresponds to Biber's notion of representativeness in terms of texts as products. The corpus is designed as representative, but not claimed to be balanced. Starting with SYN2015, the concept of writing was narrowed down only to the language printed and publicly published. Thus, SYN2020 does not contain, for example, inscriptions in public space, private letters, posters, or other ephemerals, and it also does not include texts published only on the Internet (for these there are special corpora of Internet Czech, e. g. NET or ONLINE" [11] (Fig. 13).

Text group	Czech corpus, %	Belarusian corpus, %
FIC: fiction	33,33	44,3
NFC: non-fiction	33,33	22,9
NMG: newspapers and magazines	33,33	32,8

Fig. 13. Comparison of the Czech and Belarusian corpora.

4 Conclusion

The latest updates to the Belarusian NooJ module have led to significant improvements in both lexical and grammatical processing capabilities. The expansion of the dictionary, the inclusion of newly identified words and forms, and the systematic correction of tagging—particularly for gerunds—have addressed key issues in morphological annotation. The introduction of new disambiguation rules and specialized grammars for homonymy, phraseological units, and numerical expressions has significantly increased the module's accuracy in automatic text analysis. The development and balancing of a new representative corpus further strengthen the reliability of linguistic research and NLP applications for Belarusian. Immediate future work will focus on updating the properties.def file to reflect all relevant dictionary categories, implementing accent and phonetic transcription data, developing structures for phonetic inflections, and continuing to refine and expand the corpus to ensure comprehensive language coverage and robust performance of the Belarusian NooJ module.

References

1. Biber, D.: Representativeness in corpus design. Literary Linguist. Comput. **8**(4), 243–257 (1993)
2. BNC User Reference Guide, http://www.natcorp.ox.ac.uk/docs/URG/BNCdes.html, Accessed 01 Sep 2025
3. Hetsevich, Y.S., Zianouka, Y.S., Latyshevich, D.I., Bakunovich, A.A., Drahun, A.Y., Kazlova, M.A.: A model of homographs automatic identification for the Belarusian language. Informatics **20**(4), 87–100 (2023). (In Belarusian: Гецэвіч Ю.С., Зяноўка Я.С., Латышэвіч Д.І., Бакуновіч А.А., Драгун А.Я., Казлова М.А. Мадэль аўтаматызаванай ідэнтыфікацыі амографаў для беларускай мовы. Інфарматыка.) https://doi.org/10.37661/1816-0301-2023-20-4-87-100
4. Liepieshaw, I.J.: Etymalagichny slownik fraziealagizmaw. BielEn, Minsk (1993). (In Belarusian: Лепешаў, І. Я. Этымалагічны слоўнік фразеалагізмаў. Мінск: БелЭн.)
5. Navigli, R., Velardi, P.: Structural semantic interconnections: a knowledge-based approach to word sense disambiguation. IEEE Trans. Pattern Anal. Mach. Intell. **27**(7), 1075–1086 (2005)
6. Reentovich, I., et al.: The first one-million corpus for the Belarusian NooJ module. In: Okrut, T., Hetsevich, Y., Silberztein, M., Stanislavenka, H. (eds.) Automatic Processing of Natural-language Electronic Texts with NooJ. NooJ 2015, Communications in Computer and Information Science, vol. 607, pp. 3–15. Springer, Cham (2016)
7. Saint-Joanis, O.: Disambiguation grammars for the Ukrainian module. In: Bartulović, A., Mijić, L., Silberztein, M. (eds.) Formalizing Natural Languages: Applications to Natural Language Processing and Digital Humanities. NooJ 2023, Communications in Computer and Information Science, vol. 1816, pp. 102–113. Springer, Cham (2024)
8. Silberztein, M.: Formalizing Natural Languages: the NooJ Approach. Wiley, Hoboken NJ, USA (2016)
9. Suprunchuk, M., et al.: Creation of parallel medical and social domains corpora for the machine translation and speech synthesis systems. In: González, M., Reyes, S.S., Rodrigo, A., Silberztein, M. (eds.) Formalizing Natural Languages: Applications to Natural Language Processing and Digital Humanities. NooJ 2022, Communications in Computer and Information Science, vol. 1758, pp. 139–150. Springer, Cham (2023)
10. Suprunchuk, M., Varanovich, V., Zianouka, Y., Hetsevich, Y.: Automatic grammatical disambiguation in Belarusian and Russian legal domain. In: Silberztein, M. (ed.) Formalizing Natural Languages: Applications to Natural Language Processing and Digital Humanities. NooJ 2024, Communications in Computer and Information Science, vol. 2443, pp. 79–90. Springer, Cham (2025)
11. SYN2020 Corpus, https://wiki.korpus.cz/doku.php/en:cnk:syn2020, Accessed 01 Sep 2025
12. The Word Paradigm Generator, https://corpus.by/wordparadigmgenerator, Accessed 19 Aug 2025

13. Van den Beukel, S., Aroyo, L.: Homonym detection for humor recognition in short text. In: Proceedings of the 9th Workshop on Computational Approaches to Subjectivity, Sentiment and Social Media Analysis, Brussels, 31 October 2018, pp. 286–291 (2018)
14. Varanovich, V., Suprunchuk, M., Zianouka, Y., Prakapenka, T., Dolgova, A., Hetsevich, Y.: Creation of a legal domain corpus for the Belarusian module in NooJ: texts, dictionaries, grammars. In: González, M., Reyes, S.S., Rodrigo, A., Silberztein, M. (eds.) Formalizing Natural Languages: Applications to Natural Language Processing and Digital Humanities. NooJ 2022, Communications in Computer and Information Science, vol. 1758, pp. 151–162. Springer, Cham (2023)
15. Agirre, E., Edmonds, P. (eds.): Word Sense Disambiguation: Algorithms and Applications. Springer, Dordrecht (2007). https://doi.org/10.1007/978-1-4020-4809-8

Describing French Simple Declarative Sentences

Max Silberztein[(✉)] [iD]

Université Marie & Louis Pasteur, 25000 Besançon, France
`max.silberztein@univ-fcomte.fr`

Abstract. This paper aims to describe French simple declarative sentences by constructing a set of formalized linguistic resources in the form of electronic dictionaries and local syntactic grammars. The sentence grammar describes sentences with structures N_0 V, N_0 V (àldelε) N_1 and N_0 V (àldelε) N_1 (àldelε) N_2. It consists of local grammars that describe predeterminers and determiners, simple noun phrases, and sentences. We tested these resources by applying them to the text *La femme de trente ans* [Balzac, 1881], provided as the default corpus in the NooJ software.

Keywords: NooJ · Syntax · Automatic Parsing · Lexicon-Grammar · Local Grammars

1 Introduction

1.1 The Project

The NooJ linguistic platform has been designed to help linguists formalize natural languages—more specifically, linguistic phenomena that must be dealt with when analyzing written texts at various levels: orthography; inflectional, derivational, and agglutinative morphology; local, structural, and transformational syntax; lexical and predicative semantics (see Silberztein [10]). While there are now many formalized linguistic resources available for over 30 languages in the NooJ formalism,[1] there have been few attempts to combine the description of phenomena of these various levels into a single module capable of describing complete sentences.

This paper describes an exercise that aims to describe sentences with the structures N_0 V (no complement), N_0 V (àldelε) N_1 (one complement) and N_0 V (àldelε) N_1 (àldelε) N_2 (two complements) from the French novel *La femme de trente ans*, [Balzac 1881], excluding sentences that contain punctuation, as punctuation markers are usually used to insert intra-sentential embedded clauses, parenthetical citations, and discourse markers (e.g., pause fillers in dialogues).

---

[1] See https://nooj.univ-fcomte.fr/resources.html.

D. Petković et al. (Eds.): NooJ 2025, CCIS 2832, pp. 65–76, 2026.
https://doi.org/10.1007/978-3-032-17103-0_6

1.2 Project Boundaries

On the one hand, my goal is to construct a grammar that covers as many sentences as possible from the novel *La femme de trente ans*. On the other hand, I do not wish the grammar to be limited to describing only the sentences that occur in this novel; therefore, I will generalize the grammar as much as possible.

- In the novel, very few sentences contain a single verb conjugated in an indicative tense, e.g., *Elle regardait la Bièvre* [She was looking at the Bièvre river]. My goal is to develop a grammar that also recognizes sentences that contain a verb conjugated in a compound tense, e.g., *Elle avait volé comme un oiseau.* [She had flown like a bird], a modal verb, e.g., *Ces Anglais veulent toujours se singulariser* [These English people always want to stand out], an aspectual verb, e.g., *Le général commença même à concevoir de sinistres pressentiments* [The general even began to have sinister premonitions.], and/or a negation, e.g., *Je ne me crois pas coupable* [I don't believe myself guilty].
- Very few noun phrases in the novel are constituted by a single determiner and a noun, e.g., *son costume* [his suit]. My goal is to develop a grammar that also recognizes noun phrases constituted by a pronoun (e.g., *elle* [she]), or noun phrases introduced by a predeterminer (e.g., *comme un léger nuage* [like a light cloud]). These noun phrases start with a nominal determiner (e.g., *mes gouttes de laudanum* [my laudanum drops], an adjectival determiner (e.g., *quelques lettres de recommandation* [a few letters of recommendation]), or an adverbial determiner (e.g., *beaucoup de ces anomalies curieuses* [many such curious anomalies]). I have also developed the following resources:
- a dictionary that contains the proper names that occur in the novel (e.g., *Hélène, la Loire*) as well as a local grammar that recognizes sequences of proper names with their titles, e.g., *Mme de Listomère, M. le baron de Mauny.*
- a dictionary that contains adverbial insertions limited to simple or multiword lexical units, e.g., *nécessairement* [necessarily] or *à la longue* [eventually], listed in the DELAC dictionary and therefore recognizable by the NooJ syntactic symbol <ADV>. However, the grammar is not designed to recognize free circumstantial complements such as *avec une politesse froide* [with cold politeness] or *où elle est partie* [where she went].
- a grammar to describe the coordination of determiners, e.g., *deux ou trois* [two or three], the coordination of noun modifiers, e.g., *une brillante et curieuse population* [a brilliant and curious population], and the coordination of nouns, e.g., *un geste et un sourire* [a gesture and a smile]. However, the grammar does not describe coordination between verbs or sentences, e.g., *Cette belle et suave contrée endort les douleurs et réveille les passions* [This beautiful and gentle land soothes pain and awakens passions].
- a grammar that describes nominal complements introduced by the main prepositions *à* and *de*, as they are usually used to introduce essential verb and noun complements, e.g., *une jeune personne à garder* [a young person to look after], *Les colonels de chaque régiment* [The colonels of each regiment]. The grammar does not describe noun phrases that have locative complements, e.g., *ce front penché vers la terre* [this forehead bowed toward the earth], nor adverbial complements, e.g., *quelques lettres*

de recommandation pour ses amies [a few letters of recommendation for her friends], nor relative complements, e.g., *la seule personne dont les services lui plaisaient* [the only person whose services she liked].

1.3 Available Resources

The module I have developed uses the following resources that were already available in the NooJ French module:[2]

- updated versions of the French electronic dictionaries "dm" (Trouilleux [11]), "DELAS" (Courtois [3]), and "DELAC" (Silberztein [9]);
- the "Prénoms" dictionary, which lists first names;
- the "Toponymes" dictionary, which contains toponyms;
- the "Adjectifs de nationalité" dictionary, which contains adjectives denoting people (ethnic groups, inhabitants, and nationalities) extracted from the DEM dictionary (Dubois and Dubois-Charlier [4]);
- the "Elisions" and "Contractions" dictionaries, which contain respectively elided and contracted French words;
- 39 local grammars used to disambiguate most grammatical words.

2 Developing the Module

The goal is to parse and syntactically annotate as many sentences as possible in the corpus that follow the structures: N_0 V, N_0 V (à|de|ε) N_1, and N_0 V (à|de|ε) N_1 (à|de|ε) N_2, with potential adverb insertions. Leclère [8] describes the classification of the French verbs in the lexicon-grammar[3] according to their syntactic properties; from that classification, I have filtered out verbs that have sentential complements (tables 1 to 19), verbs with frozen or semi-frozen constituents (tables Cx), and verbs that require complements introduced by a preposition other than *à* or *de* (e.g., table 35ST).

N_0 V	31H, 31R
N_0 V N_1	32NM, 32CV, 32RA, 32A, 32H, 32PL, 32L, 32R2
N_0 V Prép N_1	34L0
N_0 V N_1 Prép N_2	36DT, 36R, 36S, 37M1, 37M1, 37M2, 37M3, 37M4, 37M5, 37M6

The NooJ grammar "Phrases declarative.nog", corresponding to this classification, is shown in Fig. 1. Note that this grammar recognizes sentences with transitive verbs (<V+N0VN1>, <V+N0VPrépN1>, and <V+N0VN1PrépN2>) that do not have any complement, as complements are considered optional.

The project consists of developing the grammars for **N_0, N_1, N_2,** and **V+x**.

---

[2] These resources are included by default in the NooJ French module and are being updated regularly.

[3] For a description of the lexicon-grammar of French verbs, see Boons, Guillet, Leclère [1], Boons, Guillet, Leclère [2], Guillet, Leclère [7], Gross, [5], Gross [6].

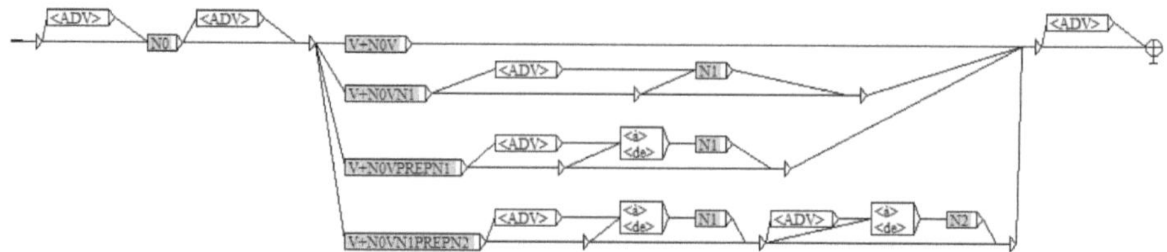

Fig. 1. Sentences with direct complements and indirect complements introduced by *à* or *de*.

2.1   Description of the Noun Phrase

In French, noun phrases are almost identical whether they function as subjects, direct or indirect objects, e.g., *Cette femme recommande cette femme à cette femme* [This lady recommends this lady to this lady]. However, some pronouns can only appear as subjects (e.g. *il* [he]), as direct complements (e.g. *le* [him]), or as indirect complements (e.g. *à elle* [to her]). The embedded graph **Pronom0** lists the pronouns that can occur in a subject position, e.g., *quelqu'un* [someone], *il* [he]. Figure 2 shows the graph that represents subject noun phrases:

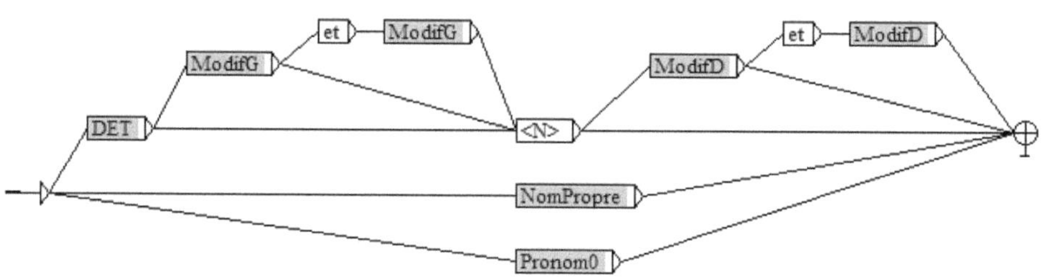

Fig. 2. Subject Noun Phrases.

NomPropre recognizes proper names, e.g., *Mme d'Aiglemont, M. le baron de Mauny*. Nouns can be modified by left modifiers (**ModifG**) and right modifiers (**ModifD**); modifiers can be coordinated, e.g., *La belle et élégante femme du général* [the beautiful and elegant wife of the general].

The local grammars for N_1 and N_2 are identical, but replace the grammar **Pronom0** with **Pronom1** and **Pronom2**, respectively. Note that direct and indirect object complements that occur as clitics before the verb are described in the **Vx** grammar, e.g., *Je le lui donne* [I give it to her].

Figure 3 displays the grammar **Déterminant** [Determiner], which is composed of more than thirty graphs, including graphs for:

- predeterminers (**Pred**), e.g., *presque* [almost];
- numerical determiners (**Dnum**), e.g., *trente-trois* [thirty-three];
- definite determiners (**Ddef**), e.g., *cette* [this];
- indefinite determiners (**Dind**), e.g., *une* [a];

- partitive determiners (**Dpart**), e.g., *de la* [some];
- nominal determiners (**Dnom**), e.g., *un morceau de* [a piece of];
- adjectival determiners (**Dadj**), e.g., *les mêmes* [the same], and
- adverbial determiners (**Dadv**), e.g., *beaucoup de* [a lot of].

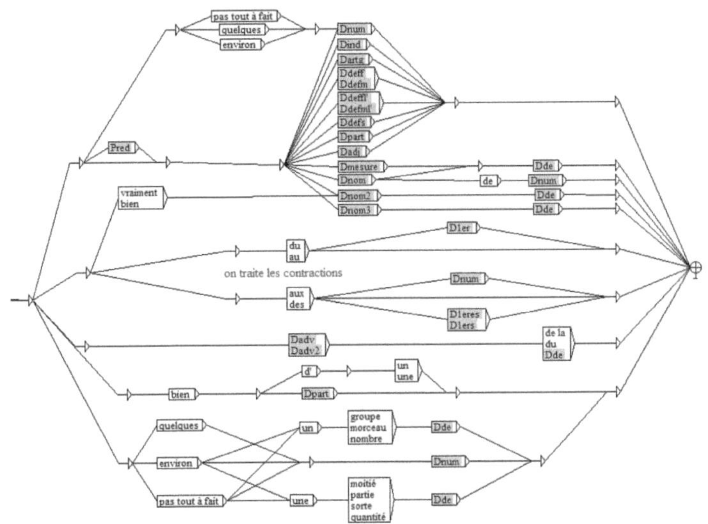

Fig. 3. Determiners

Figure 4 displays the grammar **Pred** [predeterminer].

The graph **Pred** primarily recognizes adverbs that are used as modifiers of determiners, e.g., *approximativement* [approximately]. Numerical determiners (described by the grammar **Dnum**) can also function as predeterminers, e.g., *à trois près tous sont venus* [all but three came]. The predeterminer *seul* [only] agrees with the determiner, e.g., *seules deux amies sont venues* [only two friends came].

Figure 5 displays the grammar **ModifD** [noun right modifier].

ModifD recognizes sequences such as (*la voiture*) *bleue de son amie* [her friend's blue car]. The syntactic symbol <A> represents adjectives, <N> represents nouns, and <ADV> represents adverbs.

Note that this grammar does not recognize noun complements introduced by other prepositions than *à* and *de*, e.g., (*la recommendation*) *pour ses amies* [a recommendation for her friends]: these complements correspond to circumstantial, rather than essential, complements of an implicit secondary verb that can be made explicit in a relative clause, e.g., (*la recommendation qui a été écrite*) *pour ses amies* [the recommendation that was written for her friends].

The grammar **ModifG** [Noun left modifier] is similar to **ModifD,** but without noun complements.

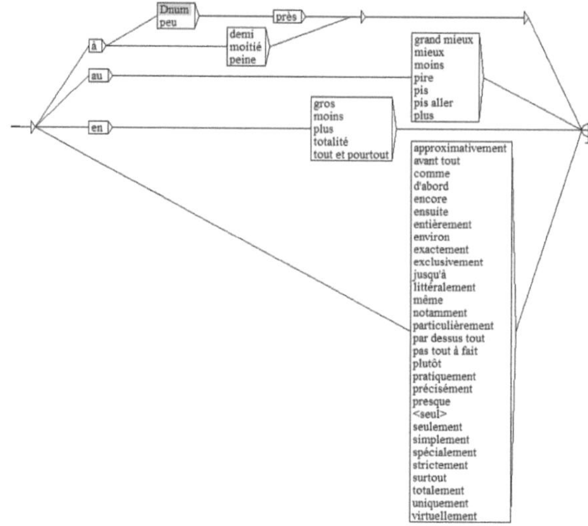

Fig. 4. Predeterminers

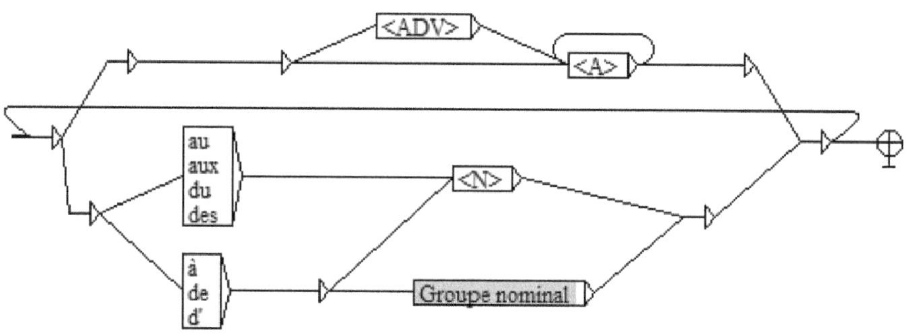

Fig. 5. Noun Right Modifier

2.2 Description of the Verb Group

In French, Verb Groups consist of a main verb conjugated in a simple or compound tense, with optional aspectual and modal verbs, negation, and clitics. Figure 6 displays a grammar for transitive verbs.

In Fig. 6, <V+a-G-INF-PP> represents all verbs conjugated with the auxiliary *avoir* (+a) that are neither in the Gerundive (-G), nor in the Infinitive form (-INF), nor in the Past Participle form (-PP), i.e., all verbs conjugated in a simple tense. Compound tenses in French are formed with a conjugated auxiliary verb, either *avoir* or *être*, followed by the verb in its past participle form (<V+PP>). Other auxiliary verbs, as defined in (Gross 1999) and listed in the lexicon-grammar table LG1, are associated with the main verb in its infinitive form (<V+INF>) and might be combined in a sequence, e.g.:

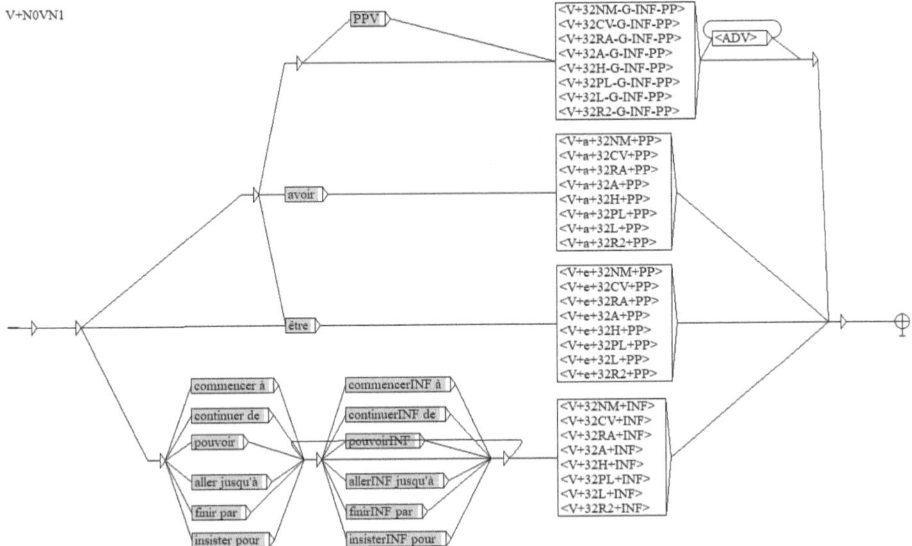

Fig. 6. Grammar of the transitive verb groups (structure $N_0 V\ N_1$)

Elle peut commencer à continuer d'insister pour finir par partir. [She may start to keep insisting and eventually leave.]

Figure 7 displays an extract of the LG1 lexicon-grammar table. The column "PREP" describes the preposition associated with each auxiliary verb. Some auxiliary verbs are transitive, e.g., *Le général alla prendre une carafe* [The General went to fetch a carafe], others are associated with the preposition *à*, e.g., *Les gens tardaient à servir le café* [People were slow to serve coffee], others are associated with the preposition *de*, e.g., *elle venait de jouer* [she had just finished playing], and others with the preposition *par*, e.g. *Le marquis d'Aiglemont finit par se persuader* [The Marquis d'Aiglemont finally convinced himself]. There are no occurrences of auxiliary verbs associated with the prepositions *jusqu'à* or *pour* in the corpus.

As an example, Fig. 8 displays the grammar that represents auxiliary verbs associated with the preposition *à*, conjugated in a simple or a compound tense.

Figure 9 displays the grammar that recognizes auxiliary verbs associated with the preposition *de*.

In French, direct and indirect complements can be pronominalized as Pre-Verbal Particles; the grammar **PPV** [Pre-Verbal Particles] is shown in Fig. 10.

The grammar **PPV** recognizes occurrences of one or two pronominalized complements. It also recognizes the negation particle *ne* and its elided variant *n'*; note that when this particle occurs, the following main or auxiliary verb may be followed by an adverb: *guère, jamais, pas, plus,* or *point*.[4] These adverbs are recognized thanks to the loop over the node <ADV> after the verb. Note that it does not recognize the pronominalized

---

[4] Verbs under negation may also be followed by a noun phrase introduced by a negative determiner, e.g., *aucun* [no] or by a negative pronoun, e.g., *personne* [nobody].

<By NooJ - [C:\Users\Max Silberztein\Documents\NooJ\fr\Lexical Analysis_Verbes LG1.dic]   —   □   ×

File   Edit   Lab   Project   Windows   Info   Max   TEXT   DICTIONARY   _ > ×

Dictionary contains 109 entries

Entrée	Aux	FLX	N0	PPV	PREP	Spec
achever	"avoir"	PESER	N0Hum		"de"	-
aller	"être"	ALLER	N0Hum			-
aller	"être"+"être"	ALLER	N0Hum		"jusqu'à"	-
aller	"avoir"+"êt...	ALLER	N0Hum		"pour"	-
aller	"être"+"être"	ALLER	-		"sans"	-
apprêter	-	AIMER	-	"se"	"à"	-
arrêter	"avoir"	AIMER	N0Hum		"de"	-
arrêter	"avoir"	AIMER	N0Hum		"de"	-
arrêter	"être"	AIMER	N0Hum	"se"	"de"	-
avancer	"être"	PLACER	N0Hum	"se"	"à"	-
aviser	-	AIMER	-		"de"	-
avoir	"avoir"	AVOIR	N0Hum		"à"	x
cesser	"avoir"	AIMER	N0Hum		"de"	-
choisir	"avoir"	FINIR	N0Hum		"entre"	-
commencer	"avoir"	PLACER	N0Hum		"à"	

0.3 sec   Cancel

Fig. 7. Dictionary for auxiliary verbs listed in Lexicon-Grammar LG1 table

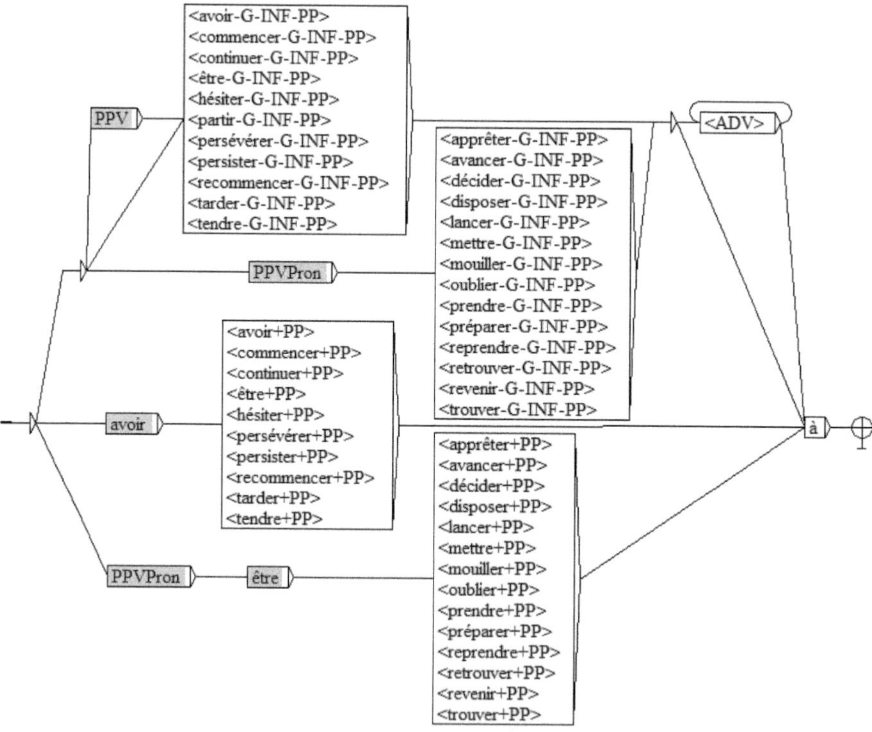

Fig. 8. Grammar "commencer à.nog" of auxiliary verbs associated with the preposition *à*

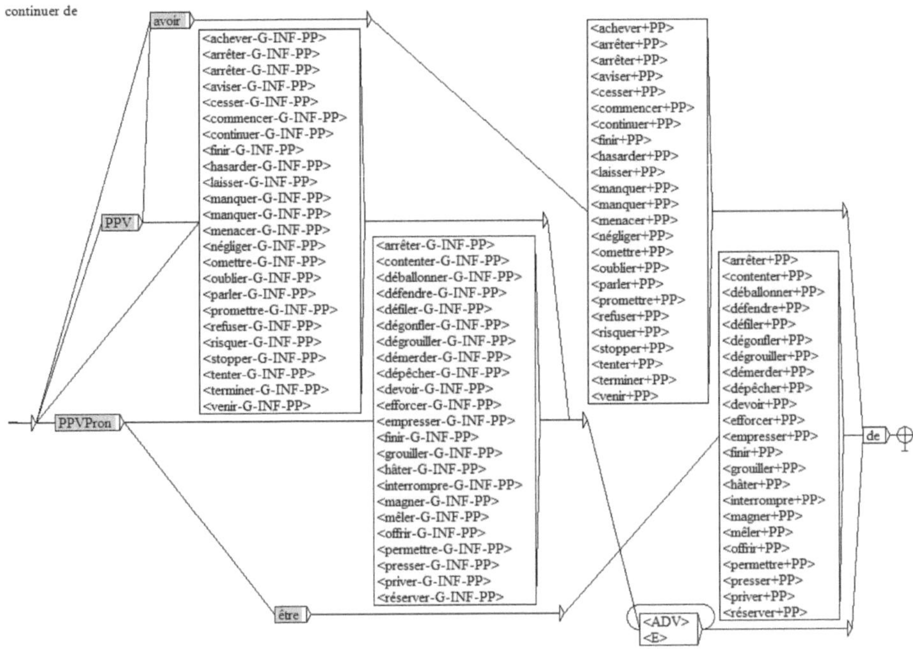

Fig. 9. Grammar "continuer de.nog" of auxiliary verbs associated with the preposition *de*

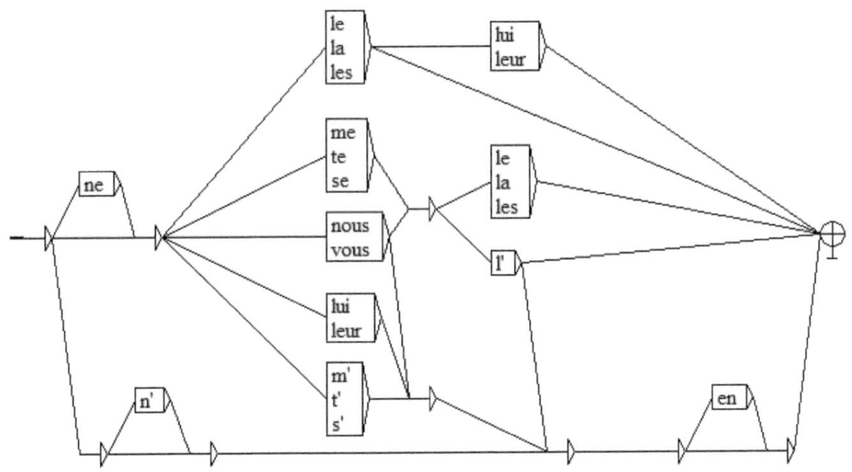

Fig. 10. Grammar of pre-verbal particles

locative complement '*y*', e.g., *il ne nous y verra plus* [he will no longer see us there], as recognizing circumstantial complements lies outside the stated goal of this project.

Some auxiliary verbs are pronominal, i.e., they must be preceded by one of the accusative pronouns *me, te, se, nous, vous, m', t',* or *s'*. The grammar **PPVPron** contains mandatory paths to these pronouns.

3   Applying the Module to the Corpus

The grammar represents sentences with 0, 1, or 2 complements, introduced either without a preposition or with the preposition *à* or *de*. Therefore, the grammar potentially recognizes $1 + 3 + 3 \times 3 = 13$ sentence structures. Applying the grammar to the novel *La femme de trente ans* [Balzac, 1881] produces 83 sentences.

- 28 sentences with no complement were correctly recognized. Note that most of them correspond to more than one lexical analysis, e.g.:

> *Le galop d'un cheval retentit soudain.*
> [The gallop of a horse suddenly resounds]
> [The gallop of one horse suddenly resounded]
> [The gallop of a horse suddenly resounds]
> [The gallop of one horse suddenly resounded]

In this sentence, the determiner *un* is lexically ambiguous (indefinite or numerical determiner), and the verbal form *retentit* is morphologically ambiguous (Present or Past tense).

- 53 sentences with one complement were recognized; however, 3 of these sentences actually contain two complements rather than one. These mistakes are caused by the fact that the prepositions *à* and *de* and the conjunction *et* can introduce both verb and noun complements:

(a) *Tout à coup un valet apporta une lettre à la marquise.* [Suddenly, a valet brought a letter to the marquise.]

In sentence (a), the preposition *à* introduces a complement of the verb *apporta* [brought] rather than a complement of the noun *letter* [letter].

(b) *La tante prit le papier et le lut.* [The aunt took the paper and read it.]

In sentence (b), the word "lut" is lexically ambiguous, as it can be a verbal form [to read] or a noun [a mixture]. Here, the sequence *le papier et le lut* has been incorrectly analyzed as a noun phrase object complement [the paper and the mixture] of the verb *prit* [took].

- 14 sentences were recognized with two complements. One sentence is actually syntactically ambiguous:

Je veux l'hospitalité de l'Arabie. [I want the hospitality of Arabia] or [I want the hospitality from Arabia].

Six sentences were incorrectly recognized because of the syntactic ambiguity of the prepositions *à* and *de* (which can introduce either a verb or a noun complement), e.g.,

La marquise avait les franches couleurs de la santé. [The marquise had the healthy complexion of good health].

This sentence contains only one complement: *les franches couleurs de la santé*, rather than two. Requiring the verbs *avoir* [have], *être* [be], *mépriser* [despise], and *vouloir* [want] to have only one complement would avoid these mistakes.

4 Conclusion

This project aims to write a syntactic grammar that recognizes all declarative sentences of the forms N_0 V, N_0 V (àldelɛ) N_1, and N_0 V (àldelɛ) N_1 (àldelɛ) N_2. Applying the grammar to the novel *La femme de trente ans* [Balzac, 1881] extracted 83 sentences, corresponding to 95 analyses, because NooJ analyzed several sentences as having both one complement and two complements. In other terms, these do not correspond to actual mistakes, but rather to "noise", which is typical of the NooJ approach.

For the development of a complete grammar for declarative sentences, the next step will therefore consist in adding precise syntactic properties from the lexicon-grammar, integrating the exact preposition for each verb into the grammar, describing precisely the preverbal pronouns accepted by each verb, and adding passive forms when they are valid.

We need to enhance the grammar of auxiliary verbs so that it recognizes sentences that contain multiple auxiliary verbs, e.g., *Elle aurait dû pouvoir finir par accepter.* [She should have been able to accept it eventually]. We also need to add other syntactic structures to the grammar to recognize sentences such as: *Cela est vrai* (N_0 V A) [this is true], *Il y a là quelqu'un* (il y *avoir* N_1) [There is somebody there], *C'est ce que je pensais* (c'est ce que Phrase) [This is what I thought], etc.

Recognizing circumstantial complements, such as locative complements (e.g., *dans la rue de Rivoli* [in the rue de Rivoli]) and temporal complements (e.g., *avant midi* [before noon]), will also allow us to treat these circumstantial complements in the same way as lexicalized adverbs.

References

1. Boons, J.-P., Guillet, A., Leclère, C.: La structure des phrases simples en français. I: Constructions intransitives. Droz Ed. Genève (1976)
2. Boons, J.-P., Guillet, A., Leclère, C. : La structure des phrases simples en français. II: Classes de constructions transitives. Université Paris 7, Paris (1976)
3. Courtois, B.L.: Dictionnaire électronique des mots simples. Lang. Fr. **87**, 11–22 (1990)
4. Dubois, J., Dubois-Charlier, F.: La combinatoire lexico-syntaxique dans le Dictionnaire électronique des mots. Les termes du domaine de la musique à titre d'illustration. Langages **179180**(3), 31–56 (2010)
5. Gross, M.: Méthodes en syntaxe. Hermann Éditions, Paris (1975)
6. Gross, M.: Sur la définition d'auxiliaire du verbe. Langages, 8–21 (1999)
7. Guillet, A., Leclère, C.: La structure des phrases simples en français: constructions transitives locatives. Droz Ed. Genève-Paris (1992)
8. Leclère, C.: Organisation du lexique-grammaire des verbes français. Langue française (87), 112–122 (1990)

9. Silberztein, M.L.: Dictionnaire électronique des mots composés. Lang. Fr. **87**, 71–83 (1990)
10. Silberztein, M.: Formalizing Natural Languages: the NooJ approach. Wiley Eds., Hoboken, NJ, USA (2016)
11. Trouilleux, F.: Le DM, a French dictionary for NooJ. Automatic Processing of Various Levels of Linguistic Phenomena: Selected Papers from the NooJ 2011 International Conference. Cambridge Scholars Publishing, pp. 16–28 (2012)

Disambiguation in Medieval Latin

Linda Mijić[1]([⊠]) [iD] and Anita Bartulović[2] [iD]

[1] Department of Classical Philology, University of Zadar, Zadar, Croatia
`lmijic@unizd.hr`
[2] Department of History, University of Zadar, Zadar, Croatia
`abartulo@unizd.hr`

Abstract. Ambiguity is an inherent feature of all natural languages and presents a particular challenge in Natural Language Processing (NLP), especially when working with historical corpora. This study addresses the identification and resolution of specific ambiguities in MedText, a historical corpus of medieval Latin last wills and testaments from the city of Zadar (13th–15th centuries). Within the corpus of approximately 500,000 tokens, around 5,800 ambiguities were identified. The analysis distinguishes three types of ambiguity: morphological, syntactic, and lexical. Special attention is given to morphosyntactic ambiguities, including overlaps between adjectives and nouns, verbs and pronouns, as well as prepositions and conjunctions. To reduce these ambiguities, the NooJ development environment was used to create context-sensitive syntactic grammars. These grammars disambiguate forms by analyzing their syntactic context, thereby improving the accuracy of morphological tagging and syntactic parsing. Although a substantial portion of ambiguous cases was resolved through syntactic grammars, some instances still require manual correction. Nevertheless, this work represents an advancement in the disambiguation of morphosyntactic structures in non-standardized medieval Latin, contributing to the field of historical language processing.

Keywords: Medieval Latin · Zadar Commune · Last Wills and Testaments · NooJ · Disambiguation

1 Introduction

Ambiguity is an inherent characteristic of every natural language and remains one of the oldest and most persistent issues in the field of Natural Language Processing (NLP). Accurate resolution of such ambiguities is crucial for reliable linguistic analysis, particularly when working with historical or specialized corpora, where standard language resources often prove insufficient. Efficient disambiguation is therefore essential for achieving correct results (see more in [1, 2]).

Compared to modern, widely studied languages, Latin is considered a low-resourced language within computational linguistics, with Medieval Latin representing a more complex variant due to its heterogeneity and diachronic variability. This study is based on the historical corpus MedText, which comprises medieval last wills and testaments written in Latin in the city of Zadar between the thirteenth and fifteenth centuries. Further

© The Author(s), under exclusive license to Springer Nature Switzerland AG 2026
D. Petković et al. (Eds.): NooJ 2025, CCIS 2832, pp. 77–88, 2026.
https://doi.org/10.1007/978-3-032-17103-0_7

details about the corpus and its formalization are provided in previous studies [3–7]. These last wills and testaments are not only valuable legal and cultural documents, but they also pose considerable linguistic obstacles. Medieval Latin exhibits notable deviations from Classical norms (see more in [8, 9]), reflecting the fluidity and variability of the language in use during that period. Such complexity results in a high frequency of both grammatical and lexical ambiguities, reinforcing the necessity for precise and adaptable disambiguation tools.

This paper examines the different types of ambiguity present in the MedText corpus and proposes a set of syntactic grammars designed to disambiguate a substantial number of these cases. It outlines the main difficulties encountered during the process and demonstrates how grammatical and lexical ambiguities can be identified and resolved with varying degrees of efficiency using the NooJ development environment [10, 11]. The proposed approach not only contributes to more reliable morphological annotation but also provides a stronger basis for subsequent linguistic analysis and interpretation.

During the lexical and morphological analysis of the MedText corpus, a considerable number of ambiguities were identified. The corpus comprises approximately 500,000 tokens, encompassing both inflected and uninflected forms. Among these, around 5,800 different ambiguity types were documented, reflecting the high degree of morphological overlap characteristic of (Medieval) Latin. Figure 1 shows the most frequent ambiguities found in the corpus.

```
NooJ - [Ambiguities]
 File   Edit   Lab   Project   Windows   Info

Select Analysis:
5830 different types of ambiguities
Freq  Annotations
1889  <qui,PRON+rel+FLX=QUI+N+s+n>  <qui,PRON+rel+FLX=QUI+Acc+s+n>  <qui,PRON+indef+FLX=QUI+N+
1100  <Iadera,N+f+top+oik+FLX=TERRA0+G+s>  <Iadera,N+f+top+oik+FLX=TERRA0+D+s>
1025  <condo,V+reg+FLX=LEGO+1+s+pr+subj+act>  <condo,V+reg+FLX=LEGO+1+s+futi+act>  <quondam,AI
970   <anima,N+f+c+FLX=FILIA+Nom+s>  <anima,N+f+c+FLX=FILIA+Voc+s>  <anima,N+f+c+FLX=FILIA+Ab+
887   <meus,PRON+poss+FLX=MEUS+Voc+p+n>  <meus,PRON+poss+FLX=MEUS+Acc+p+n>  <meus,PRON+poss+FI
856   <parvus,A+de+FLX=PARVUS+G+p+m+pp>  <parvus,A+de+FLX=PARVUS+G+p+n+pp>
846   <testamentum,N+n+c+FLX=VERBUM+Nom+s>  <testamentum,N+n+c+FLX=VERBUM+Acc+s>  <testamentum
790   <cum,PREP>  <cum,C+subord>
764   <suus,PRON+posref+FLX=CERTUS0+Voc+p+n>  <suus,PRON+posref+FLX=CERTUS0+Acc+p+n>  <suus,PF
754   <bona,N+n+c+FLX=ARMA+D+p>  <bona,N+n+c+FLX=ARMA+Ab+p>  <bonus,A+de+FLX=BONUS+D+p+m+pp>  <
753   <is,PRON+dem+FLX=IS+G+s+m>  <is,PRON+dem+FLX=IS+G+s+f>  <is,PRON+dem+FLX=IS+G+s+n>
701   <suus,PRON+posref+FLX=CERTUS0+Ab+p+n>  <suus,PRON+posref+FLX=CERTUS0+D+p+n>  <suus,PRON+
676   <qui,PRON+rel+FLX=QUI+Acc+s+f>  <qui,PRON+indef+FLX=QUI+Acc+s+f>  <quam,C+subord>
656   <meus,PRON+poss+FLX=MEUS+Voc+s+n>  <meus,PRON+poss+FLX=MEUS+Acc+s+n>  <meus,PRON+poss+FI
642   <omnis,A+FLX=UTILIS0+Nom+p+n>  <omnis,A+FLX=UTILIS0+Acc+p+n>  <omnis,A+FLX=UTILIS0+Voc+p
```

Fig. 1. The list of the most common ambiguities exported from the corpus in NooJ.

To better understand their distribution and linguistic nature, Sect. 2 offers an overview of ambiguity types in Latin. This is followed by proposed solutions for reducing the most frequent morphosyntactic ambiguities (divided into three categories) using the NooJ platform in Sect. 3, and an outline of results and future work in Sect. 4.

2   Overview of Ambiguity Types in Latin

The corpus reveals three types of linguistic ambiguity: morphological, syntactic, and lexical.

Morphological ambiguity is extensively attested in Latin, where a single form may correspond to several grammatical categories. For instance, the form *mala* can be interpreted as nominative, vocative, or ablative singular feminine; nominative, accusative, or vocative plural neuter of the adjective *malus* ('bad'); or as the noun *malum* ('apple').

Syntactic ambiguity arises when the grammatical function of a word or phrase within a sentence is unclear, i.e., whether a constituent should be analyzed as subject or object. In languages like Latin, where word order is relatively flexible, grammatical relations are not always signaled by position alone, which complicates syntactic interpretation.

Lexical ambiguity, by contrast, emerges when a single lexical item possesses multiple semantic values. An illustrative example is the Latin word *bonum*, which may denote an abstract moral quality ('good') or, alternatively, a concrete possession ('a good' or 'a piece of property').

At the current stage of analysis, the primary emphasis is placed on reducing grammatical or morphosyntactic ambiguities, which are especially frequent in highly inflected Latin. These ambiguities can be broadly classified into two categories: intra-category and inter-category ambiguities.

Intra-category Ambiguities.   They occur when identical forms are found within the same word class, typically due to overlapping inflectional endings. A classic example is illustrated in the declension of first- and second-declension adjectives, where a single surface form may simultaneously correspond to multiple case-number combinations. For example, the form *bona* may correspond to the nominative, vocative, or ablative singular feminine.

This phenomenon gives rise to considerable interpretative difficulties, demonstrated by the sentence bellow:

(1) *Magistra bona consilia bona dat.* "A good teacher gives good pieces of advice."

In this example, *bona* simultaneously functions as an attribute of *magistra* (nom. sg.) and of *consilia* (acc. pl.). Moreover, when substantivized, *bona* may assume various syntactic roles – subject, object, or vocative – thereby further increasing the degree of ambiguity. Such issues are not restricted to adjectives: Latin nominal declensions also display extensive morphological overlap. For instance, in all declensions, the dative plural form coincides with the ablative plural, while the nominative plural form is identical to the vocative plural.

Inter-category Ambiguities.   They appear when identical forms belong to different word classes. This type of ambiguity is particularly challenging because it impacts both syntactic parsing and semantic interpretation. For the purposes of this study, we further subdivided inter-category ambiguities into three subtypes: 1) ambiguities between two flective word classes, 2) ambiguities between an inflective and a flective word class, 3) ambiguities between two inflective word classes.

In the following sections, we present examples of representative ambiguity types identified in the corpus and propose a set of NooJ syntactic grammars designed to systematically identify and resolve such cases.

3   Ambiguities in the MedText Corpus

3.1   Ambiguities Between Two Flective Word Classes

Within this group, the most frequent ambiguities manifest between adjectives and nouns, with less frequent cases involving combinations such as numerals and nouns, nouns and verbs, and verbs and pronouns.

Adjective – Noun (e.g., bonus, bonum, Bona; clarus, Clara; parva, Parva).   A very high number of ambiguities in the corpus were recorded among the forms of the adjective *bonus* ('good'). Its neuter form *bonum* may also appear as a substantivized noun (*bonum* = 'a good'), or take on the role of proper names (a female name *Bona*, a masculine nickname *Bono*). Similarly, substantivized forms of the adjectives *clarus* and *parvus* can be female proper names (*Clara, Parua*)[1] in the feminine singular case forms or a masculine nickname (*Paruus*) in the masculine singular forms. This polysemy is compounded by morphological similarity and requires contextual clues for correct disambiguation. In the tagging system (TAS), such forms generate multiple potential annotations (see Fig. 1).

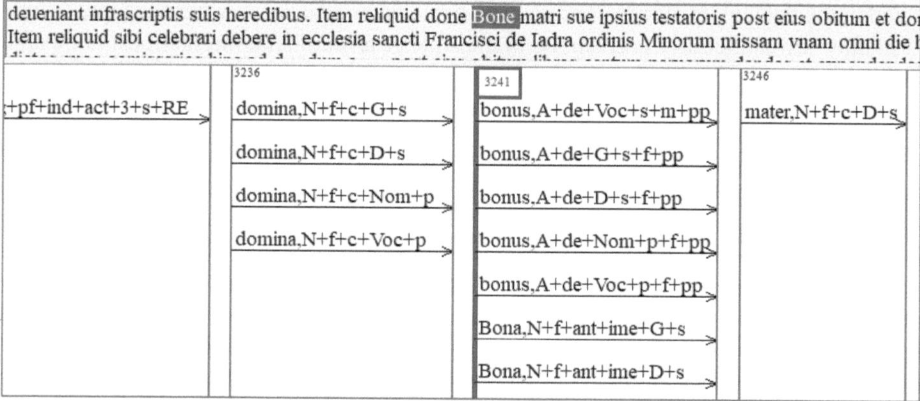

Fig. 2. Annotations of *Bone* before disambiguation.

Through the development of syntactic grammars in NooJ (Fig. 2), many of these cases were resolved. In addition to ambiguity caused by substantivization within the group, an additional layer of complexity arises from their derived adverbial (uninflected) forms (see Sect. 3.2). One such case involves a form overlap across three distinct word categories (adverb – adjective – noun), illustrated by *clare, clare, Clare*, which were also incorporated into the syntactic grammars.

---

[1] Although *Parua* is a phonetic reflection of the Croatian female name *Prva* ('First'), the name was included in the syntactic grammar because it follows the declension pattern of the Latin first declension.

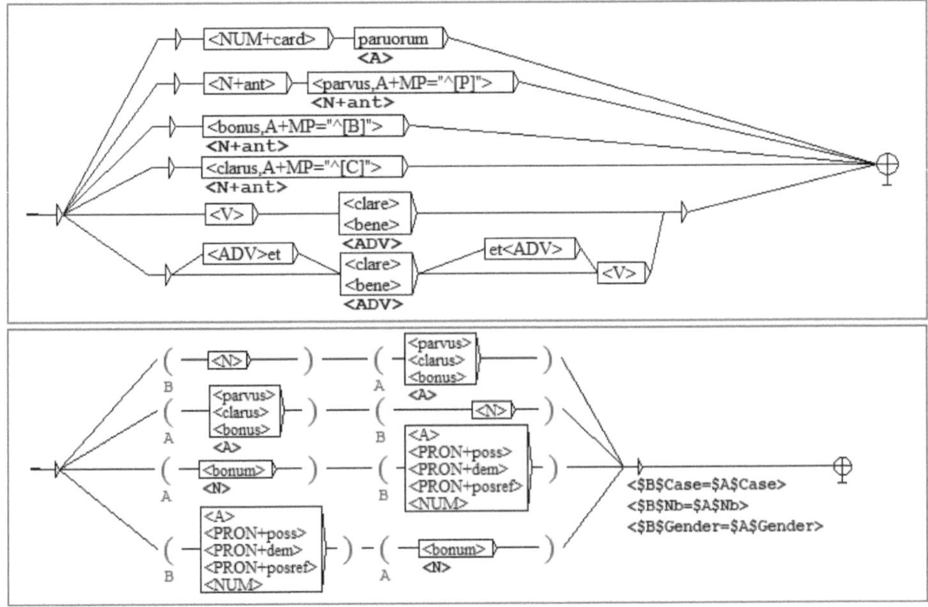

Fig. 3. Two syntactic grammars for the disambiguation of *parvus, clarus* and *bonus*.

After applying two syntactic grammars specifically created for these numerous ambiguities (Fig. 3), with the first assigned higher priority, the number of cases in this subcategory was significantly reduced. After we added/removed annotations, the grammar resolves more than 5600 tags.

Numeral – Noun (e.g., decima). In the MedText corpus, the word *decima* may function either as an ordinal numeral in the nominative, vocative, and ablative singular feminine forms, or take on the role of a substantivized noun meaning 'tenth part' or 'tithe'.

Since *decimus*, when used as an ordinal number, frequently occurs in the ablative of time, the syntactic grammar (Fig. 4) includes the most common constructions found in date expressions. In the second part, the grammar proposes solutions to distinguish cases in which *decima* (also *decimum*) appears as a noun from those where it acts as an attribute – namely, an ordinal number. The grammar disambiguates a total of 683 ambiguous forms (Fig. 5).

Single Case Ambiguities. Some ambiguities are not particularly demanding, at least within the MedText corpus, because certain theoretical ambiguities never actually occur. For instance, the form *curas* is never derived from the verb *curo, 1.* ('to care'), but always from the noun *cura* ('care'). The form *parte* consistently stems from the noun *pars, partis, f* ('part') and never from the verb *pario, 3.* ('to give birth'). *Missis* is always a form of *missa, ae, f* ('mass') and not from *mitto, 3.* ('to send'), since it was common for testators to allocate funds for masses offered for the salvation of their souls. Similarly, *eam* is always accusative singular of the pronoun *ea* ('she, that'), and never a form of the verb *eo, ire* ('to go').

Before	Seq.	After
incarnationis Christi millesimo trecentesimo secundo,	indictione quinta decima/<NUM>	, presentibus Micha de Scolatura et
libras XXV dimitto capitulo Iadrensi	pro decimis/<N>	.... defraudatis. Item fratri Stephano, filio
incarnationis Christi millesimo trecentesimo primo,	indictione quinta decima/<NUM>	, presentibus Cernilo fabro et Stephano
et pietatis, et eciam monasterio	decime Semelnici/<N>	, quam dominus archiepiscopus et capitulum
comissarios meos de bonis meis	ipsa decima/<N>	, et si ipsam .... soluatur. Item
annis incarnationis Christi millesimo trecentesimo,	indictione tercia decima/<NUM>	, presentibus Madio de Uaricassis et
incarnationis Christi millesimo trecentesimo primo,	indictione quinta decima/<NUM>	, presentibus Iohanne condam Iurgii et
incarnationis Christi millesimo trecentesimo primo,	indictione quarta decima/<NUM>	, presentibus dompno Martino, presbitero ecclesie
priori sancti Martini de Iadra	pro decima/<N>	. Item legauit dono Dobre sancte
mei habeant pro eorum labore	decimum denariorum/<N>	de precio eorum quod ipsi
ipsi vendiderint de bonis meis <	in qua decima parte/<NUM>	eos meos instituo heredes>. Item
precio dictorum bonorum sibi extrahant	decimum denariorum/<N>	prout superius dictum est. Et
mensis ianuarii secunda die intrante,	inditione decima/<NUM>	, Iadere. Temporibus equidem domini Iacobi

Fig. 4. Syntactic grammar for the disambiguation of *decima.*

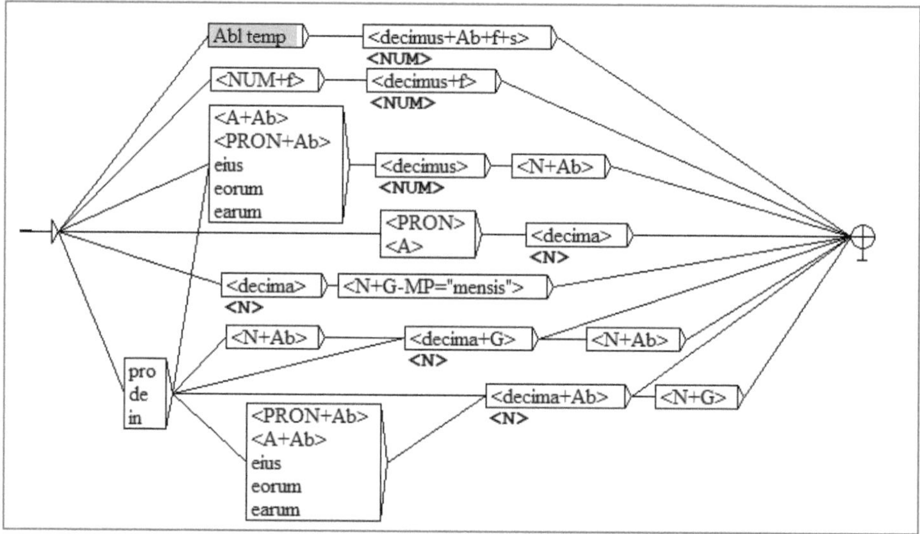

Fig. 5. Annotation results using a syntactic grammar for *decima.*

3.2 Ambiguities Between an Inflective and a Flective Word Class

Within the MedText corpus, six types of ambiguity arise between inflective and flective word classes, including the following combinations:

1. preposition – noun
2. preposition – numeral
3. adverb – verb
4. adverb – adjective
5. preposition – verb
6. conjunction – pronoun

Preposition – Noun (e.g., gratia). In Latin, the word *gratia* can be used as a noun meaning 'grace' or 'thanks', appear within prepositional phrases expressing meanings 'for the sake of' or 'because of' (e.g., *gratia salutis* 'for the sake of salvation'), or occasionally function as a proper name. MedText corpus contains 395 occurrences of the word *gratia*.

After analyzing the concordances, we found that it does not serve as a preposition in any of these cases. Instead, it consistently occurs either in the role of a noun, or a proper name. To disambiguate these uses, we created a syntactic grammar in NooJ (see Fig. 6). This grammar identifies *gratia* as a noun when immediately followed by a noun in genitive case; in all other contexts, it is tagged as a proper name (Fig. 7).

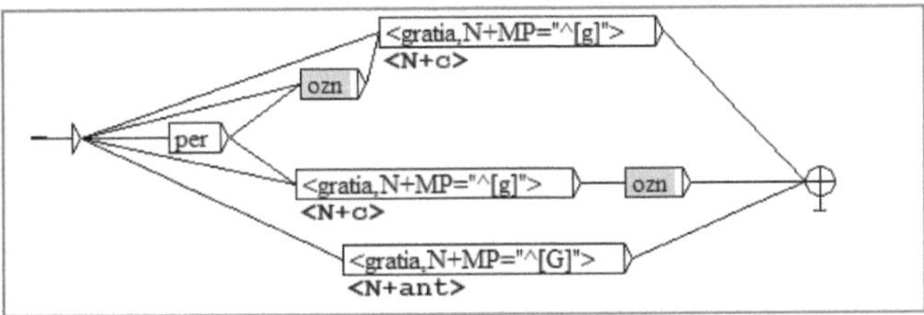

Fig. 6. Syntactic grammar for *gratia*.

By applying this grammar, we were able to eliminate incorrect tags and improve the accuracy of morphosyntactic annotation.

Before	Seq.	After
ivitani iardinarii, habitatrix Iadre, sana	per gratiam Iesu Christi/<N+c>	mente et sensu, licet languens
temporibus domini nostri Petri Çiani	Dei gracia/<N+c>	incliti ducis Venecie, Dalmacie atque
licet infirma corpore sanam tamen	per Dei graciam/<N+c>	habens mentem, memoriam et intellectu
licet infirmus corpore sanam tamen	per Dei graciam/<N+c>	habens mentem, memoriam et intellectu
graui corporis oppressa sanam tamen	per Dei graciam/<N+c>	habens mentem integrumque sensum, p
res denariorum paruorum; item sorori	Gracie/<N+ant>	de Betono priorisse monasterii sancti
Çiualellis egra corpore, sana tamen	per gratiam Iesu Christi/<N+c>	mente, intellectu, memoria atque sensu
languens, set mente et intellectu	per graciam Iesu Christi/<N+c>	compos et sanus suorum bonorum
ondam Viti marangoni habitatrix Iadre	per Dei graciam/<N+c>	mente et sensu sana, licet
condam Francisci de Çadulinis sana	per gratiam Iesu Christi/<N+c>	mente et senssu, licet corpore
ino nostro naturale domino Lodouico	Dei gratia/<N+c>	inclito rege Hungarie, tempore reuerenc
y de Matafaris decretorum doctorum.	Dei et sancte sedis apostolice gracia/<N+c>	archiepiscopi Iadrensis, ac magniffici e

Fig. 7. Annotation results using a syntactic grammar for *gratia*.

Preposition – Numeral (e.g., secundum). Secundum can be either a preposition governing the accusative, meaning 'according to', or a form of the numeral *secundus*, 3 ('second', 'the other'). Theoretically, in the phrase *secundum Deum, secundum* could be interpreted as a numeral ('second God'). However, this interpretation is absent from the MedText corpus, which contains last wills and testaments of medieval Catholic testators. For this reason, we excluded it in the first path of the rule (see Fig. 8 and 9).

Adverb – Verb (e.g., condam). The adverb *condam* appears with high frequency due to the large number of proper name formulas in which the father is referred to as 'deceased'

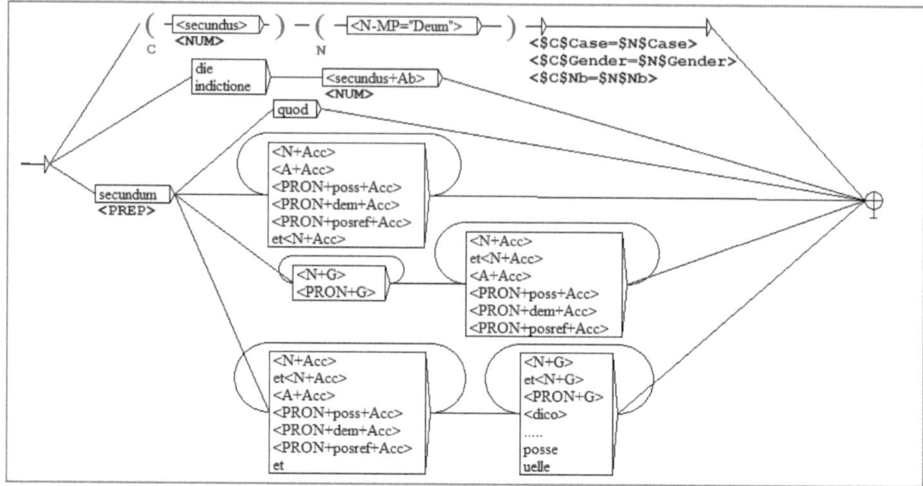

Fig. 8. Syntactic grammar for *secundum*.

Before	Seq.	After
Iadra, famulum dicti testatoris, qui	secundum quod/<PREP>	dictus testator fecerit et ord
dare ipsas libras centum paruorum	secundum quod/<PREP>	dictus testator eidem ordina
biectionem temporalis dominii Iadre	secundum statuta et ordinamenta ciuitatis Iadre/<PREP>	, quousque idem dictus frate
pposite iurisdictioni temporali Iadre	secundum statuta et ordinamenta Iadre/<PREP>	ad hoc loquentia. Et si
redditibus seruiat pro anima mea,	secundum suam possibilitatem/<PREP>	, in uita sua donec uidua
mee, ut seruiat de redditibus	secundum suum posse/<PREP>	et uelle. Et ita hoc
icte Palmucie, remaneat pauperibus	secundum tenorem testamenti dicte/<PREP>	condam Palmucie. Item reli
pro anima mea et tua,	secundum tuam possibilitatem ..../<PREP>	obitum ipsa mea vinea prop
difficare et fundare vnum hospitalle	secundum uoluntatem et conscientiam/<PREP>	infrascripti, cui ordinatum f

Fig. 9. Annotation results using a syntactic grammar for *secundum*.

or 'late'. However, it can also be the subjunctive form of the verb *condo, 3.* ('to establish'). The grammar (Fig. 10) resolves more than 1000 ambiguities (specifically, 1,037). An examination of the concordances (Fig. 11) reveals that none of these instances were verb forms.

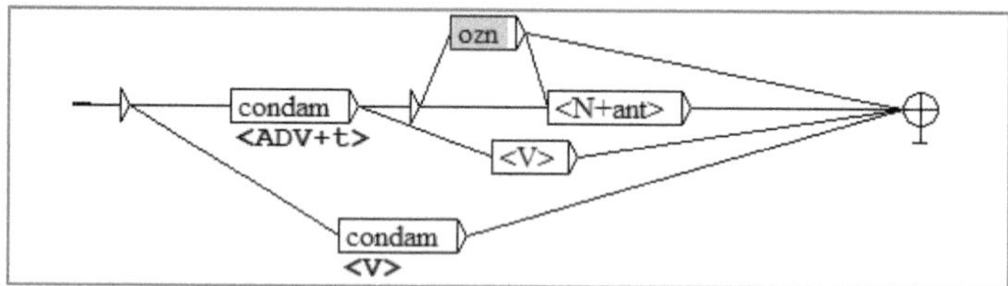

Fig. 10. Syntactic grammar for *condam*.

Other Cases of Ambiguity. Regarding additional ambiguities in the corpus, a total of 661 cases were eliminated through two syntactic grammars developed for *sine* (435) and

Before	Seq.	After
ad Osdrignum in terra heredum	condam Cerne/<ADV+t>	de Mergya, quas uero uineas
quam habere debeo de bonis	condam dicti Iurgii/<ADV+t>	patris mei, que tenet et
quam habeo in terra heredum	condam Cerne/<ADV+t>	de Mergia ad dicendum et
; 10. 7. 1294 Testamentum Stane uxoris	condam Çane/<ADV+t>	de Salbe Factum In Christi
ego quidem Stana Iadratina, uxor	condam Çane/<ADV+t>	, filii Uolcinne de Salbe, sana
mense septembri, presentibus Phylippo	condam Grisogoni/<ADV+t>	de Mauro et Petro de
a Radoscio calegario Iadrensi, filio	condam Radochne/<ADV+t>	quas ...., de quibus libris i
libras quinquaginta paruorum a Micha	condam Clementis/<ADV+t>	, Iadratino, quas per cartam mil
Et alie nepti mee, filie	condam Iacobi/<ADV+t>	filii mei, iudico et dimitto
Cerne de Cande Matheo, filio	condam Detaydi/<ADV+t>	de Copagna, Iadrensibus, et al
etc. Ego quidem Creste, 79 filius	condam Mathey/<ADV+t>	de Georgio Iadratinus, licet inf
et uxorem meam Mariam, filiam	condam Marini/<ADV+t>	de Labe, et fratres meos
que fuit empta de dimissoria	condam domini Andree/<ADV+t>	.... iudico et dimitto comu

Fig. 11. Annotation results using a syntactic grammar for *condam*.

cetero (226), respectively. The word *sine* may function either as a preposition governing the ablative or as the imperative form of the verb *sino, 3.* ('to allow'). However, similar to *condam* (used exclusively in its adverbial role), all occurrences of *sine* in the corpus were identified as prepositions. The word *cetero* exhibits both adverbial and adjectival usage.

An exceptionally high number of ambiguities is associated with *quod*, within the conjuction–pronoun category. For now, we have set aside the issue of ambiguity between the conjuctions *quod* and *quam*, which overlap with forms of the relative pronoun *qui, quae, quod*. This ambiguity must be addressed within the framework of sentence-level syntax.

3.3 Ambiguities Between Two Inflective Word Classes

In this final group, Latin prepositions – including *prope, supra, infra* – exhibit ambiguities due to their additional use as adverbs. Ambiguities are also present within preposition–conjuction category.

Preposition – Adverb (e.g., prope, supra, infra). Latin prepositions typically govern specific cases – the accusative, ablative, or both. Only two prepositions require the genitive case; *gratia*, mentioned in Sect. 3.1, is one of them.

Prepositions *prope* ('close to'), *supra* ('above', 'over') and *infra* ('below', 'beneath') are followed by the accusative case. Using two syntactic grammars (see example for *infra* et *supra* in Fig. 12), a total of 127 ambiguities were resolved (see results for *infra* et *supra* in Fig. 13).

Preposition – Conjunction (e.g., cum). The preposition *cum* is commonly used with the ablative case, but it can also be a conjunction with different meanings depending on the sentence context: *cum causale* ('since', 'because') or *cum historicum* ('when'). A problem arises when a noun in the ablative immediately follows *cum*, even though the sentence does not express a causal or temporal relationship. This is evident in the following example:

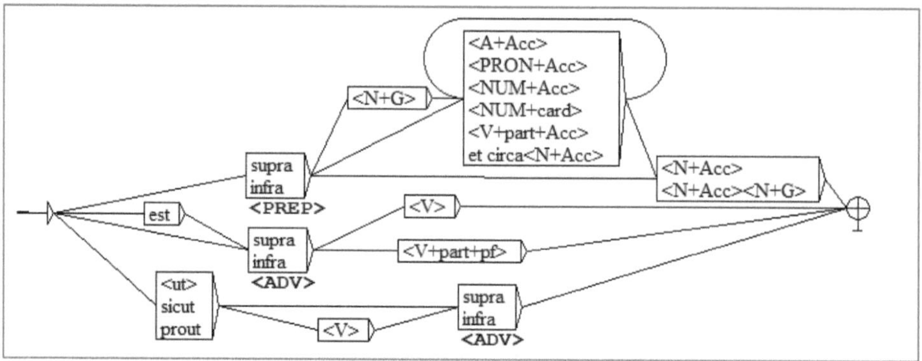

Fig. 12. Syntactic grammar for *infra* and *supra*.

Before	Seq.	After
nil sit cercius et cetera	ut supra/<ADV>	. Idcirco ego quidem Francisca, uxor
predicti ex ea nascituri decederent	infra etatem/<PREP>	legittimam, tunc ipsis filiis suis
legauit libras centum ad grossos,	ut supra continetur/<ADV>	, usque quo idem Franciscus peruenerit
peruenerit ad etatem legitimam, nec	infra dictum tempus/<PREP>	dictus Franciscus uel alius pro
im uel nasciturorum aliquis decederet	infra etatem/<PREP>	legitimam et sine liberis, tunc
nascituri sibi decederent sine liberis	infra etatem/<PREP>	legitimam, tunc et eo casu
anima sua, prout de aliis	supra ordinauit/<ADV>	. Item uoluit et legauit Crucore
predictum aliud testamentum, de quo	supra fit/<ADV>	mencio, cassauit et nullius valoris
postumorum ei heres erit et	infra quintum decimum annum/<PREP>	intestatus decesserit, dictam Marizam ei
olivariis pluribus in ea, posita	supra portum/<PREP>	Sancti Iacobi, districtus Iadre, gognayorum
disposuit, voluit et mandavit quod	supra funus/<PREP>	et occasione funeris et sepulture
predictas libras CCCC eciam statim	infra unum annum/<PREP>	postquam nubisset habeant dicta quatuor

Fig. 13. Annotation results using a syntactic grammar for *infra* and *supra*.

(2) *Cum morte nil sit certius et nil incertius* (…) "Since nothing is more certain or uncertain than death (…)"

In this sentence, *morte* is linked to the nominal predicate *nil sit certius et nil incertius*, in which the predicate nouns *certius* et *incertius* are comparatives that, in Latin syntax, require the ablative of comparison, here *morte*. Therefore, we included a rule in the syntactic grammar instructing that *cum* followed by *morte* should be annotated as a conjunction rather than a preposition (see Figs. 14 and 15). Using this grammar, a total of 781 ambiguities were eliminated. However, further syntactic refinement is needed to fully address the causal and temporal functions expressed by the conjunction *cum*.

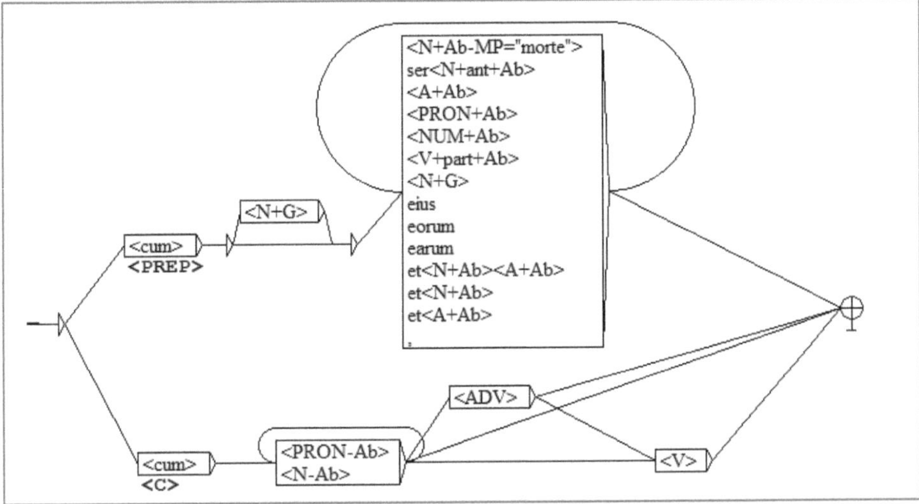

Fig. 14. Syntactic grammar for *cum*.

Before	Seq.	After
ptum residuum MCCC librarum	cum conscilio et uoluntate/<PREP>	dicti Uiti, fratris mei, ubi
de Drasimerio, Iadrensibus, et aliis.	Cum/<C>	morte nil sit cercius etc
meis facio et ordino testamentum	cum uoluntate et assensu sororis/<PREP>	mee Dobrane et ad hoc
ad affictum domum meam lapideam	cum coquina, curia et ballatoria/<PREP>	in .... et de ipso affictu
quod habeo super eos, et	cum ipsa dote mea/<PREP>	.... manutenere filios meos Bartholome
rtholomeum et Damianum, quos habeo	cum dicto Nicolao, uiro meo,/<PREP>	quos mihi heredes instituo in
unus succedat alteri, quos dimitto	cum dictis bonis meis/<PREP>	.... in cura et comissaria suprascripte
... dimissionem et quietacionem	cum pena/<PREP>	et qualibet firmitate, et omnia
mini Marini Superancii, egregii comitis.	Cum/<C>	morte nil sit cercius etc
.... Uitum et Andream .... stare	cum ea,/<PREP>	et dare sibi reuerenciam et
de Drasimerio, Iadrensibus, et aliis.	Cum/<C>	morte nil sit cercius etc
sine furno et loco meo,	cum suis pertinenciis/<PREP>	.... in confinio sancti Petri Ueteris

Fig. 15. Annotation results using a syntactic grammar for *cum*.

4 Results and Future Work

For practical reasons, we chose not to merge all syntactic grammars for resolving ambiguities into a single one, since some grammars significantly slowed down NooJ's processing. Instead, we developed twelve targeted grammars to recognize specific word meanings in context, thereby reducing ambiguity and improving the accuracy of linguistic analysis. In this way, we automatically disambiguated and removed over 9,000 annotations, while the remaining cases were manually extracted from the TAS.

Despite these improvements, disambiguation continues to pose a persistent and complex challenge in the computational analysis of Latin, particularly in its medieval variants, which are less standardized and often contextually dense. Nevertheless, numerous issues remain, especially in analysis of sentence-level syntax, which requires deeper contextual modeling.

References

1. Jurafsky, D., Martin, J.H.: Speech and Language Processing: An Introduction to Natural Language Processing, Computational Linguistics, and Speech Recognition. Prentice Hall (2008)
2. Kwong, O.Y.: New Perspectives on Computational and Cognitive Strategies for Word Sense Disambiguation. Springer, Heidelberg (2013)
3. Mijić, L., Bartulović, A.: Formalizing latin: an example of medieval latin wills. In: Bekavac, B., Kocijan, K., Silberztein, M., Šojat, K. (eds.) Formalising Natural Languages: Applications to Natural Language Processing and Digital Humanities. NooJ 2020, Revised Selected Papers, pp. 24–36. Springer, Cham (2021)
4. Bartulović, A., Mijić, L.: NooJ anotacije antroponima i toponima iz zadarskih srednjovjekovnih oporuka. In: Botica, I., Galović, T., et al. (eds.) Zbornik u čast Mirjane Matijević Sokol, vol. II, pp. 677–691. Književni krug Split, Split (2025)
5. Mijić, L., Bartulović, A.: Pridjevi i prilozi srednjovjekovnih latinskih oporuka u NooJ format (Manuscript under review)
6. Bartulović, A., Mijić, L.: Latin pronouns, numerals and prepositions in the NooJ tool. In: Bartulović, A., Mijić, L., Silberztein, M. (eds.) Formalizing Natural Languages: Applications to Natural Language Processing and Digital Humanities. NooJ 2023, Revised Selected Papers, pp. 39–50. Springer, Cham (2023)
7. Mijić, L., Bartulović, A.: Recognizing verbs in medieval Latin. In: Formalizing Natural Languages: Applications to Natural Language Processing and Digital Humanities. NooJ 2024, Revised Selected Papers, pp. 16–27. Springer, Cham (2024)
8. Moorwood, J.: Latin Grammar. Oxford University Press (1999)
9. Stotz, P.: Handbuch zur lateinischen Sprache des Mittelalters. Bedeutungswandel und Wortbildung, vol. 2. Verlag C.H. Beck, München (2002)
10. Silberztein, M.: Formalizing Natural Languages: The NooJ Approach. Wiley-ISTE, London (2016)
11. Silberztein, M.: Disambiguation tool for NooJ. In: Váradi, T., Kuti, J., Silberztein, M. (eds.) Applications of Finite-state Language Processing. Selected Papers from the 2008 International NooJ Conference. Cambridge Scholars Publishing, Newcastle upon Tyne (2008)

Transformations and Paraphrases of Quechua Interrogative Sentences

Maximiliano Duran[1,2](✉)

[1] C.R.I.T., University of Franche-Comté, Besançon, France
duran_maximiliano@yahoo.fr
[2] LIG, UGA, Université de Grenoble, Grenoble, France

Abstract. In this paper, I first present a formalized classification of question sentences and a study on the automatic generation of paraphrases of interrogative sentences. These results can be applied at different levels in NLP for the Quechua language. Interrogative sentences are an important part of communication, since they allow one to obtain information, engage in conversation, or show curiosity. But in Quechua, how many forms can be formed correctly? What are the different types of interrogative sentences in Quechua? For this study, we gathered texts from ancient chronicles, contemporary publications, and transcriptions of oral recordings of native speakers. The analysis of this corpus allowed us to identify some morphosyntactic and semantic patterns and forms of interrogation. Then, using the NooJ platform, we formalized the grammatically valid transformations and developed grammars that can generate paraphrases of a given Quechua interrogative sentence.

Keywords: transformational analysis · Paraphrasing interrogative sentences · interrogative sentences

1 Introduction

In this paper, I first present a formalized classification of question sentences, followed by a study on the transformations and automatic generation of paraphrases of interrogative sentences. These findings can be applied at different levels in NLP for the Quechua language. Interrogative sentences are a key part of communication, as they help us gather information, engage in conversations, or express curiosity. In how many ways can they be correctly formed? What are the different types of interrogative sentences? What are the syntactic transformations that can be used to create grammatical paraphrases from a direct sentence?

In surveying existing Quechua grammar literature, we have not found a formalized answer to these questions. To fully address them, we would need to analyze syntactic patterns in a comprehensive written corpus. Unfortunately, Quechua remains a "poorly endowed language," so written documents are very scarce. For this study, we have compiled a corpus that includes texts such as: Avila, Francisco de, Dioses y hombres de Huarochiri [1], Guaman Poma de Ayala, Felipe, (Extract of texts in Quechua from)

D. Petković et al. (Eds.): NooJ 2025, CCIS 2832, pp. 89–100, 2026.
https://doi.org/10.1007/978-3-032-17103-0_8

Nueva Coronica y Buen Gobierno [4], Guardia Mayorga, Cesar, Pakpaku chayñawan rimanakun. Conte [5], Itier, César, Transcription des émissions de Radio Quispillaqta [6], Lira, Jorge, Cuentos del Alto Urubamba [7], Meneses, Porfirio, Sept contes en quechua [8], Oregón Morales, José, Loro Ccolluchi [9], Taylor, G., Ritos y Tradiciones de Huarochiri [12], and transcriptions of several hours of recordings among native Quechua-speaking people in Peru.

The resulting compilation constituted a relatively large corpus of different kinds of interrogative sentences, which allowed us to identify the interrogative patterns of the language. Below, we can see two extracts from this corpus:

"ajoyrakichu koya rakiriwanchik tiyuyrakichu ñusta rakiriwanchik sikllallai chinchirkuma kaptiikichu umallaipi sonjo rurullaipi apaykachaikiman unoi rirpo llullam kanki yakui rirpo palljam kanki maitaj sallaiwan jay niikunichu chay pallja mamaikim wañuipaj rakijninchikja chay auja yayaikim wakchajninchikja wajai nijlla wayta, sonjoyujchu tiyanki" (Guaman Poma [4]).

We can note that punctuation marks such as the question mark ("?") are absent, as these texts come from ancient manuscripts. To identify the interrogative sentences, we had to rely on context in order to extract the interrogative phrases, such as: *ajoyrakichu koya rakiriwanchik* (is the infortune my princess that splits us?).

In the more contemporary documents where the question mark ("?") is present, we used several syntactic local grammars in NooJ, a linguistic platform created by Max Silberztein [10], to isolate those phrases. We can see some examples in the following extract from *Yupinta jatispa*, a story by Meneses [6]:

"jasi sachapa sikinpi samarikuchkaptin iskay warmikuna jispiykamunku hanaymanta. Payan kajta tapukuptin kay kutichikun:

— Imaynach kanpas, tayta. Markaspija uyarini huk wanka negociantemanta: wañurachinmansi kasja huk payhina waka rantij wantinuta. Qunjaitas rumiwan chamjanman kasja purunpi, jaja patanpi. Hinaspansi sijaykachisja jaja ukuta...

— Runataja hapirurakuchu? Maypitaj pamparunku ayataja?

— Manachus-hinam hapinkuchu wañuchijnintaja. ....

— Yau, tayta. Hinaptin imayna kajtataj tarirjankichik?"

We have obtained numerous interrogative phrases like the ones listed below:

Gervasiochu kuyan Romildata?

runataja hapirurankuchu?

maypitaj pamparunku ayataja?

pitaj kachkanki ?

paywanchu kaypi karja?

imaina kajtataj tarirjankichik?

pamparurankichikchu?

sinka apiki?

imaynanpim yachanki?

paywanchu kaypi karja?

samaykachiwankimanchu asllata?

pitaj kachkanki?

imatam niwanaiki kachkan?

Imaniwasjantaj sunjuita tiyachinman karja?

may qoanaiiki?

2 Finding Syntactic Patterns in a Written Corpus

The analysis of this corpus has enabled us to identify some morphosyntactic and semantic patterns across the interrogative sentences. We identified various forms and types of interrogation, which are presented below:

*Gervasio**chu** kuyan Romildata?*	CHU
*runataja hapiruranku**chu**?*	CHU
*ichaja warmiita rijsinki**chu**?*	CHU
*pamparurankichik**chu**?*	CHU
*mamaita rijsinki**chu**?*	CHU
*yacharankichik**chu**?*	CHU
*paywan**chu** kaypi karja?*	CHU
*samaykachiwankiman**chu** asllata?*	CHU
***may** quanaiiki?*	**ADV**
***maypitaj** pamparunku ayataja?*	**ADV**
***manachu** ajallaiki kan?*	**ADV**
***manachu** jampa karja?*	**ADV**
***imaynanpim** yachanki?*	PROI
***pitaj** kachkanki?*	PROI
***imatam** niwanaiki kachkan?*	PROI
***imaniwasjantaj** sunjuita tiyachinman karja?*	PROI
***imaynanpim** yachanki?*	PROI
***paywanchu** kaypi karja?*	PROI
***imaina** kajtataj tarirjankichik?*	PROI
sinka apiki?	**VOIX**

Where CHU stands for the suffix *chu*, ADV for adverb, PROI for interrogative pronoun, VOIX for voice.

3 Forms of Interrogation

We have found four forms of interrogative sentences in the corpus:

*Gervasio**chu** kuyan Romildata?* [Does Gervasio love Romilda?]	CHU
***pitaj** kachkanki?* [who are you?]	PROI
***may** quanaiiki?* [what about that thing you had to give me?]	ADV
sinka apiki? [almost drunk?]	VOIX

3.1 Form Chu: Sentences Containing the Suffix "chu"

This suffix may be agglutinated to any part of speech (PoS) that functions as the head of the phrase. For example:

- To a noun (common or proper): *Gervasiochu riman* [Is it Gervasio who talks?]. The noun Gervasio is the head and therefore ends in -*chu* (Nchu + head modifier).
- To an adjective: *yuraqchu wayta*? [Is the flower white?] (Achu + head modifier). Here, -chu appears at the end of the adjective, the head of the phrase.
- To a pronoun: *paykunachu tusuj rinku*? [Did they go to dance?] (PROchu + head modifier). The suffix -chu occurs at the end of the pronoun, which is the head of the phrase.
- To an adverb: *paqarinchu hamunki*? [Will you come tomorrow?] (ADVchu + head modifier). -chu is at the end of the adverb that is at the head of the phrase.

It is interesting to note that "*chu*" may also be agglutinated to any inflected form of these PoS. In Fig. 1, for instance, we show the corresponding grammars for verbal forms and noun phrases.

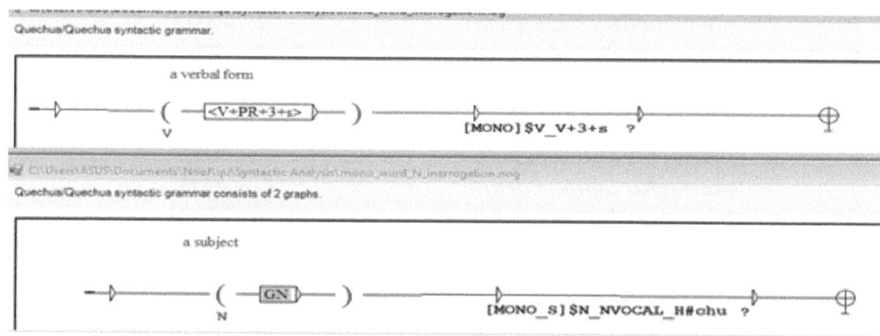

Fig. 1. Grammars that generate interrogative forms out of verbal and noun inflected forms.

For example, below are some interrogative forms of the verb *rimay* [to talk] and the proper noun Gervasio automatically generated by the second grammar:

rimanchu, EN = does he talk? + SP = habla él?
rimanjachu, EN = will he talk? + SP = hablará él?
rimarjachu, EN = did he talk? + SP = habló él?
rimankichu, EN = are you going to talk? + SP = vas a hablar?
Gervasiochu, EN = is it Gervasio? + SP = Es Gervasio?
Gervasiopaqchu, EN = is it for Gervasio? + SP = Es para Gervasio?
Gervasiowanchu, EN = is it with Gervasio? + SP = Es con Gervasio?
Gervasiopaqraqchu, EN = is it preferably for Gervasio? + SP = Es de preferencia para Gervasio?

3.2   Use of Interrogative Pronouns or PROI-Form

The family of fundamental interrogative pronouns contains only five elements:

PRO_INT = {*ima* [what], *may*[which], *mayqin* [which one (animated)], *hayka* [how many], *pi* [who]]}.

as illustrated in the following extracted sentences:

ima niwasjantaj sunjuita tiyachinman karja? [among the things he said, what comforted me?] (PROI)

    imaina kajtataj tarirjankichik? [In what condition did they find him?] (PROI).

    imainanpim yachanki? [How do you know?] (PROI).

    mayqinmi chakrapi llamkarqa? [Which of you worked in the fields?] (PROI).

    mayqintaq llullakun [who is the one who is lying?] (PROI).

    mayqintataq akllanqa [who will he choose instead?] (PROI).

    hayka runam qamusqa? [How many people had come?] (PROI).

    pita maskanki? [who are you looking for?] (PROI).

We note that the fundamental interrogative pronouns also occur in inflected forms bearing one or more adverbial suffixes like: (h)ina, mi, ta. This property makes it possible to generate many additional interrogative pronouns. In Sect. 5, we examine this phenomenon in detail.

3.3 Form Containing Interrogative Adverbs ADVI

The set of fundamental interrogative adverbs is also small:

    ADVI = {may, imay, mayqin, hayka}.

    may [which one (object)], imay [when], may[what], mayqin [which one (person)], hayka [how much].

3.4 Subject Inversion Form

An affirmative verbal phrase of the form subject-predicate (S-PRED) may become an interrogative one by inverting the word order and suffixing the suffix *-chu* to the inflected verbal form:

    Carlos rirjan → *rirjanchu Carlos*? [Carlos went → did Carlos go?].

    allju anyachkan → *anyachkanchu allju*? [The dog is barking → is the dog barking?].

3.5 Change of Intonation

When neither the suffix *-chu* nor the PROI elements or interrogative adverbs are present, a question can still be formulated in spoken communication by changing the intonation: the final word is pronounced with a rising pitch:

    Aw tayta? [Isn't it true, my father?].

    Qamjá, wauqe?[What about you, my friend?].

    Mikurunña? [Did he already eat?].

4 Formalizing Interrogative Pronouns Morphology

In Sect. 2, we noted that the set of interrogative pronouns PRO_INT contains only five elements, which seems to be very modest for a language if we want to construct complex interrogative sentences. Let us see in detail how Quechua manages to enhance this vocabulary through the use of a special set of pronominal suffixes.

PROI_SUF = (*hina, kama, m, má, man, manta, mi, nta, ninta, niq, niraq, p, pa, paq, pi, POS[1], puni, rayku, raq, ri, ta, taq, wan*).

The first level of inflection is obtained by directly adding one of these suffixes to each interrogative pronoun. We apply one of the following grammars to generate them automatically, depending on whether the pronoun ends in a vowel (PROI_V_1) or in a consonant (PROI_C_1):

PROI_V_1 = :GEP |:GEPA|:HINA| :KAMA| :MAA| :MAN|:MANTA| :MM |:NIQ |:NTA |:NTIN |:NIRAQ| :PAJ |:PI|:POSV |:PUNI|:TA|:TAQ| :WAN;

PROI_C_1 = :GEPA |:HINA |:KAMA |:MAA |:MAN |:MANTA |:MI|:NINTA |:NINTIN |:NIRAQ|:PAJ|:PI |:POSC |:PUNI |:RAYKU|:RI |:RAQ|:TA |:TAQ |:WAN;

Examples like *mayqinmi, mayqinta*, and *pita* appear in Sect. 2.

We now seek the corresponding formulas to obtain the inflected forms that contain combinations of two of these suffixes, such as the form *mayqin**tataq*** [who instead], which also appears in Sect. 2, where the suffixes *ta* and *taq* are grammatically combined. Following Duran [2], we have constructed the matrix shown in Fig. 2, where "1" represents a valid combination between the element listed on the left (row) and the one at the top (column), as in the form *tataq*.

PROI_V	GEP	GEPA	HINA	KAM	MAA	MAN	MAN	MI	MM	NTA	NINT	NIQ	NIRA	PAJ	PI	POSV	POSV	POSC	POSC	PUNI	RAYK	RAQ	RI	TA	TAQ	WAN
GEP	0	0	0	0	0	0	0	0	0	0	0	0	0	0	0	0	0	0	0	0	0	0	0	0	0	0
GEPA	0	0	1	1	1	1	1	0	1	1	0	1	1	1	1	0	0	0	0	1	0	1	1	1	1	1
HINA	0	1	0	1	1	1	1	0	1	1	0	0	0	1	1	1	1	0	0	1	1	1	1	1	1	1
KAMA	0	0	1	0	1	0	0	0	1	0	0	0	0	0	0	0	0	0	0	1	0	1	1	0	1	0
MAA	0	0	0	0	0	0	0	0	0	0	0	0	0	0	0	0	0	0	0	0	0	0	0	0	0	0
MAN	0	0	1	0	1	0	0	1	0	0	0	0	1	0	0	0	0	0	0	1	0	1	1	0	1	1
MANTA	0	0	0	0	1	0	0	0	1	0	0	0	0	0	0	0	0	0	0	1	0	1	1	0	1	1
MI	0	0	0	0	0	0	0	0	0	0	0	0	0	0	0	0	0	0	0	0	0	0	0	0	0	0
MM	0	0	0	0	0	0	0	0	0	0	0	0	0	0	0	0	0	0	0	0	0	0	0	0	0	0
NTA	0	0	0	0	1	0	0	0	1	0	0	0	0	0	0	0	0	0	0	1	0	1	1	0	1	1
NINTA	0	0	0	0	0	0	0	0	0	0	0	0	0	0	0	0	0	0	0	0	0	0	0	0	0	0
NIQ	0	1	1	1	1	1	1	1	0	0	1	0	0	1	1	0	0	0	0	1	0	1	1	1	1	1
NIRAQ	0	1	1	1	1	1	1	1	0	0	1	0	0	1	1	0	0	0	0	1	0	1	1	1	1	1
PAJ	0	0	1	0	1	0	0	1	0	0	0	0	0	0	0	0	0	0	0	1	0	1	1	0	1	0
PI	0	0	1	0	1	0	0	0	1	0	0	0	0	0	0	0	0	0	0	1	1	1	1	0	1	1
POSV_v	0	1	1	1	1	1	1	0	1	0	0	1	1	1	1	0	0	0	0	1	1	1	1	1	1	1
POSV_c	0	1	1	1	1	1	1	1	0	0	1	1	1	1	1	0	0	0	0	1	1	1	1	1	1	1
POSC_v	0	0	0	0	0	0	0	0	0	0	0	0	0	0	0	0	0	0	0	0	0	0	0	0	0	0
POSC_c	0	0	0	0	0	0	0	0	0	0	0	0	0	0	0	0	0	0	0	0	0	0	0	0	0	0
PUNI	0	1	1	1	1	1	1	0	1	0	0	1	1	1	1	0	0	0	0	0	1	1	1	1	1	1
RAYKU	0	0	0	0	1	0	0	0	1	0	0	0	0	0	0	0	0	0	0	1	0	1	1	0	1	0
RAQ	0	0	0	0	1	0	0	1	0	0	0	0	0	0	0	0	0	0	0	0	0	0	0	0	1	0
RI	0	0	0	0	0	0	0	0	0	0	0	0	0	0	0	0	0	0	0	0	0	0	0	0	0	0
TA	0	0	1	0	1	0	0	0	1	0	0	0	0	0	0	0	0	0	0	1	0	1	1	0	1	1
TAQ	0	0	0	0	0	0	0	0	0	0	0	0	0	0	0	0	0	0	0	0	0	0	0	0	0	0

Fig. 2. PROI Boolean matrix

This matrix generates all (171) valid combinations of two PROI suffixes, some of which appear in the following morphological grammar:

PROI_V_2= :GEPAHINA |:GEPAKAMA |:GEPAMAA |:GEPAMAN|:GEPAMM |:GEPAMANTA |:GEPANTA |:GEPANIQ |:GEPANIRAQ |:GEPAPAJ |:GEPAPI |:GEPAPUNI |:GEPARAQ |:GEPARI |: |:MANTAPUNI |:MANTARAQ ... |:RAQTAQ |:TAHINA |:TAMAA |:TAMM |:TAPUNI |:TARAQ |:TARI |:TATAQ |:TAWAN |:WANHINA |:WANMAA |:WANMI |:WANPUNI |:WANRAQ |:WANRI |:WANTAQ ;

---

[1] The set of possessive suffixes, for pronouns ending in a vowel is POSV = {*i, iki, n, nchin, iku, ikichik, nku*} and for pronouns ending in a consonant is POSC = {*nii, niiki, nin, ninchin, ni iku, niikichik, ninku*}.

When applied to the set PRO_INT and parsed, we obtain 429 new inflected interrogative pronouns (ending in a vowel) as shown in Fig. 3.

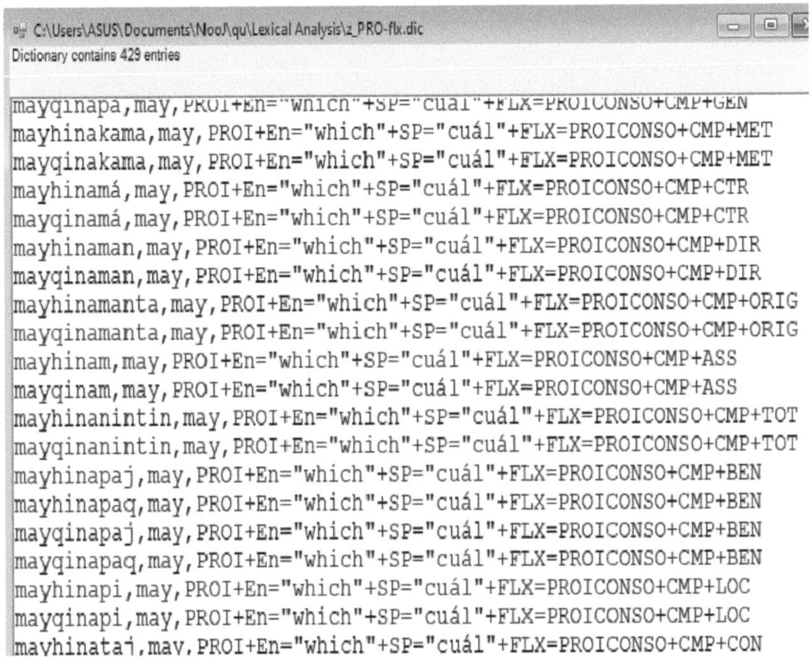

Fig. 3. New interrogative pronouns resulting from the inflection of PROI.

The English and Spanish translations of some of them are provided below:

haycap, PROI + En = when? + SP = cuándo?

mayqinkuna, PROI + En = which of them? + SP = cuáles?

mayqinniikichik, PROI + EN = who among all of you? + SP = "quién entre vosotros?".

mayta, PROI + EN = where to go? + SP = "a dónde?".

maytaq, PROI + EN = where is it? + SP = "dónde está?".

pikuna, PROI + EN = who (plural)? + SP = "quiénes?".

piman, PROI + EN = to whom? + SP = "a quién?".

pipaq, PROI + EN = for whom? + SP = "para quién?".

It is interesting to note that, as with nouns and adjectives, interrogative pronouns can also be inflected through combinations of three pronominal suffixes. The grammatical combinations of these suffixes were obtained using the method of Duran [2]. An excerpt of the resulting new interrogative inflected pronouns (more than 13,000) is shown in Fig. 4. We are currently working on their automatic translations for use in our machine translation project.

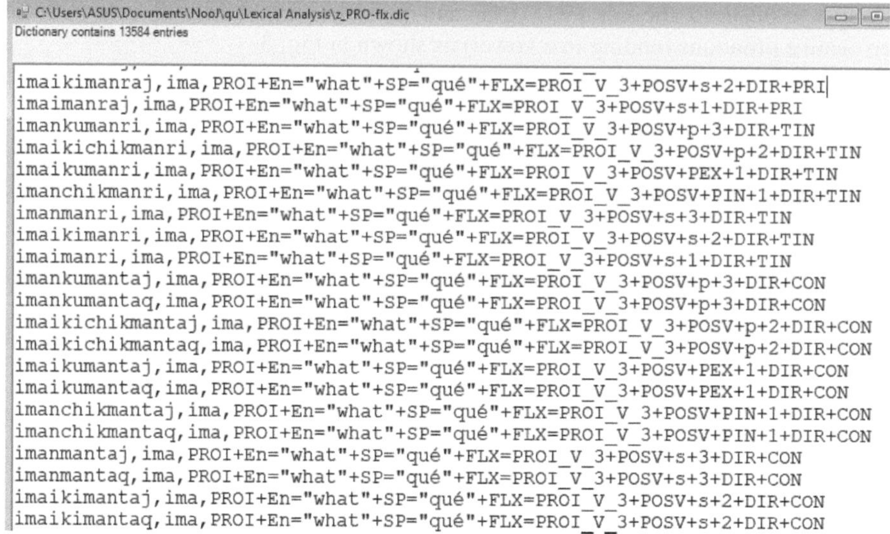

Fig. 4. Interrogative inflected pronouns with three suffixes.

5   The Inflection of Interrogative Adverbs

Similarly, interrogative adverbs can also be inflected using one or a combination of two or three adverbial suffixes. The following grammar applies to adverbs ending in a consonant (for details on the description of the presented paradigms, see Duran [3].

ADV_C_1 =:CHAA |:CHIK |:CHIKI |:CHUN |:KAMA |:LLA |:MAA |:MANTA |:MI |:NINTA |:ÑA |:PAQ |:PUNI |:QA |:RAQ |:RI |:SIC |:TA |:TAQ |:WAN |:YAA;

This grammar generates new adverbs or phrasal adverbs, including new interrogative adverbs or phrasal adverbs, such as:

haykap, ADVI + SP = "cuándo?" + EN = "when?".

haykapraj, ADVI + SP = " cuándo será?" + EN = "we don't know when?".

haykachá, ADVI + SP = "no se cuándo será?" + EN = "I really don'n know?".

haykaya, ADVI + SP = "no se sabe cuándo será?" + EN = "when will be?".

haykapchá, ADVI + SP = "no sé cuándo será?".

maypitaj ayaja, ADVI + SP = "donde está el difunto".

maypitaj pamparunku ayataja, ADVI + SP = "donde enterraron el difunto".

imayna kajtataj tarirjankichik,ADVI + SP = "en qué estado lo encontraron?".

Location modifiers: *maypi, maymanta, mayninta, mayta, maykama, mainintataj, maymi,...*

maypi [in what place?].

maymanta [where from?].

mayninta [which way do you want to follow?].

mayta [towards which place?].

maynintataj rirja? [which way he went?].

Tense modifiers: *imaykama, haykapmi, haykapmantaraq, haykaptaq, haykapllaraq,*

...

imaykama [until when?].
haykapmi [when exactly?].
haykapmantaraq [from what period in the past?].
haykaptaq karqa [when did it hapen?].
Quantity modifiers: *haykata, haykam, haykapmi,…*
haykata [how many?].
haykatam munanki [How many exactly do you want?].
haykapmi chayamunqa [when exactly will it arrive?].

6 Interrogative Forms Using Dubitative Adverbial Suffixes

An interesting type of transformation of a direct sentence into a question involves the use of adverbs of doubt (*yaja, yajapas, icha, ichapas,…*) preceding the transformed sentence, as shown in Fig. 5.

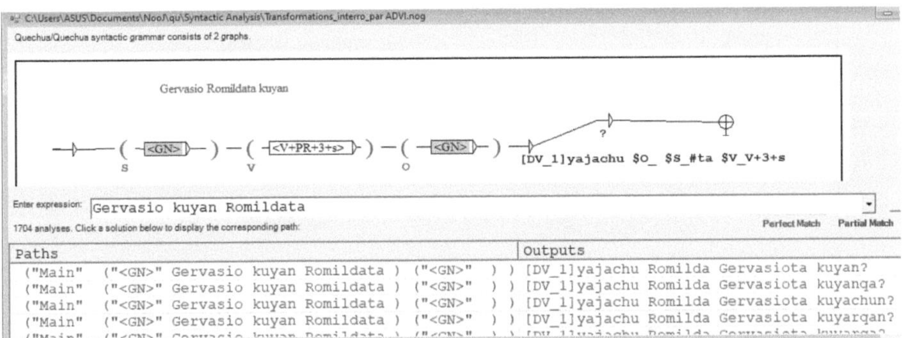

Fig. 5. The dubitative interrogation: *yajachu* [may it be possible].

7 Transforming a Direct Phrase into Interrogative Forms

As Silberztein [11] noted, an essential component of the formalization of the Quechua language is its transformational grammar. Let us take a direct sentence such as *Gervasio Romildata kuyan* [Gervasio loves Romilda] and apply some transformations. Each pair of the following sentences is associated with an interrogative transformation, indicated in brackets.

[QuestPi] *Gervasio Romildata kuyan* [Gervasio loves Romilda] → *pitaq kuyan Romildata?* [who loves Romilda] (**Uses the inflected form of the interrogative pronoun pi**).

[QuestVPr] *Gervasio Romildata kuyan* [Gervasio loves Romilda] → *kuyanchu Romildata Gervasio?* [does Gervasio love Romilda] (**Uses the form CHU applied to the verb**).

[QuestN1] *Gervasio Romildata kuyan* [Gervasio loves Romilda] → *Romildatachu Gervasio kuyan?* [is Romilda that Gervasio loves?] (**Uses the form CHU applied to the noun N1**).

98   M. Duran

[QuestN0] *Gervasio Romildata kuyan* [Gervasio loves Romilda] → *Gervasiochu Romildata kuyan?* [is Gervasio that loves Romilda?] (**Uses the form CHU applied to the noun N0**).

[QuestPro0] *Gervasio Romildata kuyan* [Gervasio loves Romilda] → *paychu Romildata kuyan?* [is he that loves Romilda?] (**Uses the form CHU applied to the pronoun pay**).

[QuestPVPassif] *Gervasio Romildata kuyan* [Gervasio loves Romilda] → *kuyasjanchu Romilda Gervasiopa?* [is Romilda loved by Gervasio?] (**Uses the form CHU applied to the passive form of the verb**).

The NooJ grammar of Fig. 6 can carry out transformational analysis and generation automatically.

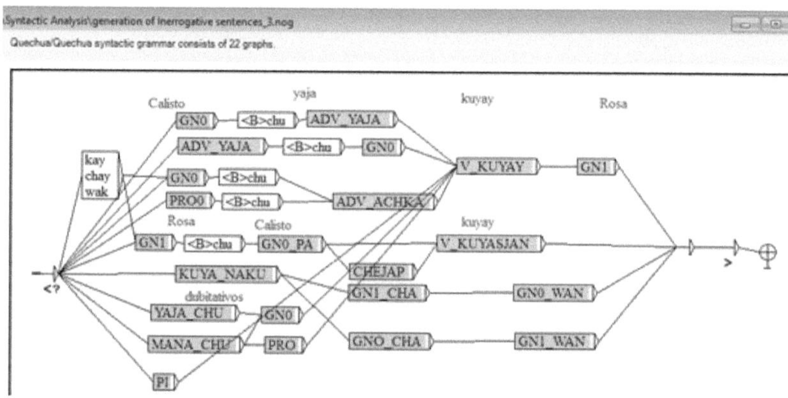

Fig. 6. Grammar: transforming a direct sentence into an interrogative one.

Parsing the sentence *Calisto kuyan Rosata* [Calisto loves Rosa] generates more than fifty thousand interrogative sentences, as shown in Fig. 7.

```
Dictionary contains 53735 entries

# Dictionary generated automatically
Calistoikichu wañuipajta kuyan Rosachata,P+Iterrogative?
Calistoikichu wañuipajta kuyan Rosata,P+Iterrogative?
icharaj Calistochalla kuyachallan paytaraj,P+Iterrogative?
icharaj Calistochalla kuyachallan paytapuni,P+Iterrogative?
kuyaykachanakunkuchu Calistochai Rosaikiwan,P+Iterrogative?
kuyaykachanakunkuchu Calistochai Rosaiwan,P+Iterrogative?
Calistochallachu sumajta kuyanraj Rosachallata,P+Iterrogative?
Calistochallachu sumajta kuyanraj Rosallata,P+Iterrogative?
Calistochallachu achka - achkata kuyarayan Rosatapuni,P+Iterrogative?
Calistochallachu achka - achkata kuyarayan Rosachallata,P+Iterrogative?
Calistochallachu achka - achkata kuyarayan Rosallata,P+Iterrogative?
Calistoikichu achkallataña kuyallan payta,P+Iterrogative?
Calistoikichu achkallataña kuyallan Rosataraj,P+Iterrogative?
Calistoikichu achkallataña kuyallan Rosatapuni,P+Iterrogative?
yachakunchikmi Calistoiku paytapuni wayllullasjanta,P+Iterrogative?
yachakunchikmi Calistoiku paytapuni wayllukullasjanta,P+Iterrogative?
yachakunchikmi Calistoiku paytapuni kuyakullasjanta,P+Iterrogative?
yachakunchikmi Calistoiku paytapuni kuyallasjanta,P+Iterrogative?
yachakunchikmi Calistoiku paytapuni munallasjanta,P+Iterrogative?
icharaj Calistochalla kuyallan payta,P+Iterrogative?
icharaj Calistochalla kuyallan Rosataraj,P+Iterrogative?
```

Fig. 7. Interrogative forms generated from a direct phrase.

Similarly, we have constructed morphosyntactic grammars to generate paraphrases of interrogative sentences, such as *Kuyanchu achkata Calisto Rosata*? [Does Calisto love much Rosa?], derived from the transformation of the sentence *Calisto Rosata kuyan* [Calisto loves Rosa]. An excerpt of the results is shown in Fig. 8.

```
Dictionary contains 53735 entries

# Dictionary generated automatically
Calistoikichu wañuipajta kuyan Rosachata,P+Iterrogative?
Calistoikichu wañuipajta kuyan Rosata,P+Iterrogative?
icharaj Calistochalla kuyachallan paytaraj,P+Iterrogative?
icharaj Calistochalla kuyachallan paytapuni,P+Iterrogative?
kuyaykachanakunkuchu Calistochai Rosaikiwan,P+Iterrogative?
kuyaykachanakunkuchu Calistochai Rosaiwan,P+Iterrogative?
Calistochallachu sumajta kuyanraj Rosachallata,P+Iterrogative?
Calistochallachu sumajta kuyanraj Rosallata,P+Iterrogative?
Calistochallachu achka - achkata kuyarayan Rosatapuni,P+Iterrogative?
Calistochallachu achka - achkata kuyarayan Rosachallata,P+Iterrogative?
Calistochallachu achka - achkata kuyarayan Rosallata,P+Iterrogative?
Calistoikichu achkallataña kuyallan payta,P+Iterrogative?
Calistoikichu achkallataña kuyallan Rosataraj,P+Iterrogative?
Calistoikichu achkallataña kuyallan Rosatapuni,P+Iterrogative?
yachakunchikmi Calistoiku paytapuni wayllullasjanta,P+Iterrogative?
yachakunchikmi Calistoiku paytapuni wayllukullasjanta,P+Iterrogative?
yachakunchikmi Calistoiku paytapuni kuyakullasjanta,P+Iterrogative?
yachakunchikmi Calistoiku paytapuni kuyallasjanta,P+Iterrogative?
yachakunchikmi Calistoiku paytapuni munallasjanta,P+Iterrogative?
icharaj Calistochalla kuyallan payta,P+Iterrogative?
icharaj Calistochalla kuyallan Rosataraj,P+Iterrogative?
```

Fig. 8. Paraphrases of Kuyanchu achkata Calisto Rosata?

8 Conclusion

The four forms of interrogative sentences have been formally defined.

1. Sentences containing the suffix *-Chu.*

Morphological single-word interrogative forms and PoS-based interrogative phrases. *wasichu* [is it the house].

2. Sentences employing or inflecting interrogative pronouns.

   pitaj rimachkan [who is speaking].

3. Sentences using interrogative adverbs and their inflections

   Jaykapmi rimanqa [When is he going to come?].

4. Sentences distinguished by intonation change

We have formalized the transformations from direct sentences into interrogative sentences. Several grammars have been developed to generate paraphrases of interrogative sentences.

In the future, we plan to continue developing paraphrase grammars and their Spanish and French transfer grammars.

References

1. Avila, F.: Dioses y hombres de Huarochiri. Quechua narrative collected by Francisco de Avila 1598(?). Arguedas, J.M. (Trans.). Lima, Perú (1966). Bilingual facsimile edition (2012)
2. Duran, M.: Formalización y tratamiento automático del adverbio en quechua. Aprendo con NooJ 2 (2022). https://doi.org/10.35305/an.vi2.11
3. Duran, M.: Dictionnaire électronique français-quechua des verbes pour le TAL. Université de Franche-Comté, Thèse de doctorat (2017)
4. Guaman Poma de Ayala, F.: Nueva Coronica y Buen Gobierno. Ed. Franklin Pease. 2 vols. Biblioteca Ayacucho, Caracas (1980)
5. Guardia Mayorga, C.: Pakpaku chayñawan rimanakun. Conte, pp. 383–384. In: Kechwa Grammar. Los Andes Editions, Lima, Perú (1973)
6. Itier, C., Meneses Lazón, P.: Contes du lever du jour. Achikyay Willaykuna. Bilingual Quechua–French. Presented and translated by C. Itier. Langues et Mondes L'Asiathèque, Paris (2001)
7. Lira, J.: Cuentos del Alto Urubamba. Centro Bartolomé de las Casas, Cuzco (1990)
8. Meneses, P.: Sept contes en quechua. Edition quechua–français by C. Itier. Langues et Mondes, Paris (2001)
9. Oregón Morales, J.: Loro Ccolluchi. Exterminio de loros y otros cuentos. Lluvia Editores, Lima (1994)
10. Silberztein, M.: Automatic transformational analysis and generation. In: Gavriilidou, Z., Chatzipapa, E., Papadopoulou, L., Silberztein, M. (eds.) Proceedings of the NooJ 2010 International Conference and Workshop, pp. 221–231. University of Thrace, Komotini (2011)
11. Silberztein, M.: Language Formalization: the NooJ Approach. Wiley (2016)
12. Taylor, G.: Ritos y Tradiciones de Huarochiri. Quechua manuscript from the beginning of the 17th century. 1st edn. IEP, Instituto Francés de Estudios Peruanos, Lima, Perú (1987)

Formalizing the Language of Young University Students

Andrea Fernanda Rodrigo(✉) ⓘ, Silvia Susana Reyes, and Mariana González

CETEHIPL, Universidad Nacional de Rosario, Rosario, Argentina
andrea.rodrigo@unr.edu.ar

Abstract. We created a corpus to identify salient features of Rioplatense Spanish within a specific community: young university students over eighteen years of age. Given the recent advances in generative artificial intelligence, it is essential that research in NLP provide this "intelligence" with access to the language varieties of all Spanish-speaking communities, so that it does not become an unreal, globalized product. Our aim has been to use the corpus in its raw form, without corrections or modifications, and to expand the dictionaries and grammars available in our Spanish Module Argentina [10] on the NooJ platform developed by Max Silberztein [9]. This has allowed us to examine the linguistic diversity of UNR students and to determine the type of language they use. A clear understanding of this linguistic landscape will enable us to enrich the Spanish Module Argentina with distinctive expressions, initially tagged as [+GRJOV], or "*gramática de jóvenes,*" youth grammar. Moreover, this knowledge will inform the development of teaching materials or even guide the creation of new discourse labels. The corpus will be made publicly available through the UNR data repository [8], facilitating future research and applications.

Keywords: NLP · Rioplatense Spanish · Youth Grammar

1 Introduction

1.1 The Aim of Our Paper

In the framework of our research project, "Towards a change in language teaching and learning using information technologies",[1] we created a corpus to identify salient characteristics of Rioplatense Spanish within a specific community: young university students over eighteen years of age.

Our guiding idea was to explore the language used by young people and to identify their own and distinctive expressions in order to valorize and empower these linguistic productions. We recognize that current advances in generative artificial intelligence make it imperative for NLP research to contribute by incorporating the linguistic diversity of

---

[1] Our four-year research project (2023–2026), hosted by the Faculty of Humanities and Arts, has been formally approved by the Supreme Council Resolution RCS No. 338/2023 of the National University of Rosario (UNR), Argentina.

© The Author(s), under exclusive license to Springer Nature Switzerland AG 2026
D. Petković et al. (Eds.): NooJ 2025, CCIS 2832, pp. 101–111, 2026.
https://doi.org/10.1007/978-3-032-17103-0_9

all Spanish-speaking communities, thereby preventing these technologies from evolving into a homogenized and artificially uniform global product.

Our aim has been to utilize this corpus, in its raw form, without corrections or modifications, and to expand the dictionaries and grammars available in our Spanish Module Argentina on the NooJ platform, developed by Max Silberztein. This allowed us to examine the linguistic diversity of UNR students and to determine the type of language they use. This linguistic knowledge will inform the development of teaching materials or even guide the creation of new discourse labels.

From the outset, a marked tendency toward oral discourse was apparent, echoing the informal dynamics of chat communications. In our 2021 publication, Rodrigo et al. [6], we reached similar conclusions, which attests to the relevance of this line of research. On that occasion, we also made the corpus freely available through the UNR data repository [7], offering authentic student productions to those in need of such materials. Engaging with youth language in real texts enables us to identify both the limitations and strengths of this "student language" and to establish an understanding of its current state. Defining a state of affairs thus constitutes an anchor point, not only rendering the present visible, but also allowing us to project future teaching materials and strategies aimed at enhancing and strengthening educational practices. Additionally, a clear grasp of this state of affairs will enrich our Spanish Module Argentina on the NooJ platform with unique expressions, initially tagged as [+GRJOV], *gramática de jóvenes*, youth grammar.

In the following sections, we will provide a purely descriptive account of the corpus (Sect. 2), and then we will proceed with its computational implementation using NooJ (Sect. 3).

2 The Corpus

Given the goals of our research project and in order to collect authentic expressions, a Google form was made available to National University of Rosario (UNR) students, inviting them to write an anecdote related to family or school. Based on the responses received, we compiled a corpus of 8,040 tokens. The sample, gathered between August and November 2024, comprises approximately eighty responses. It is worth noting that the corpus will be made publicly available through the UNR data repository [8], thereby facilitating future research and applications.

A range of salient features emerged from the corpus, as detailed below:

  (i) A marked relaxation of subject-verb agreement rules.
 (ii) A reduction in the use of punctuation marks and capitalization.
(iii) A marked relaxation in spelling rules.
(iv) The use of their own lexical terms along with terms from other Latin American varieties of Spanish (*americanismos*) and even from English.
 (v) The use of inclusive language.

Next, we will provide examples of the above-mentioned features to make a general analysis of the corpus.

2.1   A Marked Relaxation of Subject-Verb Agreement Rules

Deficiencies in spelling play an essential role in disrupting subject-verb agreement. To account for the relaxation of agreement rules, let us examine the following examples:

*2.1.1. **Ella** me **menciono** que yo me comía las "s"* [**She mention** to me that I used to swallow the "S's"].

In *ella…menciono,* subject-verb agreement is violated. The verb *menciono* stands for the first-person singular of the present indicative. However, the verb is misspelled, for it should have a written accent on the last vowel, *mencionó,* to indicate the third-person singular of the past indicative and to agree with the third-person singular pronominal subject *ella.*

*2.1.2. **Sucedió** que **me presente** en seis ocasiones al final de la materia y venía desaprobado los cinco intentos anteriores, cuando **me presente** por sexta si bien aprobé, se me aprobó por redondeo y cuando se me dise eso, me dejan ver los errores que tuve.* [(It) **happened** that (I) **take** six times for the final exam of the course and (I) had been failing the previous five attempts, when (I) **take** it for the sixth time, although (I) passed, I was approved through rounding and when I was told that, they let me see the mistakes (I) made].

As in *2.1.1,* subject-verb agreement is violated. In the subordinate noun clause functioning as subject of *sucedió,* the verb *me presente* may indicate the first or third-person singular of the present subjunctive. However, the verb is misspelled, for it should have a written accent on the last vowel, *me presenté,* to indicate the first-person singular of the past indicative and to agree with the first-person singular pro-drop subject *yo.*

2.2   A Reduction in the Use of Punctuation Marks and Capitalization

When a mode of writing closer to chat is adopted —leaning more toward orality than written form—, this feature becomes highly relevant. In chat communication, the use of full stops is not necessary; pauses are instead conveyed through intonation or, more precisely, through the fragmentation of utterances. The same applies to capital letters: the speed of writing takes precedence over time-consuming conventions. In chat language, the use of capital letters often requires switching to a different keyboard layout and therefore entails greater effort, which explains why they are frequently omitted. When transposed into written text, this practice results in a reduction in the use of punctuation marks and capital letters. Let us consider Example *2.2.1:*

*2.2.1. Al final cuando salimos al recreo me tuve que escapar por una ventana porque la puerta estaba cerrada con llave, y mis compañeras le dijeron a la profesora que yo estaba ahí, y ella pensó que me estaba muriendo asfixiado, por eso fue corriendo a buscarme pero yo ya no estaba. **tuve** que firmar una amonestación, aunque no me había metido por voluntad propia.* [In the end, when (we) went out for recess, (I) had to escape through a window because the door was locked, and my classmates told the teacher that I was there, and she thought that (I) was suffocating to death, so (she) ran to find me. But I was already gone. (I) had to sign a reprimand, although I had not gone in there of my own free will].

The omission or reduction of punctuation (particularly full stops) is clearly evident, resulting in a very long first sentence. Furthermore, the second sentence (*tuve…*) does not begin with a capital letter. The same phenomenon is noticeable in Example *2.2.2:*

*2.2.2. Esto fue finalizando el último año de la secundaria, dudando si venir a estudiar a **casilda** o quedarme en **rosario** y buscar otra alternativa de estudio, al final tomé la decisión de venir y me inscribí en la carrera de medicina veterinaria, el tema era que me inscribí 2 días antes de que cierre la entrega de los papeles de la inscripción, al otro día tuve que ir a sacar turno para certificar mi dni, ponerme la antitetanica y demás fotocopias, al final pude completar todo ese mismo día y al siguiente llevarlos a casilda!* [This happened toward the end of my final year at high school, doubting whether to come to study in **casilda** or stay in **rosario** and look for another study alternative, in the end (I) made the decision to come and (I) enrolled in the veterinary medicine career, the issue was that (I) enrolled 2 days before the deadline for submitting the registration paperwork, the next day (I) had to schedule an appointment to certify my dni, get the tetanus shot and other photocopies, in the end (I) managed to get everything that same day and the following day to take to **casilda**!].

As in *2.2.1*, full stops are often replaced by commas. Moreover, the absence of capital letters is particularly evident—not only at the beginning of sentences, but also in the marking of proper names. For instance, *Casilda* and *Rosario* are written in lowercase, despite being city names in the province of Santa Fe.

2.3 A Marked Relaxation in Spelling Rules

This subsection is related to what was presented in 2.1. Example *2.3.1.* illustrates the extent to which these features are present:

*2.3.1. Luego, al año siguiente me entero por amigas que están **rr**ecursando la materia que se **corrigio** lo que yo **plantee** en aquel momento.* [Then, the following year, (I) found out through friends who were **r**etaking the course that what I raised at that time was corrected.]

It is striking that a word begins with double *rr*, which is not permitted by orthographic rules, even when it is pronounced as a multiple vibrant 'r', as in *perro*, dog. This might indicate an area of opacity, as the rule prohibiting the use of 'rr' at the beginning of a word was not acquired at the appropriate stage in primary school, or it may simply reflect typographical carelessness.[2] Such carelessness, together with the omission of written accents on the last vowels (e.g., *corrigio, plantee*), recurs across various productions. Example *2.3.2.* also illustrates this tendency:

*2.3.2. A los once años me regalaron mi propio **petiso**, al que fuimos a buscar a un campo vecino, que era donde vivia. Más o menos una **legua**, como se decía entonces; son aproximadamente cinco **kilometros**.* [When I was eleven, I was given my own pony, which we went to fetch from a neighboring field, where (it) lived. More or less a league away, as people used to say back then; that's roughly five kilometers.]

---

[2] We cannot overlook the fact that we are going through a post-pandemic educational context. The implications of that period of isolation, during which schools were closed at critical stages of literacy acquisition, may be a factor not to be underestimated when interpreting this relaxation in reading and writing. In Example *2.3.1*, the acquisition of the rule prescribing the use of a single *r* at the beginning of a word clearly represents an area of opacity. This cannot be simply attributed to the systematic use of chat language; rather, it must, in our view, be analyzed within a broader context.

Without exception, every proparoxytone word in Spanish must bear an accent mark on the antepenultimate syllable, e.g., *kilómetros*. This example is also rich in lexical details, such as *petiso* and *legua*, which point to the rural context characteristic of the Argentine Pampas.

2.4   The Use of Local Lexical Terms Alongside Terms from Other Latin American Varieties of Spanish (*americanismos*) and Even from English

Examples *2.4.1.* and *2.4.2.* place us at a point of convergence between two emerging phenomena: on the one hand, globalized language (through the incorporation of English terms within a Spanish grammatical framework), and on the other, the use of expressions characteristic of "Latin American" Spanish:

2.4.1. Cuando digo reacción me refiero a las reacciones que se pueden dejar en los mensajes de **Whatssap**. [When (I) say reaction (I) refer to the reactions[3] that can be left on Whatssap messages.]

Example 2.4.1 includes an English term. Notably, the spelling of 'WhatsApp' has been modified, reflecting a graphic adaptation to the Spanish language context.

2.4.2. Lo peor es no poder decir nada, porque si decís algo quedás como la **forra** *que no sabe trabajar en grupo.* [The worst part is not being able to say anything, because if (you) say something, (you) look like the bad woman who doesn't know how to work in a group.]

Example *2.4.2* includes a distinctly Argentine term, *forra* [3], as well as the second-person singular inflection characteristic of Rioplatense Spanish—most notably, the *voseo* form *quedás*. Let us examine another example:

2.4.3. las emociones se volcaban de euforia, arrepujones y shimones en las pantor-rilla por la pelea del balón, y de repente, ¡Goooool! [Emotions spilled over with euphoria, shoves and kicks to the calves in the struggle for the ball, and suddenly, Goooal!]

Example *2.4.3* includes *arrepujones* as a variant of *arrempujones,* and *shimones* as a variant of *chimones* [5]. Meanwhile, the presence of the words *balón* and *gol* alludes to football, one of the most popular sports in Latin America and Argentina, and contributes a distinctive cultural marker to the corpus.

2.5   The Use of Inclusive Language

Let us examine the fifth and final feature observed in our corpus:

2.5.1. Ya pertenecía a un grupo hermoso y enorme de **varixs compañeres** *que se habia generado por WhatsApp, con el que habiamos compartido varios encuentros así que los nervios no jugaban el partido, sin embargo, llegué sobre la hora y se me hizo un poco difícil encontrar el salón.* [(I) already belonged to a beautiful and large group of **various companions** that had been generated through WhatsApp, with which we had shared several gatherings, so nerves weren't playing the game; however, (I) arrived in time and had a bit of trouble finding the room.]

---

[3] 'Reactions' may mean the emoji-based responses that users attach to individual WhatsApp messages.

Inclusive language is not used uniformly, as the [-x] marker for non-binary gender alternates with [-e]. *Varixs compañeres* is an example of inclusive usage: it avoids binary gender inflection by substituting 'x' and 'e' for the traditionally gendered inflections 'o' (masculine) and 'a' (feminine). This example also connects with example *2.4.1* through the inclusion of the popular term WhatsApp, although in this instance, its English spelling is retained.

3 Work in NooJ

We now turn to corpus processing with NooJ. We will briefly review the changes introduced in the Spanish Module Argentina in order to accurately account for the features observed in the productions of university students.

3.1 Changes in Properties' Definition

We modified the Properties' Definition file to incorporate inclusive endings for both nouns and adjectives, based on the patterns observed in our corpus. Additionally, we added the tag [+ingl] to nouns.

- N_género = masc I fem I g_inv I neutro Iinclus;
- N_origen = ingl;
- ADJ_género = masc I fem I g_inv I neutroI inclus;

3.2 A New Dictionary

We created a youth dictionary to record the distinctive features of young students' writing without altering our main dictionary. Each new entry was tagged as [+GRJOV]. Since no orthographic corrections were applied, we accepted variants that diverge from standard Spanish spelling. As a result, the youth dictionary includes verbs without accent marks and words with non-normative spellings.

3.2.1 Verbs

- *veia*, V + pi + 3a + sg + ind + GRJOV
- *rrecursando*, V + ger + GRJOV
- *corrigio*, V + pps + 3a + sg + ind + GRJOV
- *hechar la reta*, V + locución + GRJOV#iniciar un partido de fútbol informal, usado en México[4]
- *hechar la cascarilla*, V + locución + GRJOV#iniciar un partido de fútbol informal, usado en México[5]

---

[4] It is important to note that NooJ allows the inclusion of user comments in the dictionary, marked with an asterisk. These comments are not processed by the system. We have employed this feature to enrich and validate our dictionary.

[5] Rioplatense Spanish is lexically enriched by terms from other Latin American countries, such as Mexico (e.g.: *pelota chimeca*). This reflects an inclusive public university education that is open to the world.

3.2.2 Nouns

- *Whatssap.* #término del inglés
- *mixeados* #término del inglés
- *faoul* #término del inglés
- *forra* #argentinismo [3]
- *arrepujones* #variante de arrempujones *(RAE)* español de México [4]
- *shimones#variante de chimón (rozadura)* en Diccionario de americanismos, español de México [5]
- *chaparro#* Diccionario de americanismos, español de México
- *choya#* Diccionario de americanismos, español de México
- *choncho#* Diccionario de americanismos, español de Puerto Rico
- *petiso#* Diccionario de americanismos, español de Argentina

3.2.3 Adjectives and Adverbs

- *al rededor*, ADV + GRJOV# old form of the adverb around (source CORDE Dictionary) [2]
- *antitetanica*, ADJ + fem + sg + GRJOV
- *chimeca#* Diccionario de americanismos, español de México
- *rapido*, ADJ + masc + sg + GRJOV

3.3 Changes in Morphological Grammars

The corpus generated from students' productions compelled us to make changes to the morphological grammars. The changes in the Properties Definition file are reflected in the modifications to the morphological grammars, particularly in the inflectional paradigms of adjectives and nouns. A new gender ending [+inclus] was added:

- FLACO = <E> /masc + sg | s/masc + pl | <B> a/fem + sg | <B> as/fem + pl |<B> x/inclus + sg|<B> xs/inclus + pl;
- PERRO = <E> /masc + sg|s/masc + pl|<B> a/fem + sg|<B> as/fem + pl|<B> e/inclus + sg|<B> es/inclus + pl;

These changes to the inflectional models allow us to inflect the entries and generate the following forms: *flaco, flaca, flacos, flacas, flacx, flacxs,* and, on the other hand, *perro, perra, perros, perras, perre, perres.*

3.4 Syntax in Our Corpus

Before presenting the new grammars we designed for our corpus, it is useful to consider some general points regarding syntax, in order to align with other works previously published by our team, where we applied the notion of the nucleus phrase proposed by Gabriel Bès [1], a guiding concept that has always been at the core of our research. From this perspective, nucleus phrases are integrated into a larger phrase.

Tense correlation is not always observed: verbs in the present tense are constantly combined with verbs in the past. Syntax becomes complex, as the corpus contains either no full stops or very few. Close to orality, word order without punctuation pushes grammaticality to its limits.

Let us begin with the noun phrase in *3.4.1*:

*3.4.1. Un grupo hermoso y enorme **de varixs compañeres** que se habia generado por WhatsApp.* [A beautiful and large group of companions that had been formed through WhatsApp.]

This noun phrase presents a challenge not only because it contains a prepositional phrase (*de varixs compañeres*), but also because it features inclusive inflections. The grammar for this noun phrase is displayed in Fig. 1.

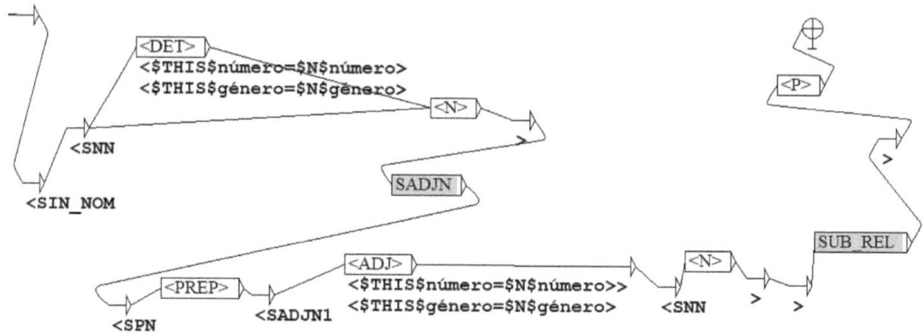

Fig. 1. Grammar for the noun phrase of *3.4.1*.

In keeping with standard practice, we used *Locate* to validate the grammar (Fig. 2).

Fig. 2. Validation of the grammar in Fig. 1 using *Locate*.

Sentence *3.4.2.* illustrates a disruption in subject-verb agreement:

*3.4.2. **Ella** me **menciono** que yo me comía las "s". [She mention to me that I used to swallow the "S's"].*

In this grammar, we observe, on the one hand, a lack of tense correlation between the verb of the subordinate clause (*comía*, imperfect tense) and the verb of the main clause (*menciono*, present tense). Additionally, there is a violation of subject-verb agreement: the verb *menciono* (I mention) indicates the first-person singular of the present indicative, but it does not agree with the pronominal third-person singular subject *ella* (she). Proper third-person singular subject-verb agreement, whether in the present or past tense, would be **menciona** or **mencionó**, respectively. It is important to note that, in many cases, the accent mark is essential for distinguishing whether a verb form expresses the present or the past tense.

When designing this grammar in NooJ, we did not consider the tense correlation rules between the verb of the subordinate clause and the verb of the main clause. Figure 3 shows how a sentence that violates agreement can be processed, and how the analysis can be validated using *Show Debug*.

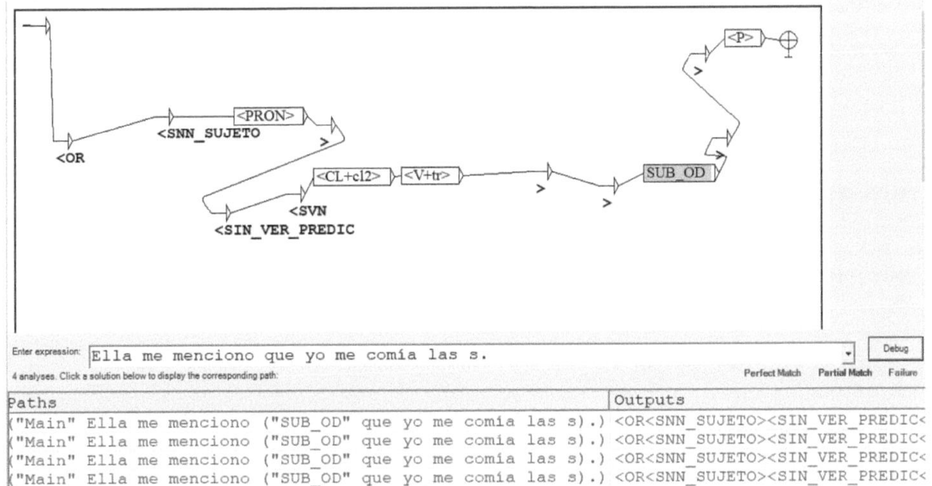

Fig. 3. Grammar and validation for *3.4.2*.

NooJ can easily process sentences with varying word order, whether following the traditional subject-predicate syntactic structure or the more emphatic predicate-subject arrangement, as in sentence *3.4.3*:

3.4.3. Estallaba de emociones resbordadas el equipo ganador. [Was Bursting with Overflowing Emotions the Winning Team.]

Figure 4 shows the grammar we designed for *3.4.3*.

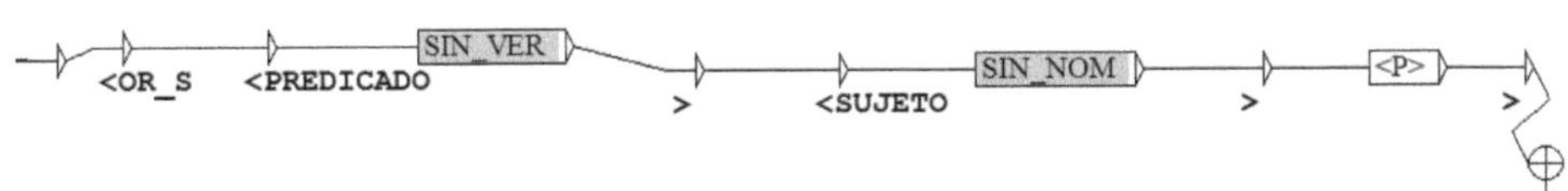

Fig. 4. Grammar for *3.4.3*.

Finally, we applied *Linguistic Analysis* to validate the grammar of Fig. 4 (Fig. 5).

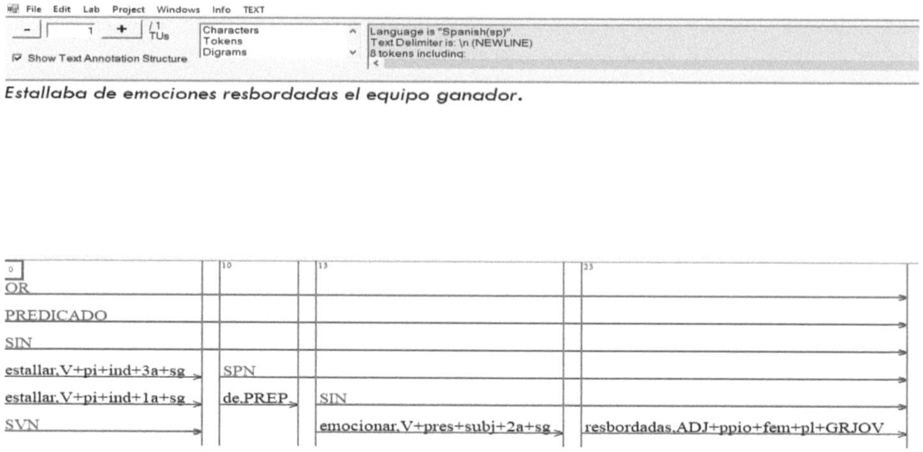

Fig. 5. Linguistic Analysis applied to the grammar of Fig. 4.

4 Conclusions

In this work, we considered several aspects related to the analysis of the corpus compiled from UNR student responses (via Google Forms). Participants were asked to narrate family or school anecdotes with the aim of capturing authentic expressions of our culture. Five features drew our attention: a marked relaxation in subject-verb agreement and in spelling rules, a reduction in the use of punctuation marks and capitalization, the use of their own lexical terms along with terms from other Latin American varieties of Spanish (*americanismos*) and even from English, and the use of inclusive language. However, we chose not to address the reduction in punctuation, given NooJ's capacity to insert punctuation marks in graphs using the <P> operator. Nonetheless, we reserve for future work an exploration of how the comma frequently replaces the full stop as the sole punctuation mark.

Our analysis revealed the need for a youth dictionary that includes lexical entries that are either typical of Argentine culture (*argentinismos*) and Latin American expressions (*americanismos*). This reflects a longstanding Argentine tradition: public universities welcome both Argentine citizens and individuals from other Latin American countries (as well as from elsewhere, of course). These new entries tagged as [+GRJOV] enrich our corpus and reinforce our commitment to developing AI resources that are not market-driven but instead nourished by Latin American idiosyncrasy. This approach preserves the authenticity of youth linguistic production and enables the study of emergent forms and deviations from normative orthography within digital and informal registers. It is worth noting that we also incorporated inclusive inflections due to NooJ's morphological flexibility, which enhanced the patterns generated by our morphological grammars. This addition also responds to the need for greater representational flexibility in gender marking, aligning with contemporary inclusive language practices.

Finally, the syntax often deviates from the typical subject-verb-object order of Spanish. This tendency is closely linked to the oral nature of chat-based communication and is particularly characteristic of youth writing. It is also highly probable that disruptions in tense agreement —often caused by the absence of accent marks on certain verb forms—occur primarily in written texts, rather than in oral discourse. As a result, students tend to demonstrate greater proficiency in oral production than in written expression.

References

1. Bès, G.G.: La phrase verbale noyau en français. Recherches sur le français parlé **15**, 237–358. Publications de l'Université de Provence (1999)
2. Corpus diacrónico del Español (CORDE) de la RAE. http://corpus.rae.es/cordenet.html. Accessed 23 Aug 2025
3. Jergozo. Diccionario de jergas hispanas. https://www.jergozo.com. Accessed 23 Aug 2025
4. Real Academia Española: Diccionario de la lengua española (23rd ed.). [Versión 23.8 en línea]. https://dle.rae.es. Accessed 23 Aug 2025
5. Real Academia Española, Asociación de Academias de la Lengua Española: Diccionario de americanismos. https://www.asale.org/damer/. Accessed 23 Aug 2025
6. Rodrigo, A., Reyes, S., Fernández Gallino, M.A.: Automatic treatment of causal, consecutive, and counterargumentative discourse connectors in Spanish. In: Bekavac, B., Kocijan, K., Silberztein, M., Šojat, K. (eds.) Formalising Natural Languages: Applications to Natural Language Processing and Digital Humanities. NooJ 2020, Communications in Computer and Information Science, vol. 1389. Springer, Cham (2021). https://doi.org/10.1007/978-3-030-70629-6_14
7. Rodrigo, A.F.: Dataset: Automatic Treatment of Causal, Consecutive, and Counterargumentative Discourse Connectors in Spanish. RDA UNR, V1 (2022). https://doi.org/10.57715/UNR/KXHJO2
8. Rodrigo, A.F.: Dataset corpus de textos escritos por estudiantes de grado de la Universidad Nacional de Rosario. RDA UNR, V1 (2025). https://doi.org/10.57715/UNR/5KKC9I
9. Silberztein, M.: Formalizing Natural Languages: the NooJ Approach. Wiley, Hoboken NJ, USA (2016)
10. Spanish Module Argentina. https://nooj.univ-fcomte.fr/resources.html. Accessed 23 Aug 2025

Formalization of Numerical Expressions in Rioplatense Spanish: A Pedagogical Application

Carmen González[(⊠)], Celina Colussi, and Iván Oliva

CETEHIPL, Universidad Nacional de Rosario, Rosario, Argentina
caar.gonzalez26@gmail.com

Abstract. This research focuses on the pedagogical application of NooJ. Drawing from the CETEHIPL (*Centro de Estudios de Tecnología Educativa y Herramientas Informáticas de Procesamiento del Lenguaje*) framework, we explore and define aspects of the Rioplatense Spanish used by a specific group: young people over the age of eighteen and university students at the UNR. This study also aims to expand the Spanish-Argentine module [8] through the automatic processing of numerals. According to the *Nueva Gramática de la Real Academia Española* [3], numerals are classified as cardinals and ordinals. Bartulović and Mijić [1] set a precedent in this field by analyzing Medieval Latin numerals to create inflectional models in the NooJ format. Although our primary goal is to describe the use of numeral expressions by this specific age group in our reference corpus [6] and any other aspects that may arise, their work serves as a starting point for us. Our research is intended to be developed as follows: first, we will seek to complete the dictionaries and inflectional grammars in the Spanish-Argentine module. Second, we will design grammars that can analyze numerical expressions similar to the ones that occur in the corpus. While these advances are preliminary, we hope to draw some conclusions based on the use of genuine expressions of Rioplatense Spanish among young people who use numerals.

Keywords: Numerals · Youth grammar · Rioplatense Spanish · NooJ

1 Introduction

This research primarily focuses on the pedagogical application of NooJ for Natural Language Processing (NLP), a linguistic environment developed by Max Silberztein[7]. We created a corpus based on the framework of our research project[1] to define key aspects and features of Rioplatense Spanish spoken by young university students over eighteen years old. Framed within the scope of the study of the CETEHIPL (*Centro de Estudios*

---

[1] This study was carried out inthe framework of our research project, "Towards a change in language teaching and learning using information technologies", Supreme Council Resolution RCS N°338 23, Faculty of Humanities and Arts, National University of Rosario, UNR, Argentina (2023–2026).

D. Petković et al. (Eds.): NooJ 2025, CCIS 2832, pp. 112–123, 2026.
https://doi.org/10.1007/978-3-032-17103-0_10

de Tecnología Educativa y Herramientas Informáticas de Procesamiento del Lenguaje), this research also seeks to explore and define aspects of Rioplatense Spanish used by a specific group. To achieve this, we started working on a corpus, taking into account a specific population: young people over the age of eighteen and university students at the UNR. The primary goal was to find out what kind of language young people speak and which expressions are their own, in order to give them value and empower these linguistic productions.

With regard to our corpus, it is important to make clear the methodology used to collect the examples produced by the university students: a Google form was used, in which they were asked to write an anecdote about family or school in order to collect genuine expressions. This form served as a resource to create a corpus containing 8,040 tokens. Students were asked to complete this Google Form from July to November 2024, and during this period, 80 responses were received.

2   Our Research

To organize our exposition, we will follow several stages. First, we will try to define what numerals in Spanish[2] are; second, we will try to characterize the written production from the corpus; and third, we will present the work in NooJ.

From a grammatical point of view, numerals present grammatical complexity because they serve different functions while also sharing similarities with other word categories such as determiners, adjectives, and even nouns. According to the *Nueva Gramática de la Real Academia Española,* numerals can be classified as **cardinal** numerals and **ordinal** numerals[3]. The question now is how to reflect this theoretical background in the corpus of reference, and what conclusions we can draw from it[4].

Taking into account the written samples provided by the young students, it was observed not only that this written corpus was quite similar to oral language, but also that, in previous works[5], this written language was quite similar to WhatsApp chat as well. Becoming acquainted with the language used by young people in real texts will enable us to account for the shortcomings and strengths of this "language used by students" and to thus establish a state of affairs. A clear understanding of this state of affairs will make it possible for us to enrich our Spanish-Argentine module in the NooJ platform with genuine expressions that, initially, will be identified with the tag [+GRJOV], *gramática de jóvenes* ('youth grammar'). Here are some examples containing numerals provided by our young students:

2.1. *Cuando yo tenía unos dos o tres años./* When I was two or three years old.

---

[2] Even though we centered our research on Rioplatense Spanish, it is necessary to clarify that we did not see significant differences between this and the Spanish spoken in the Iberian Peninsula.

[3] According to this bipartite classification, cardinal numerals are used to express quantities, whereas ordinal numbers indicate position or rank within a sequence or order.

[4] Bartulović and Mijić [1] set an important antecedent in this field: they analyzed Medieval Latin numerals, using tags to create inflectional models in NooJ.

[5] Specifically, Rodrigo et al. [4] analyzed texts provided by primary school teachers and early childhood educators, and Rodrigo, Andrea [5] published the data on which the research was based.

2.2. *Hace dos años* / Two years ago.
2.3. *Dos hechos relacionados con lo paranormal* / two facts related to the paranormal.
2.4. *En primer lugar, sufrimos un corte de luz./* First, we experienced a power outage.
2.5. *Primero hablamos de las montañas./* First, we talked about the mountains.

3   Working in NooJ

In the automatic processing of NooJ, several stages were followed. This work is intended
to be developed as follows:

- Check that the Properties' Definitions contain all the necessary definitions required
  to address structures using numerals.
- Complete the dictionaries and inflectional grammars in the Spanish-Argentine
  module.
- At the syntactic level, design grammars that can analyze and generate typical
  expressions such as those found in the corpus.

3.1   Changes in the Properties' Definitions

We noticed that the numerals appearing in our corpus were classified as adjectives with
a clear nominal nucleus, instead of quantifiers referring to countable items. Thus, we
needed to check whether the ordinal and cardinal numeral categories are included in the
definitions of adjectives. After confirming that these categories were not included, we
made a series of changes:

ADJ_tipo = num|rel|gentil;
ADJ_tipo_num = ordinal|cardinal;

3.2   Changes in Dictionaries

A series of lexical entries attested in our corpus was included:

3.2.1 uno,ADJ + num + cardinal + sg
3.2.2 dos,ADJ + num + cardinal + pl
3.2.3 2,ADJ + num + cardinal + pl + GRJOV[6]
3.2.4 tres,ADJ + num + cardinal + pl
3.2.5 cuatro,ADJ + num + cardinal + pl
3.2.6 cinco,ADJ + num + cardinal + pl
3.2.7 primer,ADJ + masc + sg + apócope + num + ordinal
3.2.8 primero,ADJ + FLX = FLACO + apocopable + num + ordinal
3.2.9 segundo,ADJ + FLX = FLACO + num + ordinal

It is worth noting that we added to our dictionary the possibility of numbers being
treated as ordinal adjectives replacing letters, as shown in 3.2.3. We verified that this
could be done in NooJ without any problems. We then extended the syntactic grammar
in the SNN (nominal phrase nucleus) that we had created with the previous lexical entry:

---

[6] We observed that in the corpus, numbers appeared as such in addition to letters. For example:
El tema era que me inscribí 2 días antes.

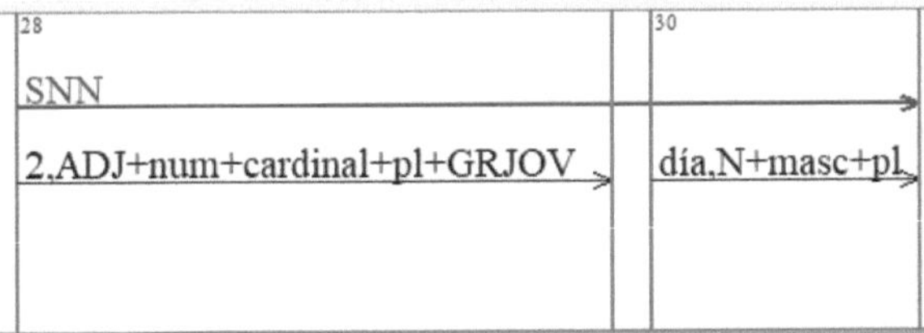

Fig.1. SNN with numbers instead of words only.

3.3 Our Grammars

In our grammars, we follow the model provided by Gabriel Bès [2] for the verbal phrase nucleus in French, in order to maintain consistency with what we propose in our Spanish Argentine module, as shown in Fig. 1. We have now developed our grammars based on the examples in Sect. 2.

First Adverbial Larger Phrase. We first processed the following example, which contains a larger adverbial phrase: *Cuando yo tenía unos dos o tres años*/When I was two or three years old. In Fig. 2, we present the grammar corresponding to this phrase:

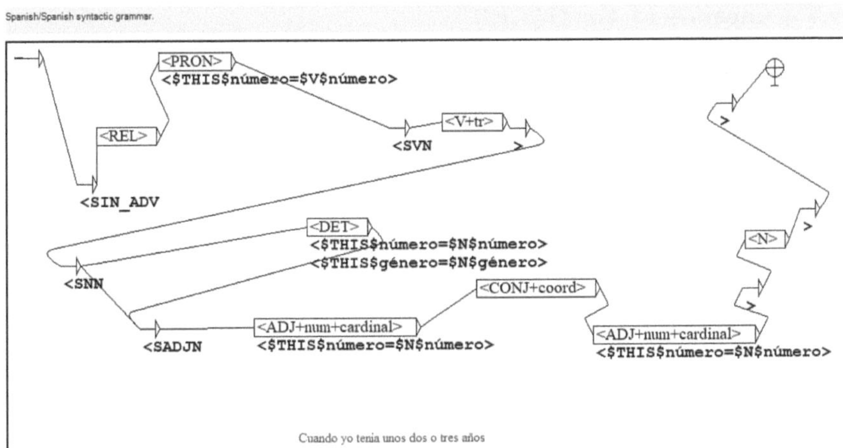

Fig. 2. SIN_ADV.

We created a grammar that reflects the order and arrangement of the constituents of this larger adverbial phrase. In this example, we see that the cardinal numeral can be preceded by a determiner within the nominal phrase nucleus, or it can be left unmodified. This, in turn, generates agreement with its nominal nucleus. The numeral can also be coordinated, as in this case, with a disjunctive conjunction. In general, the cardinal numeral integrates an adjectival phrase nucleus inside a nominal phrase nucleus. The cardinal numeral can be preceded by a determiner (e.g., *unos*), but it cannot be followed by another adjective, such as a qualifying adjective.

Now, to validate this grammar, we use *Locate*, as shown in Fig. 3:

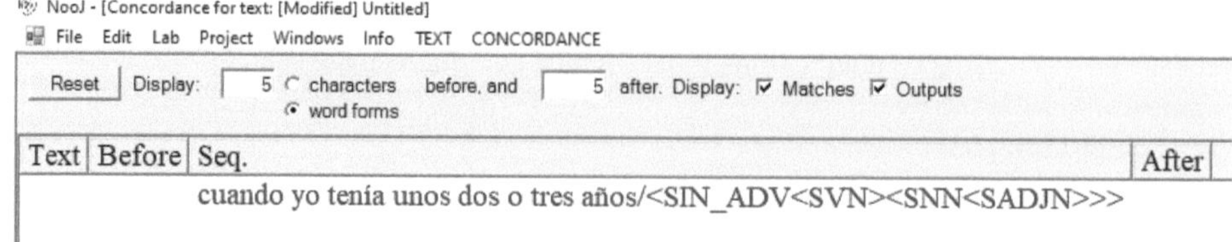

Fig. 3. *Locate* to validate the grammar

Use of Cardinal Numerals in Impersonal Expressions. In this example, we present a grammar that allows us to process the impersonal expression: *Hace dos años*/Two years ago. To process it, we had to follow two steps:

First step: check that *Properties´ Definition* includes minor sentences, i.e., sentences which do not have a clause as one of their constituents:

O_clase = B | U |C |S | SUBORD | COORD;

Second step: check that the Spanish verb *hacer* is included for use in impersonal expression structures:

hacer,V + impers + FLX = HACER

Next, we show in Fig. 4 a grammar used for impersonal expressions and validation with *Show debug:*

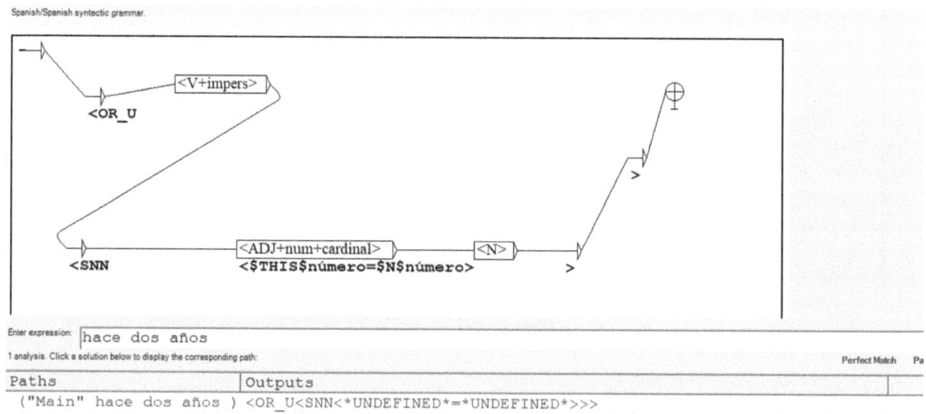

Fig. 4. Grammar for an impersonal sentence (OR_U) containing a cardinal numeral.

Grammar for the Noun Phrase with Cardinal Numerals. This example allows us to present a grammar for a larger nominal phrase, SIN_NOM, that contains a larger adjectival phrase, SIN_ADJ: *dos hechos relacionados con lo paranormal/* two facts related to the paranormal. See Fig. 5

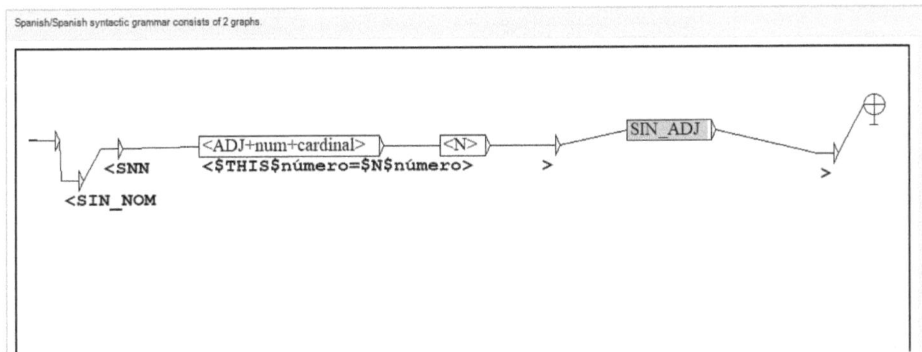

Fig. 5. Grammar for a SIN_NOM.

To validate the grammar of Fig. 5, we used the *Linguistic analysis,* as shown in Fig. 6:

dos hechos relacionados con lo paranormal					
SIN					
SNN		SIN			
dos.ADJ+num+cardinal+pl	hecho.N+masc+pl	relacionado.ADJ+ppio+masc+pl	SPN		
dos.CUANT+num+masc+pl	hacer.V+tr+ppio+masc+pl	SADJN	con.PREP	SADJN	
dos.CUANT+num+fem+pl	hacer.V+intr+ppio+masc+pl			lo.CL+cl3+3a+sg+masc+ac	
	hacer.V+impers+ppio+masc+pl			lo.DET+artdet+sg	

Fig. 6. Grammar validation of Fig. 5.

The grammar has to reflect that the nucleus noun phrase *dos hechos* ('two facts') is concatenated with a larger adjective phrase (SIN_ADJ) *relacionados con lo paranormal* (as shown in the embedded graph of the main grammar). The numeral is placed in front of a nominal nucleus, just as in the previous examples. This example shows that the nominal nucleus can be followed by a SIN_ADJ.

Pro_Drop Subject Sentence Including an Ordinal Numeral. In this example, we present the grammar of a sentence containing an ordinal numeral: *En primer lugar, sufrimos un corte de luz* ('First, we experienced a power outage'). See Fig. 7:

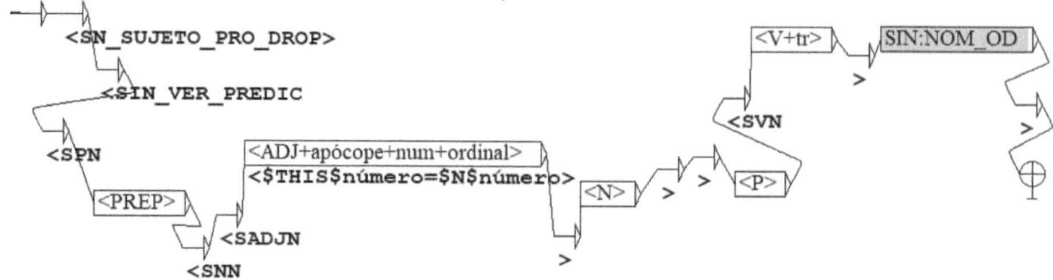

Fig.7. Grammar of a Pro_Drop subject sentence

Again, we need to validate the grammar; however, in this case, we need to use *Locate*. In Fig. 8 Grammar validation Fig. 7:

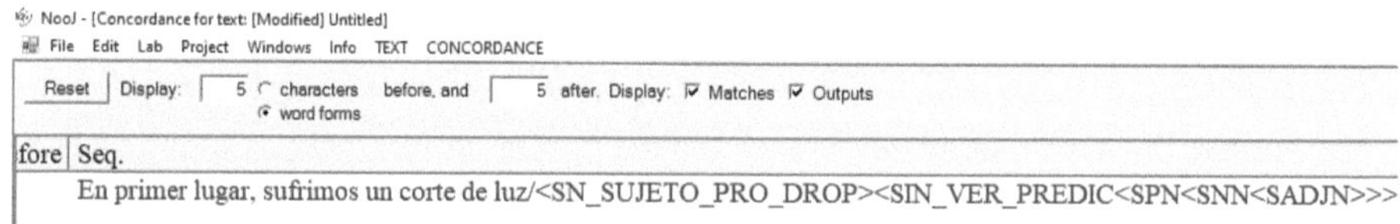

Fig. 8. Validation of the grammar

Prototype for the Expressions Using Cardinal Numerals. We continue to build a prototype grammar that can subsume the cardinal numerals found in our corpus. See Fig. 9:

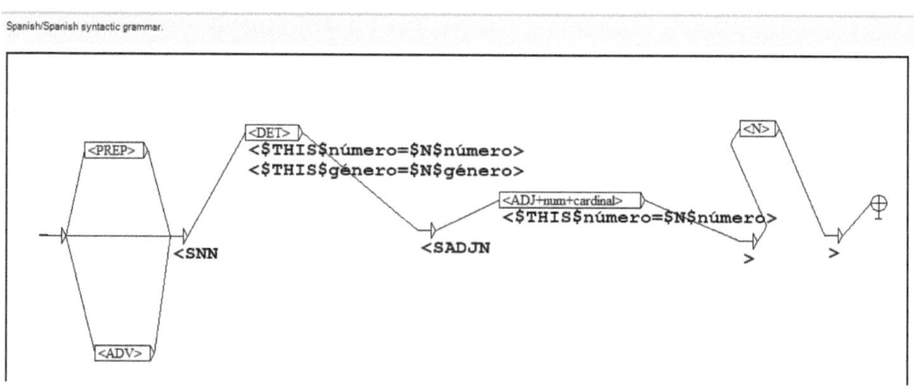

Fig. 9. Prototype for expressions with cardinal numerals.

By using *Locate* in our corpus, we obtained a considerable number of occurrences that correspond to the format shown in Fig. 9. See Fig. 10:

Text (Before)	Seq.	After
Río Turbio, cuando apenas tenía	siete años	, me separé del grupo de
la profesora se había ido,	dos chicos	me agarraron y me metieron
recibí de Trabajadora Social. Hace	dos años	me inscribí nuevamente y acá
día me pasó que teníamos (	cinco compañeras	y yo) planear un encuentro
un documento en común. Restaban	solo cuatro días	para el encuentro. Solicité ayuda
dinámica y solo recibí algunas	de dos compañeras	. Del resto nada. Terminé la
del encuentro cuando yo hacía	tres días	que les venía pidiendo que
dije que a las únicas	dos personas	que persigo en esta vida
para que hagan algo, son	a mis dos hijos	. El resto que se haga
no había pared, así que	entre tres personas	lo corrimos y dimos con
atrapada'. El curso se dividía	en dos grandes	equipos: uno de varones y
de sangrar porque me partí	las dos paletas	. No había llegado a poner
compuesta x mi esposo y	mis siete hijos	.Cuatro son Universitario y dos
esposo y mis siete hijos.	Cuatro son	Universitario y dos están en
para lograr un acuerdo. Uno	de los dos pregunta	¿vas a llamar a mi
estudiando, ingresé como ayudante alumno	en tres cátedras	, sin expectativas económicas. A tres
tres cátedras, sin expectativas económicas.	A tres meses	de haber comenzado con esta
llamado a concurso en una	de las tres cátedras	. Me presento, y gano el
a mi padre, también Jaime	de nueve años	de edad. En 1990 me fui
directora porque me habían desaprobado	dos veces	matemáticas en la secundaria Una
que se hizo por más	de cien años	. En nuestro caso, intentando volver

Fig. 10. *Locate* based on the application of the prototype for cardinal numerals.

A *Statistical Analysis* of cardinal numeral occurrences was applied based on the output of the *Locate*. See Fig. 11:

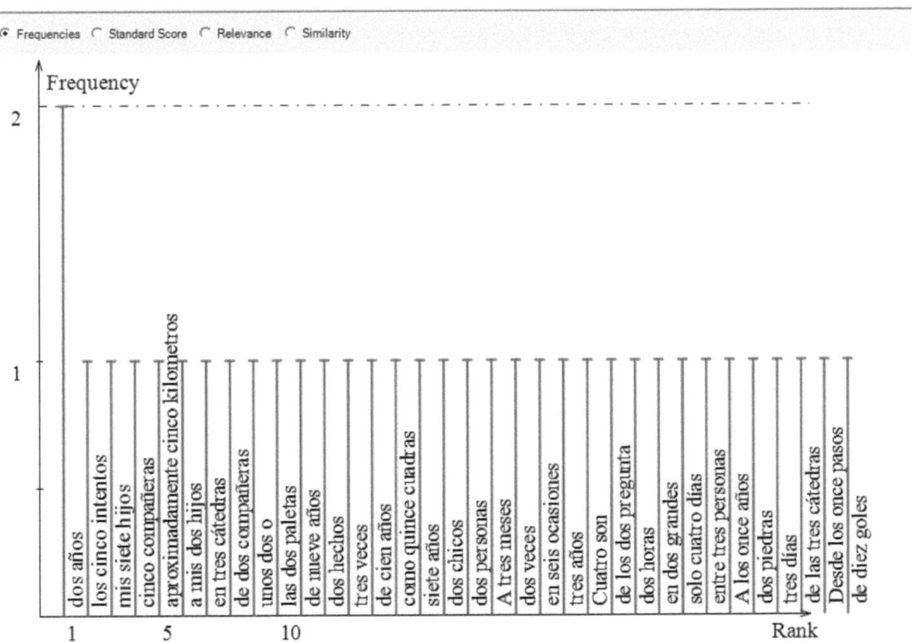

Fig. 11. *Statistical Analysis* of the output in Fig. 10

From Fig. 10, we understand that cardinal numeral adjectives usually come before a nominal nucleus and agree with the noun phrase. They can be preceded by a determiner, preposition, or adverb.

Prototype for Expressions Using Ordinal Numerals.   We continue to build a prototype grammar that can subsume the ordinal numeral expressions found in our corpus. See Fig. 12:

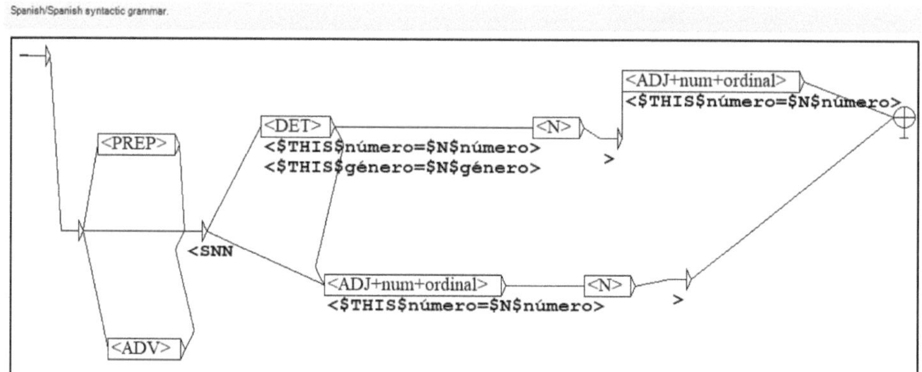

Fig. 12. Prototype for expressions with ordinal numerals.

By using *Locate* in our corpus, we obtained a considerable number of occurrences that correspond to the format shown in Fig. 12. See Fig. 13:

Text	Before	Seq.	After
intentos anteriores, cuando me presente		por sexta si	bien aprobé, se me aprobó
el partido con el anhelado		primer gol	. Minutos más tarde, caían más
de repente cambió de portería		al quinto gol	. Todo era sudor, fuerza y
anécdota va a estar dirigida		a el primer día	que pisé la facultad, allá
la facultad, allá por el 2022,		primera clase	presencial post pandemia. Ya pertenecía
relacionados con lo paranormal sucedieron:		en primer lugar	, sufrimos un corte de luz
tendido eléctrico con la casa;		en segundo lugar	, se produjo al día siguiente
entorno familiar con cierta inquietud.		La primera vez	que ingresé a Humanidades fue
formal o estricta. Cuando dieron		esta primera charla	nos separaron por carreras y
su experiencia universitaria. A partir		de esos primeros días	de cursada encontré casi una
la ropa a la basura.		En segundo año	de la secundaria, un día
agregué que se supone que		en un cuarto año	, uno ya sabe la dinámica
momento que sonó el timbre.		Mi primer recuerdo	en una institución escolar: Me
de mi niñez ,infancia . Recuerdo		las primeras lecturas	junto a la estufa de
veía un testículo. Anécdota familiar		sobre las primeras vacaciones	de la familia completa las
tradición de que los estudiantes		de quinto año	se despidan de la escuela
cuando tenía 10 años y cursaba		cuarto grado	de la escuela primaria. Tenía
semana uno de esos libros.		Al séptimo día	, debíamos llevar una reseña propia

Fig. 13. *Locate* based on the application of the prototype for ordinal numerals.

A *Statistical Analysis* of ordinal numeral occurrences was applied based on the output of *Locate*. See Fig. 14:

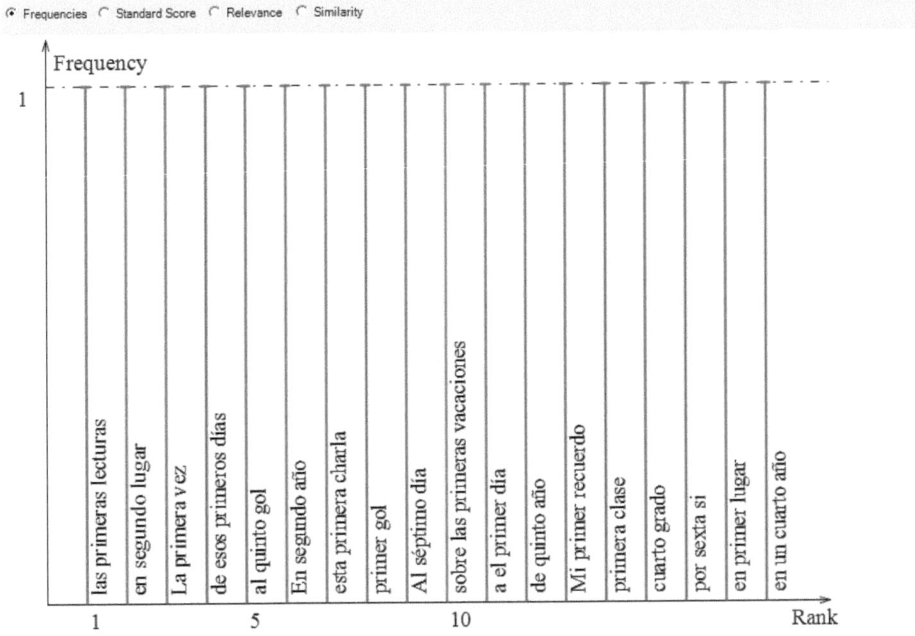

Fig. 14. *Statistical Analysis* of the output in Fig. 13

Integrating the Two Prototypes. We integrated both prototypes to achieve a greater generalization. See Fig. 15:

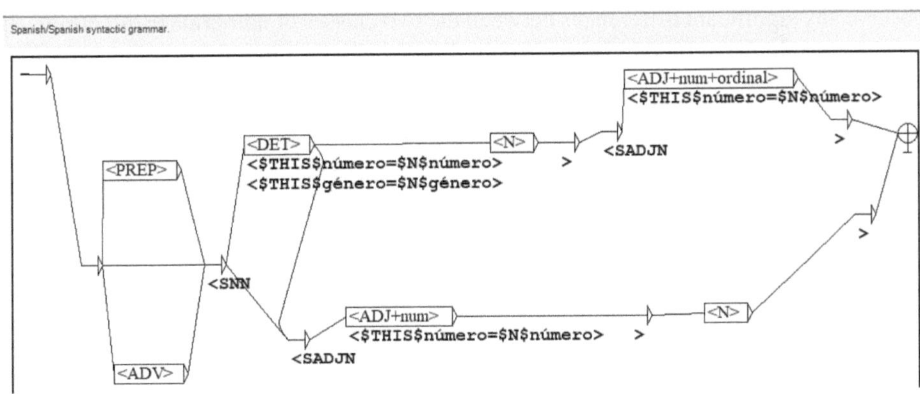

Fig. 15. Prototype grammar for two types of numerals.

Generation of the Integrated Prototype. We continued to develop the generation process based on the integrated prototype. See Fig. 16:

```
# Language is: sp
#
# Alphabetical order is not required.
#
# Use inflectional & derivational paradigms' description files (.nof), e.g.:
# Special Command: #use paradigms.nof
#
# Special Features: +NW (non-word) +FXC (frozen expression component) +UNAMB (unambiguous lexical entry
#                   +FLX= (inflectional paradigm) +DRV= (derivational paradigm)
#
# Special Characters: '\' '"' ' ' ',' '+' '-' '#'
#
#
# Dictionary generated automatically
#
<DET> <N> <ADJ+num+ordinal>,<SNN+<$THIS$número=$N$número>+<$THIS$género=$N$género>>+<$THIS$número=$N$nú
<DET> <ADJ+num> <N>,SNN+<$THIS$número=$N$número>+<$THIS$género=$N$género>+<$THIS$número=$N$número>
<ADJ+num> <N>,SNN+<$THIS$número=$N$número>
<PREP> <DET> <N> <ADJ+num+ordinal>,<SNN+<$THIS$número=$N$número>+<$THIS$género=$N$género>>+<$THIS$númer
<PREP> <DET> <ADJ+num> <N>,SNN+<$THIS$número=$N$número>+<$THIS$género=$N$género>+<$THIS$número=$N$númer
<PREP> <ADJ+num> <N>,SNN+<$THIS$número=$N$número>
<ADV> <DET> <N> <ADJ+num+ordinal>,<SNN+<$THIS$número=$N$número>+<$THIS$género=$N$género>>+<$THIS$número
<ADV> <DET> <ADJ+num> <N>,SNN+<$THIS$número=$N$número>+<$THIS$género=$N$género>+<$THIS$número=$N$número
<ADV> <ADJ+num> <N>,SNN+<$THIS$número=$N$número>
```

Fig. 16. Generation with the prototype of Fig. 15

4   Conclusions

Throughout this work, we observed the numeral expressions in the corpus created for this project. As can be observed, the grammar used by young people follows rules of order and agreement of constituents with respect to the nominal nucleus. Despite the differences between ordinals and cardinals—for example, the fact that ordinals can be shortened (e.g., *en primer lugar*/in the first place), or that they inflect along with the nominal nucleus—we created an integrated prototype that allows us to extract numeral expressions from the corpus using *Locate*. The following categories appear before numeral expressions: DETERMINER, ADVERB, and PREPOSITION. At this stage, we did not observe any significant differences between the two classes of numerals in our corpus. In order to enable the numeral classes, we modified the definition of properties to include the different subclasses.

Nowadays, we know that advances in generative Artificial Intelligence make it essential for research in Natural Language Processing to "feed" these "intelligences" with the language varieties of all Spanish-speaking communities, so as not to turn them into an artificial, globalized product. This is the central objective of our research.

References

1. Bartulović, A., Mijić, L.: Latin pronouns, numerals and prepositions in the NooJ Tool. In: Bartulović, A., Mijić, L., Silberztein, M. (eds.) Formalizing Natural Languages: Applications to Natural Language Processing and Digital Humanities. NooJ 2023, Communications in Computer and Information Science, vol. 1816, Springer, Cham (2024). https://doi.org/10.1007/978-3-031-56646-2_4
2. Bès, G.G.: La phrase verbale noyau en français. Recherches sur le français parlé **15**, 273–358 (1999)
3. Real Academia Española: Nueva Gramática de la Real Academia Española, Capítulo 21. Los numerales, pp. 1503–1552. Espasa Libros S.L.U., Madrid (2009)

4. Rodrigo, A., Reyes, S., Fernández Gallino, M.A.: automatic treatment of causal, consecutive, and counter argumentative discourse connectors in Spanish. In: Bekavac, B., Kocijan, K., Silberztein, M., Šojat, K. (eds.) Formalising Natural Languages: Applications to Natural Language Processing and Digital Humanities. NooJ 2020, Communications in Computer and Information Science, vol. 1389, Springer, Cham (2021). https://doi.org/10.1007/978-3-030-70629-6_14

5. Rodrigo, A.F.: Dataset: automatic treatment of causal, consecutive, and counterargumentative discourse connectors in Spanish. RDA UNR, V1 (2022). https://doi.org/10.57715/UNR/KXHJO2

6. Rodrigo, A.F.: Dataset corpus de textos escritos por estudiantes de grado de la Universidad Nacional de Rosario. RDA UNR, V1 (2025). https://doi.org/10.57715/UNR/5KKC9I

7. Silberztein, M.: Formalizing Natural Languages: the NooJ approach. Wiley, Hoboken NJ, USA (2016)

8. Spanish module Argentina at the NooJ platform, https://nooj.univ-fcomte.fr/resources.html, Accessed 27 Aug 2025

Disambiguation of Rromani Adjective-Noun Phrases

Masako Watabe[(✉)] [iD]

Université Marie Et Louis Pasteur, CRIT (UR 3224), 25000 Besançon, France
`masako.watabe@univ-fcomte.fr`

Abstract. This article aims to present Rromani morphosyntactic studies and the formalization of syntactic grammars on the NooJ platform for the disambiguation of Rromani Adjective-Noun phrases.

Keywords: Adjective-Noun (AN) Phrase · Formal Grammar · Morphosyntax · NooJ · Rromani Language

1 Morphosyntax of Rromani

The inflectional morphology of adjectives and nouns in Rromani is governed by two genders (masculine and feminine), two numbers (singular and plural), and two cases (direct and oblique). Adjectives agree according to number, gender, and case of the noun. In general, adjectives precede nouns[1].

1.1 Two Cases: Direct and Oblique

How do the two cases function in Rromani?

Concerning human nouns and most animal nouns, one can use the direct case as a subject, whereas the oblique case is used as an object or with several complements introduced by postpositions.

[1] *Thule bakră soven.* [Fat ewes are sleeping.]
[2] *Bikinav thule bakrěn.* [I sell fat ewes.]
[3] *Phirav thule bakrěnça.* [I walk with fat ewes.]

For example, *thule bakră* [fat ewes] in the direct case functions as a subject, *thule bakrěn* [fat ewes] in the oblique case functions as an object, and the identical phrase *thule bakrěn* [fat ewes] in the oblique case functions as an instrumental complement with the postposition *-ça* [with].

Concerning inanimate nouns and some animal nouns, one can use the direct case as a subject or an object, whereas the oblique case is used only with a postposition.

---

[1] An adjective following a noun has an emphatic value, *e.g.*, *amari gudli daj* [our gentle mother] *vs. amari daj gudli* [our GENTLE mother].

© The Author(s), under exclusive license to Springer Nature Switzerland AG 2026
D. Petković et al. (Eds.): NooJ 2025, CCIS 2832, pp. 124–136, 2026.
https://doi.org/10.1007/978-3-032-17103-0_11

[4] *Gudle phabaja peren.* [Sweet apples fall.]
[5] *Kidav gudle phabaja.* [I pick sweet apples.]
[6] *Pekav tòrta gudle phabajença.* [I make a cake with sweet apples.]

For example, *gudle phabaja* [sweet apples] in the direct case functions as a subject or an object, and *gudle phabajen* [sweet apples] in the oblique case functions as an instrumental complement with the postposition *-ça* [with].

2 Morphosyntactic Ambiguity

Combining three properties (gender, number, and case) produces eight inflected forms of adjectives. However, most adjectives have no more than three inflectional endings [1, 3, 4]. This results in a large number of inflectional homonyms.

For example, the adjective *thulo* [fat] has three endings: -o, -i, and -e, producing eight forms: *thulo* in the masculine singular direct, *thuli* in the feminine singular direct, and *thule* in the plural direct of both genders and the oblique of both genders and numbers.

Table 1 presents the inflected forms of four adjectives, each of which is associated with a specific inflectional paradigm: *thulo* [fat] is a vocalic oxytonic[2] adjective, *aver* [other] is a consonantal oxytonic adjective, *lùngo* [long] and *sociàlo* [social] are vocalic non-oxytonic adjectives. We can observe several homonymic forms. For example, *thule* is ambiguous in six cases.

Table 1. Inflected forms of adjectives.

	[fat]	[other]	[long]	[social]
m + sg + dr	*thulo*	*aver*	*lùngo*	*sociàlo*
m + pl + dr	*thule*	*avera*	*lùngi*	*sociàlo*
m + sg + ob	*thule*	*avere*	*lungone*	*socialone*
m + pl + ob	*thule*	*avere*	*lungone*	*socialone*
f + sg + dr	*thuli*	*aver*	*lùngo*	*sociàlo*
f + pl + dr	*thule*	*avera*	*lùngi*	*sociàlo*
f + sg + ob	*thule*	*avere*	*lungone*	*socialone*
f + pl + ob	*thule*	*avere*	*lungone*	*socialone*

Tables 2 and 3 present inflected forms of nouns: *bakro* [sheep] and *bakri* [ewe] are vocalic oxytonic animal nouns, *kher* [house] and *phabaj* [apple] are consonantal oxytonic inanimate nouns, *studènti* [male student] and *studènta* [female student] are vocalic non-oxytonic human nouns.

---

[2] Stress positions affect inflectional morphology in Rromani. Borrowed words are generally non-oxytonic.

Regarding masculine nouns, there are no homonymic forms, whereas some homonymic forms can be observed in the feminine. For example, *bakră* and *phabaja* are ambiguous in two cases.

Table 2. Inflected forms of masculine nouns.

	[sheep]	[house]	[male student]
m + sg + dr	*bakro*	*kher*	*studènti*
m + pl + dr	*bakre*	*khera*	*studèntă*
m + sg + ob	*bakres*	*kheres-*	*studentes*
m + pl + ob	*bakren*	*kheren-*	*studenten*

Table 3. Inflected forms of feminine nouns.

	[ewe]	[apple]	[female student]
f + sg + dr	*bakri*	*phabaj*	*studènta*
f + pl + dr	*bakră*	*phabaja*	*studènte*
f + sg + ob	*bakră*	*phabaja-*	*studenta*
f + pl + ob	*bakrĕn*	*phabajen-*	*studenten*

Consequently, a phrase composed of an adjective and a noun can be ambiguous too. For example, *thule bakră* can mean "fat ewes" in the plural direct, or "fat ewe" in the singular oblique.

Suppose a user wants to analyze an adjective-noun (AN) phrase *thule bakră* on the NooJ platform [6]. In that case, NooJ will systematically make six annotations, including incorrect ones for the adjectival form *thule* and two annotations for the nominal form *bakră*, without syntactic grammar, due to ambiguity (see Fig. 1) [5].

3   Syntactic Grammar for Disambiguation

How can ambiguities in such phrases arising from inflectional homonymy be resolved? We have developed two syntactic grammars on the NooJ platform that describe the agreement between adjectives and nouns.

3.1   Masculine aN Phrases

We observed that homonymy does not exist in masculine AN phrases despite the presence of homonymic forms of adjectives (see Tables 1 and 2). Each of the four AN phrases in the example below (*thulo bakro* in the singular direct, *thule bakre* in the plural direct, *thule bakres* in the singular oblique, and *thule bakren* in the plural oblique) is distinct from the others.

[7] *Thulo bakro sovel.* [A fat sheep is sleeping.]
[8] *Thule bakre soven.* [Fat sheep are sleeping.]
[9] *Bikinav thule bakres.* [I sell a fat sheep.]
[10] *Bikinav thule bakren.* [I sell some fat sheep.]

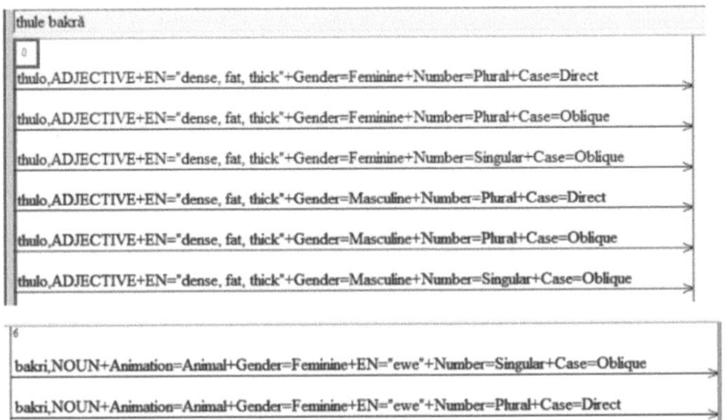

Fig. 1. *Thule bakră* annotated by NooJ without syntactic grammar.

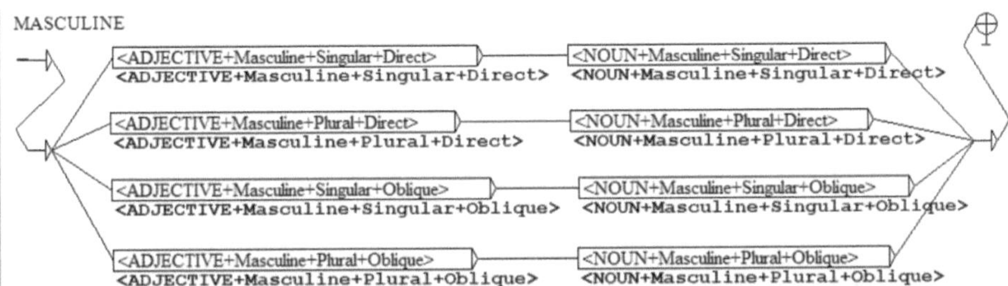

Fig. 2. Syntactic grammar for the disambiguation of masculine AN phrases.

Figure 2 shows the syntactic grammar for the disambiguation of masculine AN phrases formalized on the NooJ platform. Each sequence represents an AN phrase. The content in a node corresponds to the category and properties of a linguistic unit, *i.e.*, an inflected form (*e.g.*, "ADJECTIVE + Masculine + Singular + Direct"), whereas the content below a node corresponds to its annotation. For example, the first sequence means that if one wants to analyze an AN phrase composed of an adjective and a noun, each in the masculine singular direct, NooJ will analyze not each word separately but the set of words as a single phrase and annotate that it is a phrase composed of an adjective and a noun, each in the masculine singular direct.

Figures 3 and 4 present the AN phrase *thule bakres* in the masculine singular oblique, annotated by NooJ before and after applying the syntactic grammar. The adjective form

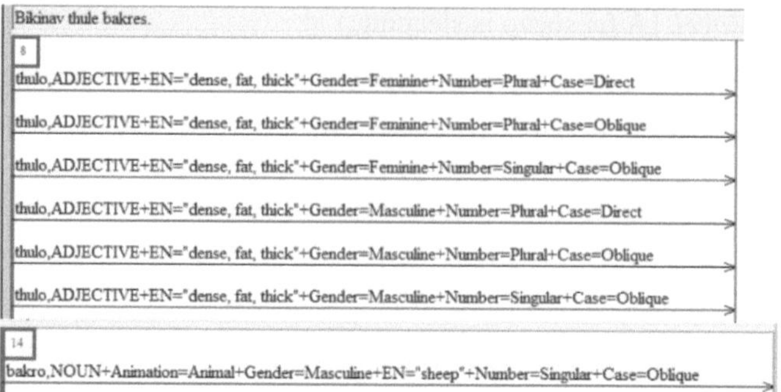

Fig. 3. *Thule bakres* annotated by NooJ without syntactic grammar.

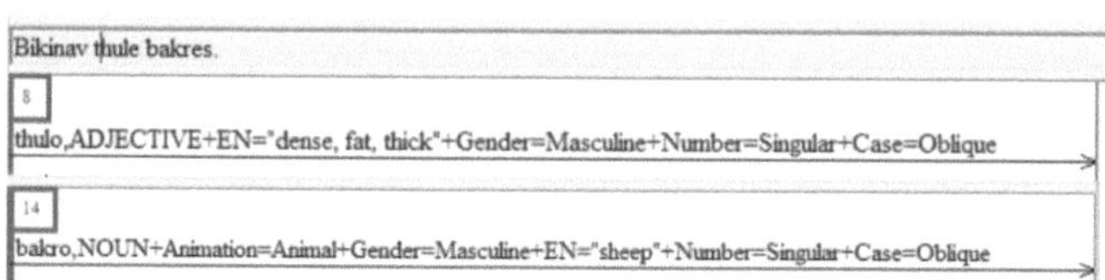

Fig. 4. *Thule bakres* annotated by NooJ with syntactic grammar.

thule is ambiguous in six cases without syntactic grammar. With the NooJ syntactic grammar, we eliminated the five incorrect annotations, thus successfully resolving ambiguities in masculine AN phrases.

3.2 Feminine aN Phrases

Figure 5 shows the syntactic grammar for the disambiguation of feminine AN phrases. We have formalized six types of feminine AN phrases.

Singular Direct and Plural Oblique. We observed that homonymy does not exist in feminine AN phrases in the singular direct and the plural oblique (see Tables 1 and 3). For example, *thuli bakri* [fat ewe] in the singular direct and *thule bakrĕn* [fat ewes] in the plural oblique are distinct from each other.

[11] *Thuli bakri sovel.* [A fat ewe is sleeping.]
[1] *Thule bakră soven.* [Fat ewes are sleeping.]
[12] *Bikinav thule bakră.* [I sell a fat ewe.]
[2] *Bikinav thule bakrĕn.* [I sell fat ewes.]

The first part of Fig. 5 concerns the disambiguation of feminine AN phrases in the singular direct and the plural oblique. For example, the second sequence means that if one wants to analyze an AN phrase composed of an adjective and a noun, each in the feminine plural oblique, NooJ will analyze it and annotate it as a phrase composed of an adjective and a noun, each in the feminine plural oblique.

Figures 6 and 7 present the AN phrase *thule bakrĕn* in the feminine plural oblique, annotated by NooJ with and without syntactic grammar. The adjective form *thule* is ambiguous in six cases without syntactic grammar. The NooJ syntactic grammar eliminates the five incorrect annotations.

Consonantal Adjective. We mentioned that there are ambiguities only in AN phrases containing a noun in the feminine plural direct and the feminine singular oblique. But what about adjectives? Only adjectives associated with a specific inflectional paradigm can be ambiguous. This paradigm is called the "BUXLO"[3] paradigm, which applies to vocalic oxytonic adjectives, *e.g.*, *buxalo* [large], *thulo* [fat], *gudlo* [sweet].

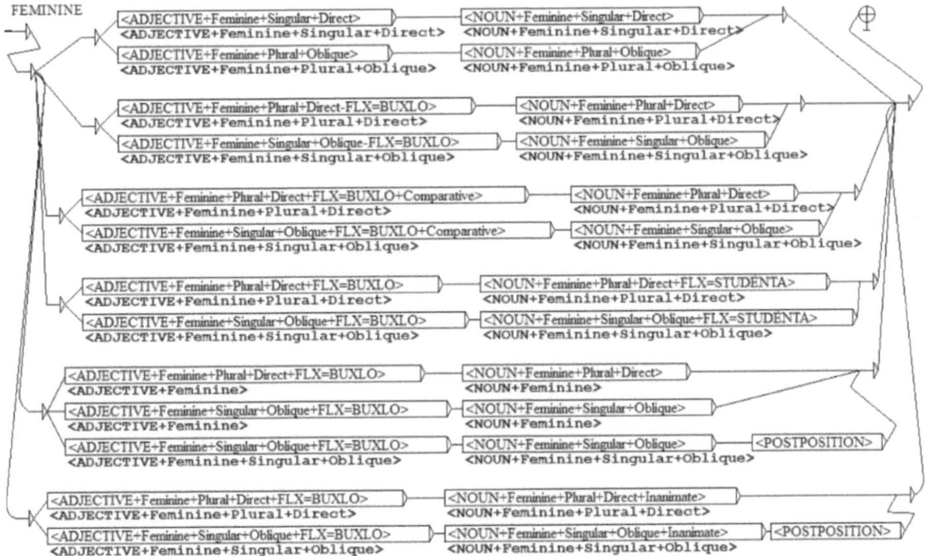

Fig. 5. Syntactic grammar for the disambiguation of feminine AN phrases.

However, there is no ambiguity in AN phrases containing other types of adjectives. For example, the adjective *aver* [other] is oxytonic but consonantal; therefore, it is not associated with the "BUXLO" paradigm. Admittedly, the noun form *bakră* [ewe(s)] is ambiguous. However, the adjective forms corresponding to *bakră* are not ambiguous, *i.e.*, *avera* in the plural direct and *avere* in the singular oblique. Each of the four AN phrases in the example below (*aver bakri* in the singular direct, *avera bakră* in the plural direct, *avere bakră* in the singular oblique, and *avere bakrěn* in the plural oblique) is distinct from the others.

[13] *Aver bakri sovel.* [Another ewe is sleeping.]
[14] *Avera bakră soven.* [Other ewes are sleeping.]
[15] *Bikinav avere bakră.* [I sell another ewe.]
[16] *Bikinav avere bakrěn.* [I sell other ewes.]

---

[3] In Rromani, *buxlo* is an adjective meaning "large." Each paradigm name is defined by a representative Rromani word and written in capital letters in the NooJ module for Rromani.

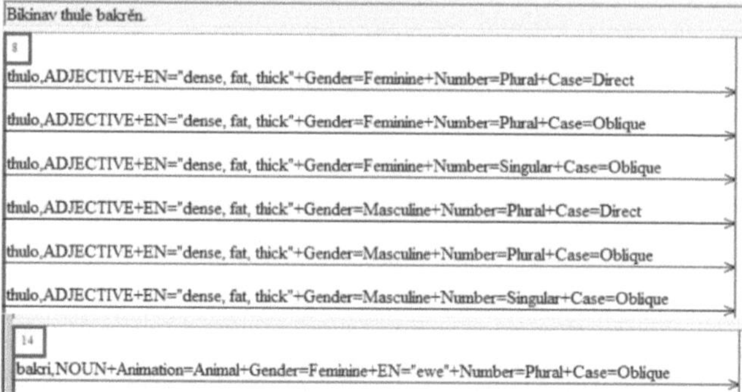

Fig. 6. *Thule bakrĕn* annotated by NooJ without syntactic grammar.

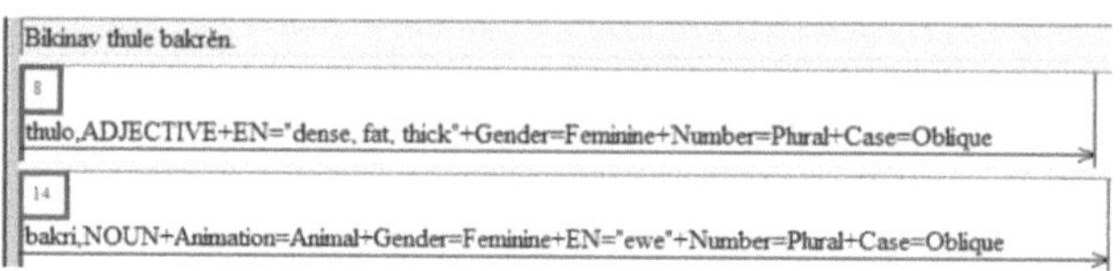

Fig. 7. *Thule bakrĕn* annotated by NooJ with syntactic grammar.

The second part of Fig. 5 concerns the disambiguation of feminine AN phrases containing an adjective not associated with the "BUXLO" paradigm. The minus sign ("–") functions to eliminate all adjectives associated with the "BUXLO" paradigm.

For example, the first sequence in this part means that if one wants to analyze an AN phrase composed of an adjective not associated with the "BUXLO" paradigm in the feminine plural direct and a noun in the feminine plural direct, NooJ will analyze and annotate it as a phrase composed of an adjective and a noun, each in the feminine plural direct.

Figures 8 and 9 present an AN phrase *avera bakră* in the feminine plural direct, annotated by NooJ with and without syntactic grammar. The adjective form *avera* and the noun form *bakră* are ambiguous without syntactic grammar. The NooJ syntactic grammar then eliminates the incorrect annotations.

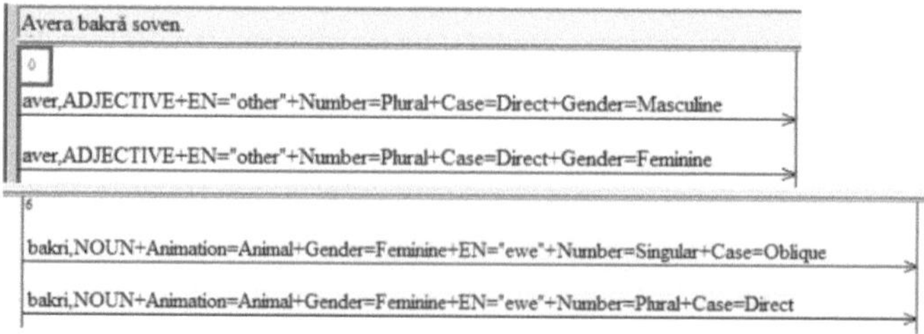

Fig. 8. *Avera bakră* annotated by NooJ without syntactic grammar.

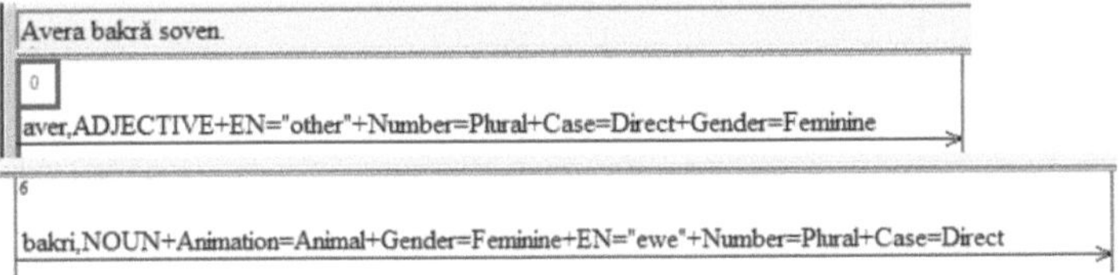

Fig. 9. *Avera bakră* annotated by NooJ with syntactic grammar.

Comparative. The comparative consists of an adjective stem and the suffix *-eder*,[4] *e.g.*, *thulo* [fat] > *thuleder* [fatter]. Even vocalic adjectives initially associated with the "BUXLO" paradigm will be associated with another paradigm in the comparative because of the suffix, which is consonantal. This paradigm is called the "TANG"[5] paradigm, which applies to consonantal oxytonic adjectives, such as *tang* [narrow], *aver* [other], *godăver* [intelligent].

There is no ambiguity in AN phrases containing the comparative. For example, the noun form *bakră* [ewe(s)] is ambiguous in the plural direct and the singular oblique. However, the comparative forms corresponding to *bakră* are not ambiguous, *i.e.*, *thuledera* in the plural direct and *thuledere* in the singular oblique. Each of the four AN phrases in the example below (*thuleder bakri* in the singular direct, *thuledera bakră* in the plural direct, *thuledere bakră* in the singular oblique, and *thuledere bakrĕn* in the plural oblique) is distinct from the others.

[17] *Thuleder bakri sovel.* [A fatter ewe is sleeping.]
[18] *Thuledera bakră soven.* [Fatter ewes are sleeping.]
[19] *Bikinav thuledere bakră.* [I sell a fatter ewe.]
[20] *Bikinav thuledere bakrĕn.* [I sell fatter ewes.]

The third part of Fig. 5 concerns the disambiguation of feminine AN phrases containing an adjective initially associated with the "BUXLO" paradigm but used in the comparative.

For example, the second sequence in this part means that if one wants to analyze an AN phrase composed of a comparative of an adjective in the feminine singular oblique according to the "BUXLO" paradigm, and a noun in the feminine singular oblique, NooJ will analyze and annotate it as a phrase composed of an adjective and a noun, each in the feminine singular oblique.

Figures 10 and 11 present the AN phrase *thuledere bakră* in the feminine singular oblique, annotated by NooJ with and without syntactic grammar. The comparative form *thuledere* and the noun form *bakră* are ambiguous without syntactic grammar. The NooJ syntactic grammar then eliminates the incorrect annotations.

Inanimate Nouns. We mentioned that inanimate nouns in the oblique do not occur without a postposition. For example, an adjective form *gudle* [sweet] and a noun form *phabaja* [apple(s)] are ambiguous between the plural direct and the singular oblique.

---

[4] According to the dialects, the adverbs *po* [more] and *maj* [more] can express the comparative instead of the suffix *-eder* [2], *e.g.*, *thuleder, po thulo, maj thulo*, each of which means "fatter."

[5] In Rromani, *tang* is an adjective meaning "narrow."

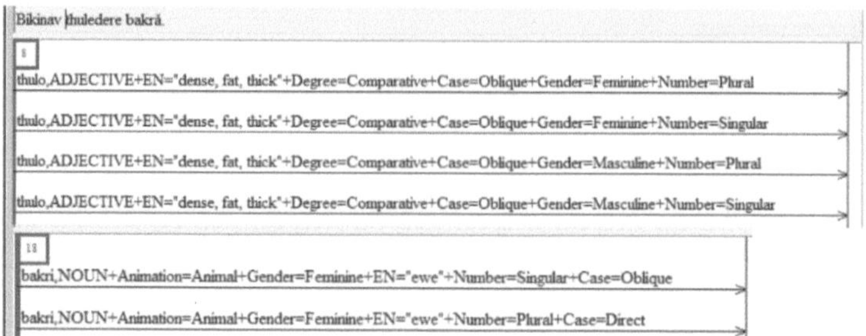

Fig. 10. *Thuledere bakră* annotated by NooJ without syntactic grammar.

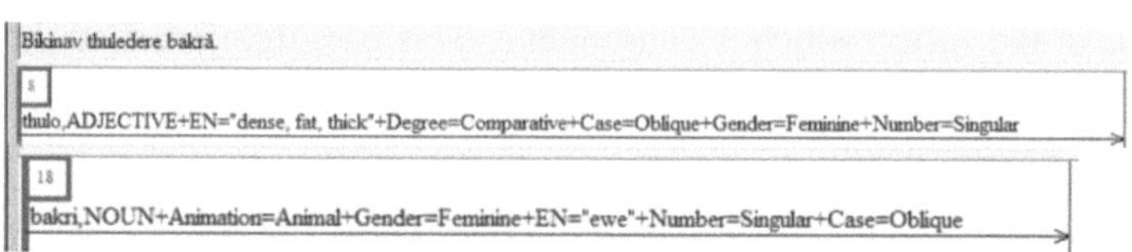

Fig. 11. *Thuledere bakră* annotated by NooJ with syntactic grammar.

However, *gudle phabaja* without a postposition should be interpreted as plural direct, and *gudle phabaja-* with a postposition should be interpreted as singular oblique. Therefore, there is no ambiguity between these types of AN phrases. Each of the six AN phrases in the example below (*gudli phabaj* in the singular direct as a subject and as an object, *gudle phabaja* in the plural direct as a subject and as an object, *gudle phabaja-* in the singular oblique, and *gudle phabajen-* in the plural oblique, the last two of which precede the postposition *-ça* [with]) functions differently from the others.

[21] *Gudli phabaj perel.* [A sweet apple falls.]
[4] *Gudle phabaja peren.* [Sweet apples fall.]
[22] *Kidav gudli phabaj.* [I pick a sweet apple.]
[5] *Kidav gudle phabaja.* [I pick sweet apples.]
[23] *Pekav tòrta gudle phabajaça.* [I make a cake with a sweet apple.]
[6] *Pekav tòrta gudle phabajença.* [I make a cake with sweet apples.]

The last part of Fig. 5 concerns the disambiguation of feminine AN phrases containing an inanimate noun. The first sequence in this part consists of an adjective and a noun in the plural direct without a postposition. The second sequence consists of an adjective and a noun in the singular oblique preceding a postposition. If one wants to analyze an AN phrase without a postposition, composed of an adjective and an inanimate noun, NooJ will analyze it and annotate it as direct. Conversely, if one wants to analyze an AN phrase composed of an adjective and an inanimate noun preceding a postposition, NooJ will annotate it as oblique.

Figures 12 and 13 present the AN phrase *gudle phabaja* [sweet apples] in the plural direct, annotated by NooJ with and without syntactic grammar. The adjective form *gudle* and the noun form *phabaja* are ambiguous without syntactic grammar. The NooJ syntactic grammar then eliminates the incorrect annotations.

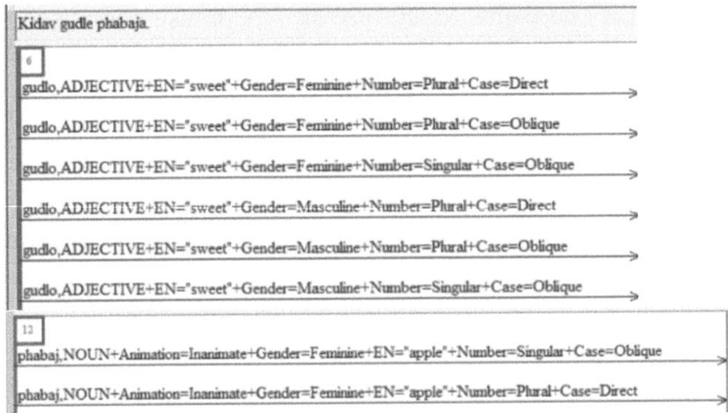

Fig. 12. *Gudle phabaja* annotated by NooJ without syntactic grammar.

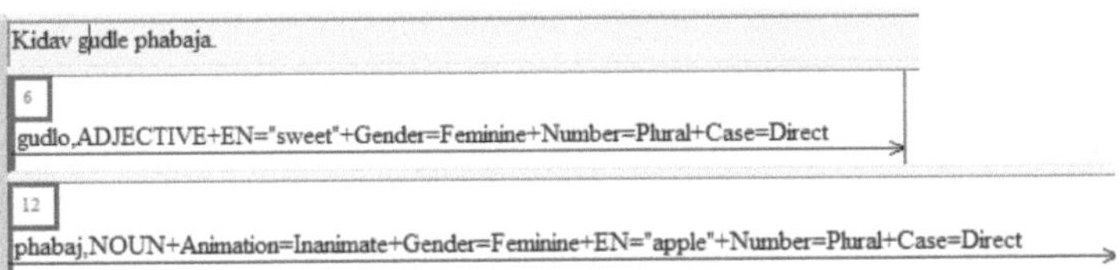

Fig. 13. *Gudle phabaja* annotated by NooJ with syntactic grammar.

Non-Oxytonic Nouns. Most words in Rromani are oxytonic, *i.e.*, the stress falls on the last syllable. A grave accent indicates the stress position, whereas there is no mark indicating the stress position of oxytonic words. For example, *studènta* [female student] in the singular direct, which includes a grave accent, is non-oxytonic, and *studenta* [female student] in the singular oblique, which does not include a grave accent, is oxytonic. NooJ recognizes them as two different forms.

We noticed that there is no ambiguity in feminine AN phrases containing a human or animal noun associated with a specific inflectional paradigm (see Table 3). This paradigm is called the "STUDÈNTA" paradigm in the NooJ module for Rromani. It applies to vocalic non-oxytonic feminine nouns, such as *studènta* [female student], *avokàta* [female lawyer].

For example, the adjective form *terne* [young] is ambiguous. However, the noun *studènta* [female student] has no homonymic form. Each of the four AN phrases in the example below (*terni studènta* in the singular direct, *terne studènte* in the plural direct, *terne studenta* in the singular oblique, and *terne studenten* in the plural oblique) is distinct from the others.

[24] *Terni studènta sovel.* [A female student is sleeping.]
[25] *Terne studènte soven.* [Female students are sleeping.]
[26] *Dikhav terne studenta.* [I see a female student.]
[27] *Dikhav terne studenten.* [I see female students.]

The fourth part of Fig. 5 concerns the disambiguation of feminine AN phrases containing a vocalic non-oxytonic human or animal noun. For example, the second sequence in this part means that if one wants to analyze an AN phrase composed of an adjective form in the feminine singular oblique and a noun form in the feminine singular oblique associated with the "STUDÈNTA" paradigm, NooJ will analyze and annotate it as a phrase composed of an adjective and a noun, each in the feminine singular oblique.

Figures 14 and 15 present the AN phrase *terne studenta* in the feminine singular oblique, annotated by NooJ with and without syntactic grammar. The adjective form *terne* is ambiguous without syntactic grammar. The NooJ syntactic grammar then eliminates the incorrect annotations. We have successfully resolved ambiguities in several types of feminine AN phrases.

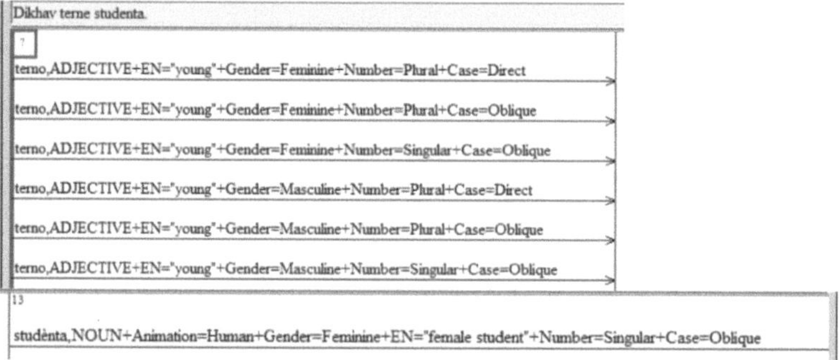

Fig. 14. *Terne studenta* annotated by NooJ without syntactic grammar.

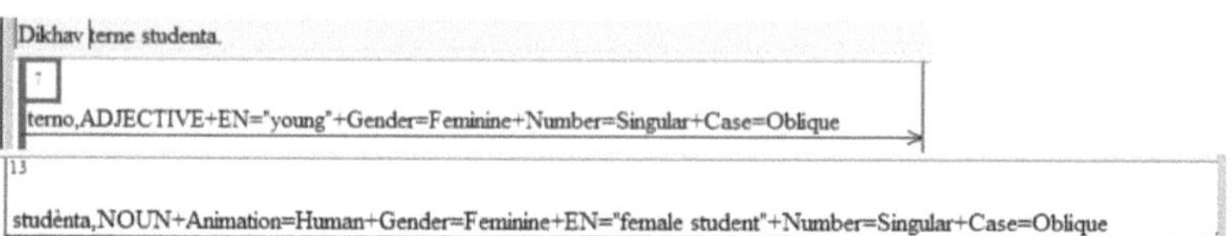

Fig. 15. *Terne studenta* annotated by NooJ with syntactic grammar.

Plural Direct and Singular Oblique. We mentioned that feminine AN phrases composed of a vocalic oxytonic adjective and a human or animal oxytonic noun (e.g., *thule bakră*) are ambiguous between the plural direct and the singular oblique, with or without postposition.

[11] *Thuli bakri sovel.* [A fat ewe is sleeping.]
[1] *Thule bakră soven.* [Fat ewes are sleeping.]
[12] *Bikinav thule bakră.* [I sell a fat ewe.]
[2] *Bikinav thule bakrĕn.* [I sell fat ewes.]
[28] *Phirav thule bakrăça.* [I walk with a fat ewe.]
[3] *Phirav thule bakrĕnça.* [I walk with fat ewes.]

We have partially formalized a syntactic grammar for the disambiguation of these types of AN phrases (see the fifth part of Fig. 5). The first sequence concerns the plural direct, the second concerns the singular oblique without a postposition, and the third concerns the singular oblique with a postposition.

For example, the third sequence means that if one wants to analyze a feminine AN phrase composed of an adjective in the singular oblique and a noun in the singular oblique preceding a postposition, NooJ will analyze and annotate it as singular oblique. Conversely, without a postposition, NooJ cannot recognize the properties of these types of AN phrases (*e.g.*, *thule bakră*) because they remain ambiguous between the plural direct and the singular oblique. At least, NooJ can recognize their gender, *i.e.*, feminine. For this reason, the first two sequences in this part do not include the number and the case of the adjective and the noun in the annotations.

Figure 16 presents the AN phrase *thule bakră*, which should be in the plural direct, annotated by NooJ with syntactic grammar. Concerning the adjective form *thule*, three incorrect annotations out of six (see Fig. 1) are eliminated thanks to the syntactic grammar. Nevertheless, the adjective form *thule* and the noun form *bakră* are still ambiguous. Moreover, an incorrect annotation, "plural oblique", for *thule* still remains.

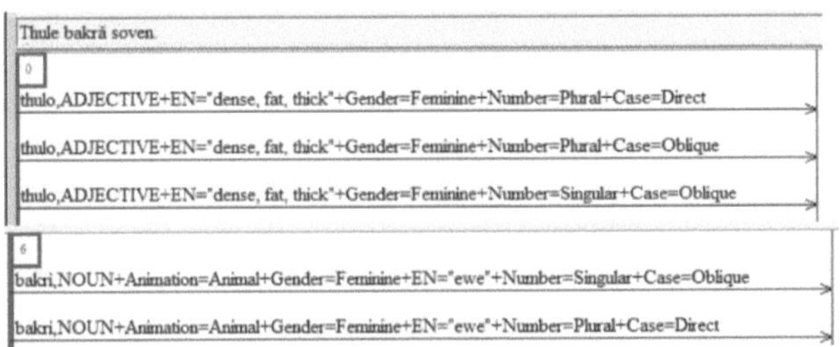

Fig. 16. Thule *bakră* annotated by NooJ with syntactic grammar.

Conclusion and Perspective. We have developed two syntactic grammars for the disambiguation of AN phrases. However, we cannot completely disambiguate some types of phrases, *i.e.*, those composed of an oxytonic vocalic adjective such as *thulo* [fat], *gudlo* [sweet], *terno* [young], and an oxytonic human or animal noun such as *bakri* [ewe], *Rromni* [Rromani woman], *phen* [sister].

The current NooJ dictionary for Rromani contains 4,524 lexical entries. Among them, 682 of the 830 adjectives are vocalic and oxytonic, and 105 of the 1,024 feminine nouns are oxytonic human or animal nouns. The proportion is not negligible.

To remove the ambiguities in these types of AN phrases (*e.g.*, *thule bakră* [fat ewe(s)]), we need to study noun phrases more comprehensively, for example, by including adjective recursion, other determiners such as the definite article, demonstratives, numerals, possessives, etc., and of course, verb phrases.

References

1. Courthiade, M.: The nominal flexion in Rromani. In: Courthiade, M., Grigore. D. (eds.) Professor Gheorghe Sarău: a life devoted to the Rromani language, pp. 157–211. Editura Universității din București, Bucarest (2016)

2. Courthiade, M., et al.: Morri angluni rromane ćhibăqi evroputni lavustik. Romano Kher, Budapest (2009)
3. Sarău, G.: Rromani Leksikologìa. Editura Universităţii din Bucureşti, Bucarest (2004)
4. Sarău, G.: Struktùre rromane ćhibăqe. Editura Universităţii din Bucureşti, Bucarest (2009)
5. Silberztein, M.: La formalisation des langues: l'approche de NooJ. ISTE Eds., London (2015)
6. NooJ Homepage, https://nooj.univ-fcomte.fr/

Foreign Workers in the Spotlight: Linguistic and Sociocultural Insights from German and Croatian Web Portals

Anja Brnjaković[1,2]($\boxtimes$), Mirela Landsman Vinković[1], and Kristina Kocijan[2]

[1] Department of German Language and Literature, Faculty of Humanities and Social Sciences, University of Zagreb, 10 000 Zagreb, Croatia
`brnjakovicanja2001@gmail.com, mlandsma@m.ffzg.unizg.hr`
[2] Department of Information and Communication Sciences, Faculty of Humanities and Social Sciences, University of Zagreb, 10 000 Zagreb, Croatia
`krkocijan@m.ffzg.unizg.hr`

Abstract. This study analyzes the discursive representation of foreign workers in Croatian and German online media. Using a corpus of 223 articles collected from ideologically diverse news portals, the research employs NooJ syntactic grammars to automatically annotate mentions of foreign workers according to four semantic roles: victim, perpetrator, user, and contributor. Results reveal contrasting national patterns: Croatian media predominantly frame foreign workers as victims, emphasizing vulnerability and marginalization, whereas German media highlight the contributor role, focusing on economic integration and labor market participation. A source-level analysis indicates that sensationalist outlets favor victim narratives, while conservative media emphasize perpetrator portrayals and downplay contributions. The findings demonstrate that media framing of foreign workers is shaped by national migration histories and editorial ideologies. This study contributes a replicable semantic role framework for cross-cultural discourse analysis and lays the groundwork for future sentiment and emotional mapping using the NRC Word-Emotion Association Lexicon.

Keywords: foreign workers · labor migration · media discourse · semantic role annotation · corpus linguistics · sentiment analysis · Croatian · German · NooJ

1 Introduction

The phenomenon of labor migration has become increasingly prominent in European societies, shaping economic, social, and political landscapes. Foreign workers constitute a significant part of the workforce in many countries, yet their representation in media discourse often reflects complex and ambivalent attitudes. Media portrayals can influence public perceptions, policy debates, and integration processes, making it crucial to understand the linguistic framing of foreign workers.

This study, building upon the research conducted in the author's master's thesis [1], examines how Croatian and German online media construct narratives around foreign

D. Petković et al. (Eds.): NooJ 2025, CCIS 2832, pp. 137–149, 2026.
https://doi.org/10.1007/978-3-032-17103-0_12

workers, focusing on the semantic roles assigned to them. Croatia and Germany represent contrasting migration contexts: Croatia is an emerging migrant-receiving country, while Germany has a long history of labor migration and institutionalized immigration policies. Comparing these two settings offers valuable insights into how media discourse is shaped by national migration histories and ideological orientations.

Using a corpus linguistics approach, this research compiles and analyzes media texts from ideologically diverse outlets. Syntactic grammars implemented in the NooJ linguistic platform enable automated annotation of foreign worker mentions, categorizing them into four semantic roles: victim, perpetrator, user, and contributor. This framework allows for systematic comparison of discursive patterns and ideological positioning in Croatian and German media.

The paper is structured as follows: after outlining the terminological framework in Section 2, the methodology of corpus construction and preprocessing is detailed in Section 3. Sections 4 and 5 present the entity recognition process and semantic role classification, respectively. Section 6 discusses automated role annotation and statistical distribution of roles, and the study concludes with a summary of findings and suggestions for future research.

2   Terminology: Defining Foreign Workers

Public attitudes toward foreign workers in Croatia and Germany reveal a complex spectrum of perceptions, highlighting the importance of precise conceptual definitions. To maintain methodological consistency in corpus analysis, this study distinguishes key terms such as migrant, immigrant, refugee, asylum seeker, and foreign worker.

Croatian legislation defines a **foreigner** as any non-Croatian citizen, including nationals of the European Economic Area (EEA), Switzerland, third countries, and stateless persons. Foreigners legally working in Croatia must hold a residence and work permit or a certificate of work registration, depending on the duration of employment. Upon registration, they are classified as **migrants**, i.e., individuals engaged in spatial mobility (Croatian Bureau of Statistics, 2024).

Germany applies a comparable definition, with a **foreigner** (*Ausländer*) being anyone without German citizenship, including stateless persons. Employment requires residence registration and a work permit. The German statistical framework further introduces the term person with a migration background (*Person mit Migrationshintergrund*), encompassing both immigrants and native-born individuals with at least one parent born without German citizenship (Statistisches Bundesamt, 2025).

Both countries use international terms such as **migrant**, **immigrant**, and **emigrant** alongside native equivalents (Croatian: *iseljenik, useljenik*; German: *Auswanderer, Einwanderer*). **Refugees** and **asylum seekers** are defined according to international conventions: refugees flee persecution, while asylum seekers await refugee status. Both Croatian and German law grant asylum seekers the right to work after three months, with recognized refugees receiving full labor rights.

Recent linguistic research by Vodanović [7] highlights the rich synonymy and semantic variation of Croatian terms for "migrant." Her analysis of newspaper usage, drawing on a NooJ-based approach, demonstrates how terms like *immigrant* are configured by contextual discourse, affecting their pragmatic connotation and symbolizing shifting perceptions of immigration in Croatian media.

For the purpose of this study, the term **foreign worker** refers to any non-national legally employed in Croatia or Germany, regardless of migration status. This category intersects with broader groups such as migrants, immigrants, and refugees, and serves as the central analytical unit in corpus annotation via NooJ grammars (Fig. 1).

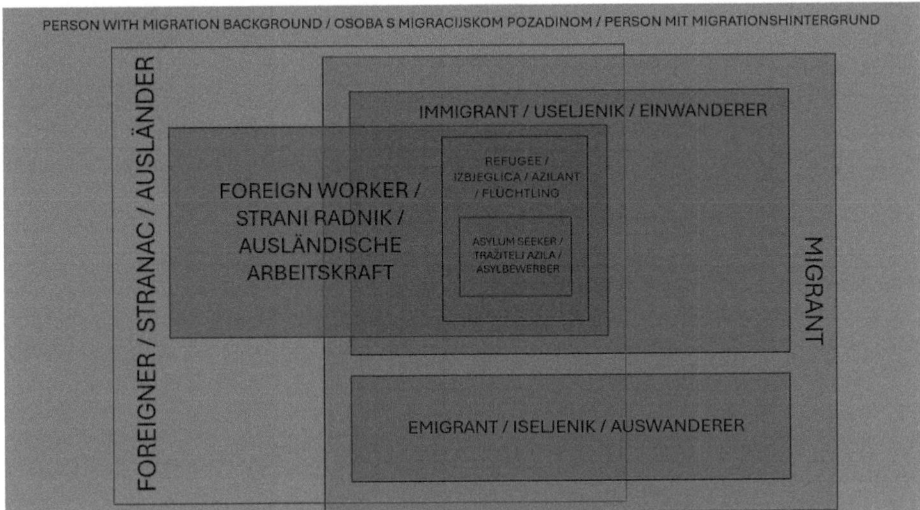

Fig. 1. Layered complexity of the term *foreign worker.*

3   Corpus Construction and Preprocessing

To explore how Croatian and German media construct discourse around foreign workers, a balanced and representative corpus was assembled. Using targeted keyword searches, *strani radnik* (Croatian) and *ausländische Arbeitskraft* (German), articles were collected from selected online news portals representing a range of political orientations (left, center, right) and publication types (serious vs. tabloid).

The German corpus includes 111 articles (81,031 tokens) from left-leaning outlets such as *Die Tageszeitung, Süddeutsche Zeitung, Frankfurter Rundschau, Die Zeit,* and *Der Spiegel,* as well as right-leaning sources like *Frankfurter Allgemeine Zeitung, Bild, Die Welt, Junge Freiheit,* and *Der Focus.* The Croatian corpus consists of 112 articles (65,623 tokens) from *24sata* (center), *Večernji list* (right), and *Novi list* (left).

Articles were published between October 1, 2024, and January 13, 2025, and collected using a custom web-scraping tool. The dataset is stored as a CSV file with metadata including title, full text, author (if available), publication date, language, source, and URL. Additionally, separate TXT files were created by language, month, and source to facilitate linguistic analysis.

Prior to analysis, the corpus underwent thorough cleaning and normalization. Typographical errors and non-standard word forms were identified using NooJ's Unknowns directory [6]. Some unknown tokens were valid but undocumented lexemes, while others were clear misspellings. Instead of expanding lexical resources, corrections were manually applied directly in the corpus to maintain semantic accuracy. Examples include Croatian corrections (*Detetektiraju* → *detektiraju, radncima* → *radnicima*) and German corrections (*Deutschand* → *Deutschland, fossilen* → *Fossilien*).

The preprocessing and annotation approach applied here builds on earlier work with the NooJ German module ([4, 5]), demonstrating the tool's adaptability across both educational and research contexts. This ensures that subsequent linguistic and sentiment analyses are based on standardized, linguistically valid input, reducing noise and improving the precision of corpus-driven insights.

4 Lexical Patterns and Entity Recognition

The first analytical step focused on identifying lexical variants and expressions referring to foreign workers. To ensure consistent entity detection across both corpora, two syntactic grammars were developed in NooJ: one for Croatian and one for German. These grammars enabled the automated annotation of noun phrases referring to foreign workers, marked as <NP+ SR> in the Croatian corpus and < NP+ AA> in the German corpus. The grammar structures are illustrated in Figs. 2 and 3.

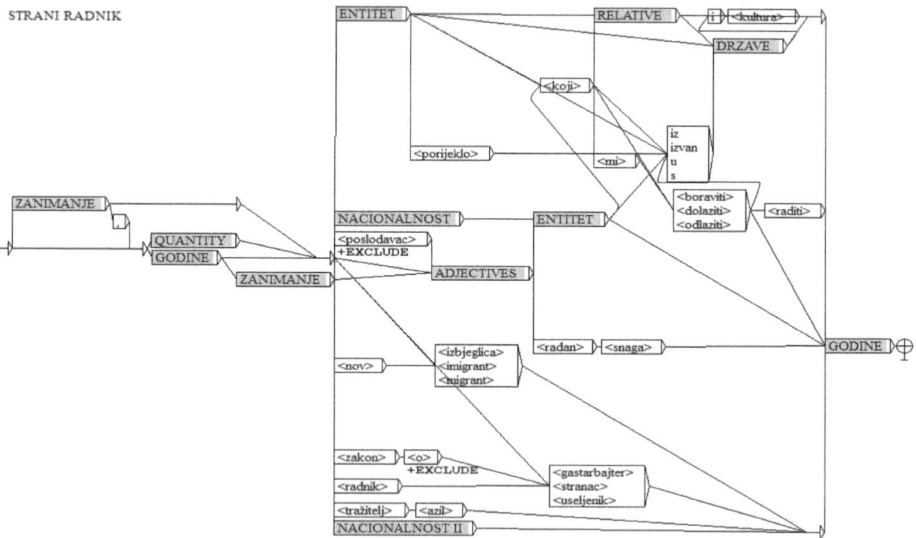

Fig. 2. NooJ syntax grammar for recognizing the entity *strani radnik* in the Croatian corpus.

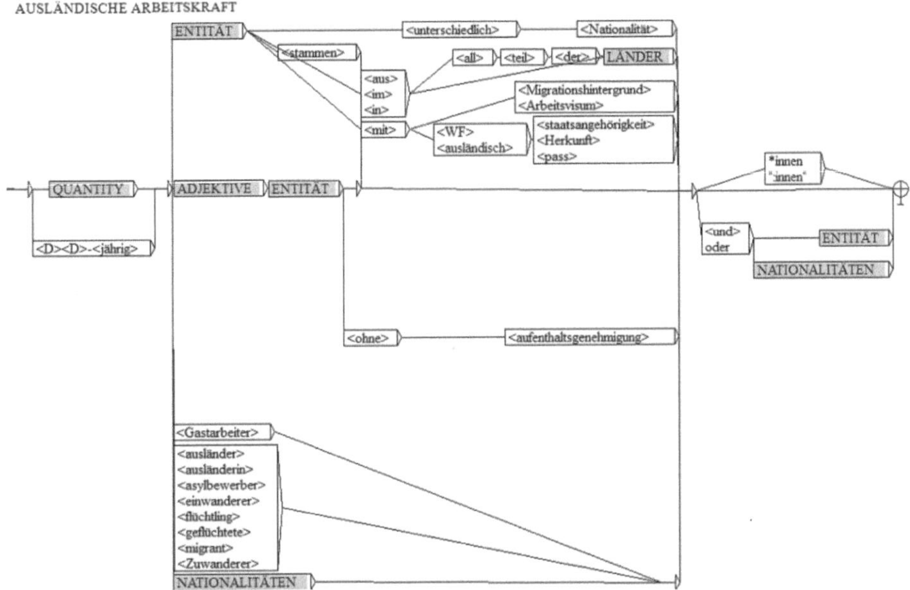

Fig. 3. NooJ syntax grammar for recognizing the entity *ausländische Arbeitskraft* in the German corpus.

The goal of this stage was to extract all relevant entities referring to foreign workers and prepare them for concordance analysis and semantic role classification. Entities were later annotated with one of four semantic roles: *victim*, *perpetrator*, *user*, and *contributor*.

4.1 Croatian Corpus

A total of **971 entities** were identified. The most frequent term was *strani radnik* (411 occurrences), comprising over 42% of all matches, indicating a relatively standardized use of terminology. Other commonly occurring terms included: *stranac* (74), *strani državljanin* (51), *Nepalac* (39), *useljenik* (38), *imigrant* (23), *migrant* (18), *državljanin trećih zemalja* (16), *Filipinac* (16), and *Indijac* (16).

The use of legal-status terms (e.g., *radnik*, *državljanin*) suggests an emphasis on regulatory identity over cultural integration. Nationality-specific terms may reflect either the visibility of particular migrant groups or targeted media attention.

4.2 German Corpus

A total of **648 entities** were identified, with more lexical variety than in the Croatian corpus. The most frequent term was *Migrant* (98), followed by *Ausländer* (88). The keyword used in article collection, *ausländische Arbeitskraft*, appeared only 33 times, indicating limited use in everyday reporting. Other frequent terms included *Syrer* (30), *Arbeitsmigrant* (21), *Einwanderer* (20), *ausländische Fachkraft* (19), *Pole* (16), *Geflüchteter* (15), and *Flüchtling* (14).

The broader lexical range reflects a more differentiated discourse in German media, distinguishing among legal status, professional qualification, and nationality. Terms like *Pole* or *Syrer* may relate to Germany's current geopolitical concerns and migration policy focus.

This entity-level analysis establishes the lexical ground for further semantic and sentiment annotation, revealing how foreign workers are named and categorized in two distinct media contexts.

5   Semantic Role Classification

Building on entity recognition, the next stage of analysis focused on classifying foreign worker representations into four semantic roles: victim, perpetrator, user, and contributor. These roles were identified within two overarching discursive domains - crime and economy - using syntactic grammars developed in NooJ. The grammars scanned for linguistic cues in the immediate environment of annotated entities, enabling systematic role attribution.

To support this classification, the NRC Word–Emotion Association Lexicon (EmoLex) was used. This widely applied resource links words to eight basic emotions (joy, trust, sadness, fear, anger, surprise, disgust, anticipation) and to overall positive/negative sentiment. The lexicon served two key functions: (a) conceptual validation of the four-role model, aligning emotional valence with discursive functions (e.g., victim aligns with sadness and fear; contributor with trust and joy), and (b) disambiguation aid for complex or ambiguous phrases that could not be conclusively classified using syntactic features alone. Each role was further divided into thematic subcategories, illustrated with representative examples from the corpora.

5.1   Victim

Foreign workers are framed as vulnerable subjects facing structural or interpersonal harm. Croatian media emphasize economic precarity and physical risk, while German outlets highlight structural exclusion and xenophobia. See Table 1 for an overview of victim subcategories and corresponding corpus examples[1].

Table 1. "Foreign worker as victim" subcategories with examples.

Subcategoriy	Example	Language
Physical assault	*...konobar iz Zadra napao i izvrijeđao stranog radnika...* en. ...a waiter from Zadar attacked and insulted a foreign worker...	Cro

(continued)

---

[1] Due to space constraints, examples for all four roles are presented in alternating order, i.e. one per subcategory from the Croatian and German corpora, respectively. This selection method does not reflect any language-specific categorization, as relevant examples were identified in both corpora for each thematic role.

Table 1. (*continued*)

Subcategoriy	Example	Language
Fear and insecurity	*...die Angst und Unruhe, die der organisierte Rechtsextremismus in Menschen aus internationalen Familien auslöst...* en. ...the fear and anxiety that organized right-wing extremism causes in people from international families...	Ger
Low wages	*Strani radnik za isti posao radi za manju plaću* en. A foreign worker earns less for the same job	Cro
Inhumane living conditions	*...leben in beengten Zimmern...* en. His employer housed him and other foreign workers in cramped rooms...	Ger
Death	*Tragedija u Osijeku: Poginuo strani radnik, ubila ga struja* en. Tragedy in Osijek: A foreign worker died after being electrocuted	Cro
Exploitation	*...Ausbeutung Tausender ausländischer Arbeitskräfte...* en. Exploitation of thousands of foreign workers...	Ger
Social invisibility	*...radnici nisu bili tema kampanja...* en. The situation of foreign workers was barely addressed in election campaigns...	Cro
Discrimination and racism	*Viele ausländische Arbeitskräfte klagen über Diskriminierung...* en. Many foreign workers complain about discrimination...	Ger

5.2 Perpetrator

This role associates foreign workers with criminality, illegality, or disruption. It is most prominent in tabloid and politically polarized sources (see Table 2 for examples).

Table 2. "Foreign worker as perpetrator" subcategories with examples.

Subcategory	Example	Language
Criminal offenses	*Sutkinja Anita Čalić kaznila Nepalca U. L. (28) i Indijca M. K. (31)...* en. Judge Anita Čalić fined Nepalese U. L. (28) and Indian M. K. (31)...	Cro
Undocumented residence	*...ohne gültigen Aufenthaltstitel...* en. ...without a valid residence permit...	Ger
Social tension and language barriers	*Na teškoće u radu sa stranim radnicima upozorili su obiteljski liječnici...* en. Family doctors reported difficulties working with foreign workers...	Cro

(continued)

Table 2. (continued)

Subcategory	Example	Language
Lack of qualifications	*Geflüchtete im Schnitt weniger qualifiziert…* en. Refugees are on average less qualified…	Ger
Deportation and rejection	*Najčešće protjerani: Ukrajina (5935), Sirija (4708), Afganistan (2396)…* en. Most frequently deported: Ukraine (5935), Syria (4708), Afghanistan (2396)…	Cro
Public skepticism and rejection	*Vorbehalte bei Arbeitgebern…* en. Reservations among employers…	Ger

5.3 User

Foreign workers are depicted as recipients of services or as passive participants in the labor market. These representations tend to be administratively neutral and lack evaluative language (see Table 3 for examples).

Table 3. "Foreign worker as user" subcategories with examples.

Subcategory	Example	Language
Wages and employment status	*Za 9000 stranih radnika bruto plaća je nešto veća od tisuću eura…* For 9,000 foreign workers gross salary is just over €1,000…	Cro
Access to education and services	*Wir erleben in unseren Beratungsstellen sehr viele Menschen mit Migrationshintergrund…* We see many people with a migration background in our counseling centers…	Ger
Social benefits and insurance	*Broj osiguranika stranih državljana iz trećih zemalja iznosio je 87.604…* The number of insured third-country nationals was 87,604…	Cro
Tax contributions	*Strani radnici koji kod nas rade i plaćaju porez…* Foreign workers who work here and pay taxes…	Ger

5.4 Contributor

This role reflects positive portrayals of foreign workers as skilled, integrated, and socially valuable. It is more prominent in German media, often aligned with economic and institutional narratives (see Table 4 for examples).

Table 4. "Foreign worker as contributor" subcategories with examples

Subcategory	Example	Language
Economic contribution	*...ljudi koji dolaze raditi i time doprinose našoj zajednici...* ...people who come to work and thereby contribute to our community...	Cro
High qualifications and work ethic	*...hart arbeitenden Migranten...* ...hard-working migrants...	Ger
Social acceptance and integration	*...najviše mi se sviđa to što su ljudi dobri prema nama Filipincima...* ...what I like most is that people are kind to us Filipinos..."	Cro
Structural dependence	*Pflegesektor mittlerweile abhängig von Arbeitskräften aus dem Ausland...* The care sector is now dependent on foreign labor...	Ger
Policy measures and recruitment strategies	*Potrebne su mjere za lakšu integraciju stranih radnika...* Measures are needed to facilitate the integration of foreign workers...	Cro

This semantic classification offers a nuanced framework for interpreting how foreign workers are ideologically positioned in Croatian and German media. The four-role model, supported by syntactic analysis and sentiment data, enables a replicable approach to multilingual discourse studies and provides a basis for mapping the emotional tone and discursive function in labor migration coverage.

6 Automated Role Annotation, Comparative Framing, and Implications

Building on the semantic role classification outlined in Section 5, this chapter presents the automated annotation process for foreign worker roles in Croatian and German media texts, followed by a comparative analysis of role distribution across national and source-level corpora.

Using the NooJ linguistic platform [6], a syntactic grammar was developed to systematically identify discursive roles attributed to foreign workers. The grammar was structured around two primary domains: the economy and crime. Within each domain, the dual-node system enabled the detection of foreign worker entities alongside role-indicative keywords in their immediate syntactic context. This facilitated the automatic annotation of four semantic roles: Contributor (<E + CONTR >), User (<E + KOR> in Croatian vs. < E + NUTZ> in German), Perpetrator (<E + PER >), and Victim (<E + VIC >).

6.1 Corpus-Level Role Distribution

In the Croatian corpus, 393 annotated instances revealed the **victim** role as the most prevalent (48.6%), indicating a humanitarian framing focused on vulnerability, exploitation, and marginalization. The **user** role accounted for 24.9%, with **contributor** and **perpetrator** roles comprising 14.5% and 12%, respectively (see Fig. 4 – left chart). This distribution reflects Croatia's position as an emerging migrant-receiving country, where ethical and empathetic narratives dominate.

Conversely, the German corpus showed 266 annotated instances, with a dominant **contributor** role (44%), emphasizing the economic utility and productivity of foreign workers. The **perpetrator** role followed at 24.8%, while **user** and **victim** roles appeared at 15.4% and 15.8%, respectively (see Fig. 4 – right chart). The prominence of perpetrator and contributor roles suggests a discourse framed by institutional and economic pragmatism, reflecting Germany's long-standing immigration infrastructure.

Fig. 4. Distribution of detected roles in Croatian (left) and German (right) corpus.

6.2 Source-Level Role Variation

Role distribution was further examined across media sources within each national corpus, revealing intra-national variation shaped by editorial orientation and journalistic style (see Fig. 5).

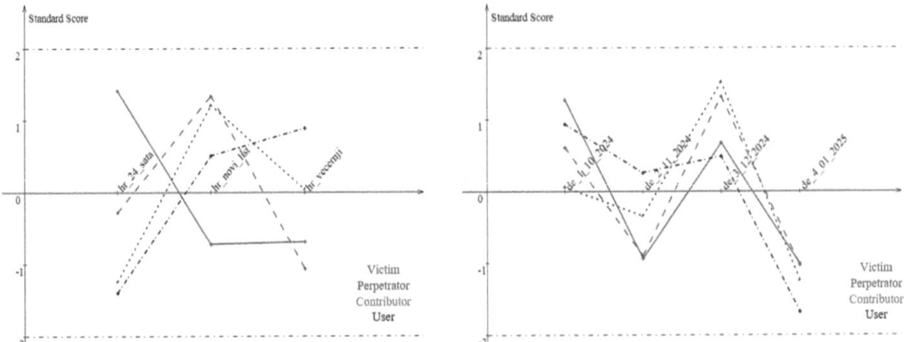

Fig. 5. Standard score (Z-score) by source for the Croatian corpus (left) and the German corpus (right).

In the Croatian corpus, three major online portals were analyzed: *24sata, Novi list*, and *Večernji list*. The **victim** role is most prominent in *24sata*, displaying a positive Z-score, while it falls below zero in the other two outlets. This pattern suggests that *24sata* emphasizes humanitarian narratives and the vulnerability of foreign workers, likely influenced by its tabloid-style discourse. Correspondingly, the **user** role, which requires more detailed reporting, is least represented in 24sata. The **perpetrator** role is most pronounced in *Novi list*, while it is underrepresented in the other outlets. The **contributor** role also peaks in *Novi list*, but is significantly lower in *Večernji list*, implying that right-leaning sources may be less inclined to portray foreign workers as contributors to society. The **user** role is most frequently observed in *Večernji list*, suggesting a focus on administrative and procedural aspects of migration.

In the German corpus, similar trends emerge. The **victim** role is most prevalent in *Bild*, consistent with its sensationalist orientation and paralleling *24sata* in the Croatian context. Conversely, the **victim** role is nearly absent in *Süddeutsche Zeitung*, known for its analytical and policy-oriented reporting. The **perpetrator** role is strongly represented in *Junge Freiheit*, while **contributor** and **user** roles are least visible in the same outlet, aligning with the outlet's conservative or far-right positioning, which tends to emphasize threat narratives over integration or productivity. The **contributor** role is highly visible in *Süddeutsche Zeitung*, and the **user** role is most prominent in *Die Welt*, indicating a more institutional and pragmatic framing of foreign labor.

These findings highlight the significant role of media ideology and format in shaping public discourse on foreign workers. The semantic role annotation and statistical modeling reveal not only national differences in framing but also important intra-national variations driven by editorial orientation. This layered approach provides a robust foundation for further sentiment analysis and comparative discourse studies, with additional educational potential for fostering students' critical thinking and media literacy in foreign language teaching [1].

6.3 Implications for Policy and Media Practice

The divergent media portrayals of foreign workers in Croatia and Germany underscore the need for more nuanced approaches in both public policy and journalistic practice. Policymakers should recognize how media framing influences public attitudes toward migrants, potentially shaping integration outcomes. Emphasizing the economic contributions and social integration of foreign workers, as seen in German media, may foster more inclusive public discourse and support policies that facilitate labor market participation and social cohesion.

For journalists and media organizations, these findings highlight the importance of balanced reporting that avoids one-dimensional victim or perpetrator narratives. Enhancing media literacy programs to critically engage audiences with diverse migrant representations can counteract stereotypes and promote a more informed public dialogue. Ultimately, fostering responsible media framing is essential for building supportive environments that recognize the multifaceted roles of foreign workers in society.

7 Conclusion

This study explored how foreign workers are framed in Croatian and German online media through the annotation of four semantic roles: victim, perpetrator, user, and contributor. The findings reveal distinct national and ideological patterns in media discourse. Croatian outlets predominantly frame foreign workers as victims, reflecting humanitarian concerns linked to Croatia's emerging status as a migrant-receiving country. In contrast, German media emphasize the contributor role, highlighting economic utility and integration challenges within a mature migration context.

Source-level analysis confirmed that tabloid outlets favor victim narratives, while conservative or right-leaning media emphasize perpetrator roles and often downplay foreign workers' contributions. These divergent portrayals underscore the media's significant role in shaping public perceptions of labor migration. By illuminating how media construct foreign worker identities, this research contributes to a deeper understanding of public perceptions that influence integration policies and societal attitudes. Greater awareness of media framing can support efforts in media literacy, promote balanced reporting, and inform policymakers engaged in migration and labor market integration strategies.

The semantic role framework developed here provides a replicable model for cross-cultural discourse analysis. Future research should further integrate emotional sentiment analysis using resources like the NRC lexicon to map the affective dimensions accompanying these roles, thereby deepening our understanding of how emotions influence migration narratives across different media and political contexts.

While this study provides valuable insights into media framing of foreign workers in Croatian and German online news, several limitations should be noted. The corpus, though balanced and representative, covers a limited timeframe and a specific selection of news portals, which may not capture the full diversity of media discourse. Additionally, the automated annotation process, while robust, relies on syntactic grammars and lexical resources that may not fully account for nuanced or implicit meanings in complex texts.

Future research could expand the dataset temporally and include additional media formats, such as television or social media, to capture broader public discourse. A deeper integration of emotional sentiment analysis using the NRC lexicon could elucidate how affect shapes audience perceptions across different media environments. Finally, investigating the impact of these media portrayals on public opinion and policy-making would further bridge the gap between discourse analysis and social outcomes.

References

1. Brnjaković, A.: The educational potential of the NooJ tool in learning and teaching German as a foreign language: a case study based on the analysis of German and Croatian online articles about foreign workers. Faculty of Humanities and Social Sciences, University of Zagreb (2025)
2. Croatian Bureau of Statistics, https://podaci.dzs.hr/2024/hr/76802, Accessed 10 Sep 2025
3. Federal Statistical Office of Germany, https://www.destatis.de/DE/Themen/Gesellschaft-Umwelt/Bevoelkerung/Migration-Integration/Glossar/migrationshintergrund.html, Accessed 10 Sep 2025
4. Landsman Vinković, M., Kocijan, K.: Preparing the NooJ German module for the analysis of a learner spoken corpus. In: Bekavac, B., Kocijan, K., Silberztein, M., Šojat, K. (eds.) Formalising Natural Languages: Applications to Natural Language Processing and Digital Humanities. NooJ 2020. Communications in Computer and Information Science. Springer, Cham, pp. 146–158 (2021)
5. Müller, R.: NooJ as a concordancer in computer-assisted textual analysis. The case of the German module. In: Koeva, S., Mesfar, S., Silberztein, M. (eds.) Formalising Natural Languages with NooJ 2013: Selected Papers from the NooJ 2013 International Conference. Cambridge Scholars Publishing, Newcastle, UK, pp. 197–208 (2014)
6. Silberztein, M.: Formalizing Natural Languages: The NooJ Approach. Wiley-ISTE, London (2016)
7. Vodanović, B.: Immigrant in the light of language production. In: Bartulović, A., Mijić, L., Silberztein, M. (eds.). Formalizing Natural Languages: Applications to Natural Language Processing and Digital Humanities. Springer, Cham, pp. 165–175 (2024)

Creation and Comparison of NooJ Grammars for Temporal Expressions in Ukrainian and Serbian

Divna Petković[1,2(✉)] [ID] and Victor Rabiet[3] [ID]

[1] Télécom Paris, 91120 Palaiseau, France
divna.petkovic@nyu.edu
[2] NYU Paris, 75005 Paris, France
[3] École Normale Supérieure, 75005 Paris, France

Abstract. This study represents the initial stage of a twofold effort: to revitalize the NooJ module for Serbian by initiating a new framework for the tagging of temporal expressions, and to enrich the already well-developed Ukrainian module through the creation of grammars for date and time expressions in both languages. This allows us to compare temporal expressions in both languages and identify patterns of concordance, as well as points of divergence. On the one hand, this work aims to enable advanced analysis of temporality-related patterns in literary texts (for example, contrasting expressions of duration with punctual expressions, such as a specific time), and on the other hand, it involves creating grammars of the same phenomena in two languages of the same branch (Slavic) but from different groups (Eastern for Ukrainian, Southern for Serbian), allowing for a closer examination of their differences (for instance, the use of an ordinal number in certain temporal expressions in Ukrainian, whereas a cardinal number is used for the same expression in Serbian). Additionally, this study highlights under-explored similarities, such as paucal numeral phrases with numbers 2, 3, and 4, as well as numbers greater than 20 that end in these digits. These paucal forms determine the case and the number of the nouns and adjectives that follow them, exhibiting inflectional features distinct from both the singular and the plural.

Keywords: NooJ · Ukrainian · Serbian · Temporal Expressions · Numeral Phrases · Paucal Phrases

1 Introduction

This paper presents a comparative analysis of temporal expression recognition using NooJ grammars for two closely related Slavic languages: Ukrainian and Serbian. A *temporal expression* in a text typically consists of a sequence of tokens (words, numbers, or symbols) that denote time, whether as a specific **point** (e.g., *now*; *today*; *1 May 1987*; *last Christmas*), a **duration** (e.g., *two hours; all week; for as long as I remember*), an **interval** (e.g., *from 9 to 5; Monday–Friday*), or a **recurrence** (e.g., *every year, on Fridays*). Understanding how these expressions are structured and used across languages

D. Petković et al. (Eds.): NooJ 2025, CCIS 2832, pp. 150–161, 2026.
https://doi.org/10.1007/978-3-032-17103-0_13

is central to a range of tasks in natural language processing, such as temporal information extraction, event and relation extraction, timeline construction, etc., as well as broader applications in areas like clinical text analysis and digital humanities.

Temporal expression recognition is a well-studied problem for high-resource languages such as English, but comparatively little work has been done for smaller Slavic languages, where resources are not as readily available, annotated datasets remain limited, and linguistic complexity poses additional challenges due to rich morphology and flexible word order.

This work is preliminary in several respects. It marks the beginning of the development of a new Serbian module in NooJ and contributes to the existing, already very developed, Ukrainian NooJ module, created by Olena Saint-Joanis (Saint-Joanis 2024). We begin with the most frequent expressions, namely date and time lexemes such as month names and hour/minute patterns, and progressively build toward more complex constructions. We first investigate how temporal expressions differ structurally between Ukrainian and Serbian, with particular attention to morphosyntactic patterns, numeral usage, and lexical variation. We hypothesize that the process of developing comprehensive NooJ grammars for both languages will expose challenges inherent to their morphological richness, such as complex inflectional paradigms and idiomatic temporal constructions, which place distinctive demands on finite-state and syntactic modelling[1]. Finally, we explore what cross-linguistic discrepancies may reveal about the relative complexity of temporal expression systems in these two Slavic languages. Beyond describing these contrasts, our goal is to provide computationally usable grammars that support temporal tagging in low-resource Slavic languages and lay the groundwork for future hybrid systems that integrate linguistic insights with data-driven methods.

The remainder of this paper is organized as follows. Section 2 situates this research within current approaches to temporal expression recognition and annotation, outlining the linguistic motivation, research goals, and the relevance of NooJ for processing low-resource languages. Section 3 details the types of linguistic classification used to design and implement the grammars in NooJ and presents the results of the contrastive analysis, with illustrative examples of temporal expressions in both Ukrainian and Serbian. Finally, Sect. 4 discusses the findings and proposes directions for future work.

2 Theoretical Framework

2.1 Temporal Expression Recognition in NLP

The study of temporal expressions has evolved into a distinct subfield of natural language processing (NLP), with its own annotation standards, evaluation campaigns, and methodologies. Temporal expressions were initially treated as a subcategory of named entities, and their identification was integrated into Named Entity Recognition (NER) systems, where dates, times, and durations were processed alongside entities such as persons and locations (Grishman & Sundheim, 1996).

---

[1] Finite-state representations are typically used for morphological and lexical processing, syntactic representations are used for higher-level grammatical structure. NooJ is explicitly built around this multi-level architecture.

The introduction of TimeML (Pustejovsky et al., 2003) established a rich markup language for annotating temporal information, and its TIMEX3 layer became the *de facto* standard framework, providing a normalized and compositional way of encoding expressions of time. Building on this foundation, the Automatic Content Extraction (ACE) program in 2004 introduced Temporal Expression Recognition and Normalization (TERN) as a dedicated representational framework, effectively distinguishing the detection and interpretation of temporal expressions from other NER tasks, and accelerating the adoption of TimeML/TIMEX3 across the field.

Since the mid-2000s, shared tasks such as TempEval (Verhagen et al., 2007, 2010) and i2b2 (Uzuner et al., 2011) have consolidated annotation practices, strengthened inter-annotator agreement protocols, and promoted TIMEX3-compatible evaluation metrics. These initiatives have advanced both the recognition and normalization of temporal expressions and have fostered a diverse ecosystem of temporal processing approaches. Nevertheless, despite these developments, languages like Ukrainian and Serbian remain underrepresented, with few available resources for temporal expression recognition and normalization—underscoring the need for rule-based frameworks like NooJ that can support resource-lean settings.

2.2   Main Approaches to Temporal Tagging

Two major paradigms dominate temporal tagging. Grammar-based approaches, which are the focus of this study, encode linguistic generalizations in an explicit and interpretable way, drawing on finite-state or context-free grammars to model morphosyntactic and lexical patterns (Strötgen & Gertz, 2010; Brucato et al., 2013; Filannino et al., 2013). These systems typically achieve high precision and transparency, making them attractive for languages with rich morphology and limited annotated resources, although their development is labour-intensive and requires substantial linguistic expertise.

In contrast, statistical and neural approaches (Ahn et al., 2007; Angeli et al., 2012) rely on large, manually annotated corpora to train sequence-labelling or classification models, excelling at recognition but often struggling with normalization, particularly in typologically diverse languages. More recently, transformer-based architectures such as BERT (Devlin et al., 2019) and domain-adapted variants (e.g., ClinicalBERT, BioBERT, etc.) have achieved state-of-the-art performance in temporal expression recognition by leveraging contextual embeddings and transfer learning (Lee et al., 2020; Bethard et al., 2022). Such systems reduce dependence on task-specific feature engineering but still require annotated data for fine-tuning, and often provide limited interpretability.

For Ukrainian and Serbian, where temporal corpora are scarce and morphosyntactic complexity is high, a grammar-first strategy is both pragmatic and theoretically informative: it delivers usable resources quickly, formalizes cross-linguistic contrasts, and lays a foundation for future hybrid systems that integrate linguistic insight with data-driven models. This is precisely where NooJ, a linguistic development environment, demonstrates potential, because it enables the construction of precise, modular grammars for tokenization, morphological and semantic analysis, and syntactic parsing.

3 Contrastive Morphosyntax of Temporal Expressions in Ukrainian and Serbian

The design of grammar-based temporal expression recognizers requires a precise understanding of the morphosyntactic structures through which time is expressed in a language. In Slavic languages, this task is particularly demanding, since lexical items denoting time are systematically reshaped by case morphology, numeral interaction, and agreement patterns.

This study adopts a contrastive approach, setting two languages side by side to bring out both their similarities and their systematic differences. Ukrainian and Serbian are typologically close as members of the Slavic language family, but they belong to different subgroups: Ukrainian to East Slavic and Serbian to South Slavic. Their selection as representatives of their respective subgroups is motivated by the fact that they share broadly comparable temporal systems, yet diverge in ways that become especially revealing when examined through the lens of numeral phrases. This makes them a particularly suitable pair for the discussion of the paucal numeral category, presented later in the paper (from Sect. 3.1 onwards).

These divergences are not merely of descriptive interest: they determine how grammars must be constructed in a system such as NooJ.

3.1 Main Syntactic Types of Temporal Modifiers

From a syntactic perspective, temporal expressions in Ukrainian and Serbian can appear in various configurations, most commonly as adverbial phrases (AdvP), prepositional phrases (PP), or noun phrases (NP). Adverbial phrases typically modify verbal predicates, as in Serbian *Јуче је дошао* and Ukrainian *Учора прийшов* ('[He] came yesterday'). Prepositional phrases express relational meaning, for example, Serbian *Радим до децембра* and Ukrainian *Працюю до грудня* ('I work until December'). Noun phrases denote nominal time references, as in Serbian *Ова недеља је била тешка* and Ukrainian *Цей тиждень був важкий* ('This week was hard'). However, there is also a special subtype of noun phrase, known as the paucal phrase, which plays a particularly important role in temporal expressions involving numerals and will be discussed in the following subsection.

Paucal Phrases and the Paucal Number. Before proceeding, it is necessary to briefly introduce the notion of the paucal number. The term derives from the Latin *paucus* 'few, small in number' and designates, in some Slavic languages such as Serbian (and BCMS more broadly), Russian, and, according to some linguistic sources[2], Ukrainian and Belarussian, the grammatical form of nouns and adjectives used in noun phrases with numerals *two*, *three*, *four*, multi-digit numbers ending in these digits, and the words meaning *both*.

The historical source of the paucal is the Old Slavic dual number, now lost in all Slavic languages except Slovenian and Upper and Lower Sorbian. Its traces, however, remain

---

[2] Note that in Ukrainian and Belarussian it is more often described as a nominative plural with a singular stress, see Stankiewicz (1986, p. 158–159).

visible in both Serbian and Ukrainian, where it triggers a specific pattern of agreement. In Serbian, the paucal is attested with nouns and adjectives of all three genders. In masculine and neuter nouns, it is characterized by the ending *-a*, which makes it homographic with the genitive singular form (and often conflated with it), although it actually represents a continuation of the old nominative, accusative, and vocative dual endings. In feminine nouns of the third declension group, the paucal is distinguished only through accentual differences.

In paucal phrases, adjectives also take the paucal rather than the definite form. This is evident in Serbian, for instance, in *од овог човека* ('from this man'), where the construction contains the preposition *од* followed by a pronominal adjective and noun in the genitive singular, contrasted with *од ова два човека* ('from these two men'), where the same preposition is followed by the pronominal adjective, the numeral *two*, and a noun, all marked for the paucal.

For a side-by-side comparison of Ukrainian and Serbian, consider the examples in Tables 1 and 2.

Table 1. Paucal NPs in Ukrainian and Serbian, model 'x *days ago*'.

Ukrainian	Serbian	English
один **день** тому	пре један **дан**	one day ago
два/три/чотири **дні** тому	пре два/три/четири **дана**	2/3/4 days ago
п'ять **днів** тому	пре пет **дана**	five days ago

Table 2. Paucal NPs in Ukrainian and Serbian, model '*clock time*'.

Ukrainian	Serbian	English
Одна **година** і двадцять одна **хвилина**	Један **сат** и двадесет један **минут**	One **hour** and twenty-one **minutes**
Дві **години** і двадцять дві **хвилини**	Два **сата** и двадесет два **минута**	Two **hours** and twenty-two **minutes**
П'ять **годин** і двадцять п'ять **хвилин**	Пет **сати** и двадесет пет **минута**	Five **hours** and twenty-five **minutes**

While these syntactic configurations are reflected in the structure of our NooJ grammars, the organization of the system itself is primarily semantic. In this preliminary stage, we focus on compiling a temporal vocabulary and constructing grammars around global semantic categories such as *date, time, duration,* and *recurrence*. These semantic distinctions guide the modular design of the NooJ temporal subsystem discussed in the following sections.

3.2 Temporal Expression Vocabulary

Within the scope of this study, we limit our vocabulary of temporal expressions to a set of lexical items, including core units of time (e.g., *second*), parts of the day (e.g., *morning*), calendric terms (days of the week, months of the year, and seasons), deictic adverbs (e.g., *today*), and numerals (both cardinal and ordinal forms). The complete list of these items is presented in Table 3.

Table 3. Core temporal vocabulary in Ukrainian, Serbian, and English.

Ukrainian	Serbian	English	Ukrainian	Serbian	English
секунда	секунда	second	понеділок	понедељак	Monday
хвилина	минут	minute	вівторок	уторак	Tuesday
година / час	сат / час	hour	середа	среда	Wednesday
ранок	јутро	morning	четвер	четвртак	Thursday
вранці	ујутру	in the morning	п'ятниця	петак	Friday
—	преподне	before noon	субота	субота	Saturday
південь	подне	noon	неділя	недеља	Sunday
—	поподне	afternoon	січень	јануар	January
вечір	вече	evening	лютий	фебруар	February
увечері	увече	in the evening	березень	март	March
день	дан	day	квітень	април	April
ніч	ноћ	night	травень	мај	May
сьогодні вночі	ноћас	tonight / last night	червень	јун	June
північ	поноћ	midnight	липень	јул	July
вікенд / вихідні	викенд	weekend	серпень	август	August
тиждень	недеља / седмица	week	вересень	септембар	September
місяць	месец	month	жовтень	октобар	October
квартал	тромесечје	quarter	листопад	новембар	November
півріччя	полугодиште	semester	грудень	децембар	December
рік	година	year	весна	пролеће	spring
століття	век	century	літо	лето	summer
ера	ера	era	осінь	јесен	fall
дата	датум	date	зима	зима	winter

(continued)

Table 3. (*continued*)

Ukrainian	Serbian	English	Ukrainian	Serbian	English
сьогодні	данас	today	вчора	јуче	yesterday
завтра	сутра	tomorrow	позавчора	прекјуче	the day before yesterday
післязавтра	прек(о)сутра	the day after tomorrow	три дні тому	накјуче	three days ago
через три дні	нак(о)сутра	in three days' time	позавчора ввечері	прексиноћ	the night before last
учора ввечері / минулої ночі	синоћ	last night	кількісні й порядкові числівники	кардинални и редни бројеви	cardinal and ordinal numbers

Many of these lexical items can participate in more than one type of temporal expression, depending on their syntactic environment and semantic function. For this reason, the vocabulary outlined above is not rigidly partitioned into discrete classes but serves as a shared resource across several temporal categories. The semantic organization of these categories is presented in the next section.

3.3 Semantic Categories of Temporal Expressions

For the purposes of grammar construction in NooJ, we distinguish four operational categories of temporal expressions: DATE, TIME, DURATION, and RECURRENCE. These categories correspond to the general types introduced in Sect. 1 (*point, duration, interval,* and *recurrence*), with the temporal *point* here subdivided into DATE and TIME, and DURATION encompassing *interval* expressions. These labels are defined with respect to the morphosyntactic behavior of Ukrainian and Serbian, and they serve as the organizing principle for the grammar modules developed in this study. Although broadly parallel to the TIMEX3 types proposed in TimeML and ISO-TimeML (DATE, TIME, DURATION, SET), the categories here are adapted to highlight features that are particularly salient in Slavic morphosyntax, such as case alternations and paucal forms.

DATE and TIME Expressions. Take, for example, the following sentence in English:
See you on Wednesday, January 28, 2026, at 15:24.
When written out in full, it reads as follows:
See you on Wednesday, the twenty-eighth of January of the year two thousand and twenty-six, at fifteen hours and twenty-four minutes.

Below are the corresponding sentences in Serbian (1) and in Ukrainian (2), with case and number markings. Agreement differences between the two languages are marked in bold.

1) Видимо се у среду *(Wednesday.Acc.SG)*, двадесет осмог *(28.Gen.SG, ordinal num.)* јануара *(January.Gen.SG)* две *(two.Gen.SG)* **хиљаде** *(thousand.paucal agreement)*

двадесет шесте *(26.Gen.SG,* ordinal num.*)* године *(year.Gen.SG)* **у петнаест** (15.invariable num.*)* **часова** *(hours.Gen.PL)* **и двадесет четири** (24.invariable num.*)* **минута** *(minutes.paucal agreement).*

2) Побачимося в середу *(Wednesday.Acc.SG)*, двадцять восьмого *(28.Gen.SG,* ordinal num.*)* січня *(January.Gen.SG)* дві *(two.Gen.SG)* **тисячі** *(thousand.Nom.PL)* двадцять шостого *(26.Gen.SG,* ordinal num.*)* року *(year.Gen.SG)*, **о п'ятнадцятій** *(15.Loc.SG, ordinal num.)* **годині** *(hours.Loc.SG)* **двадцять чотири** *(24.Gen.SG)* **хвилини** *(minutes.Nom.PL).*

Notable differences include the treatment of the hour indication as a quantity requiring an ordinal number in Ukrainian, whereas in Serbian it takes a cardinal number, which, except for *one, two,* and (archaically) *three* and *four*, is invariable. This difference affects the declension of the noun *hour*: in Ukrainian, it appears in the locative singular, while in Serbian it occurs in the genitive plural (here following *fifteen*). However, if the numeral ended in *2, 3,* or *4* (except *12, 13,* and *14*), Serbian instead uses a special paucal form, as seen in the examples following the numerals *2* in *two thousand* and *24* in *twenty-four minutes*. Ukrainian likewise exhibits a special agreement pattern for numerals ending in *2, 3,* or *4*, as seen when contrasting the construction *24 min* ('двадцять чотири **хвилини**'), where the noun *minutes* appears in the nominative plural, with, for example, *25 min* ('двадцять п'ять **хвилин**'), where *minutes* is in the genitive plural. However, not all Ukrainian grammars agree on the exact status of this special form; for a discussion of this issue, see Breu (2020).

To further illustrate this contrast, Figs. 1 and 2 show two NooJ grammars of hours (sub-grammars within the DATE and TIME) for Ukrainian and Serbian, respectively:

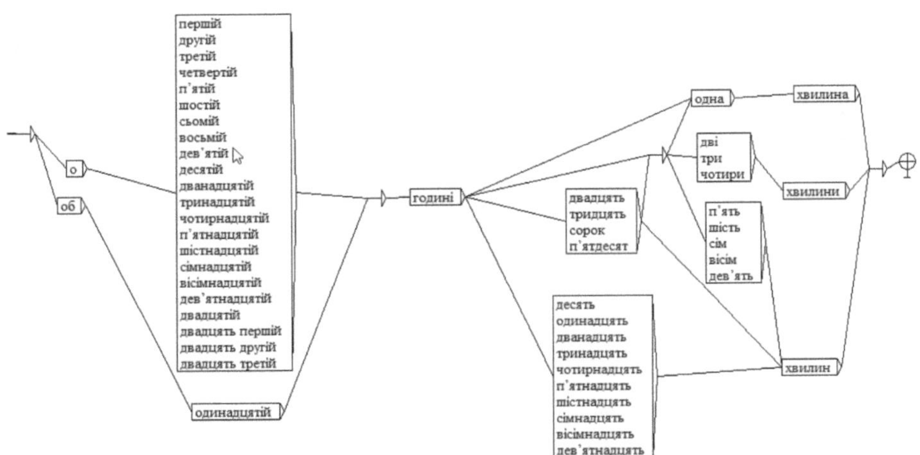

Fig. 1. A NooJ grammar of hours in Ukrainian.

DURATION Expressions. These expressions indicate the extent or length of an event or state. In both Ukrainian and Serbian, they are typically realized through genitive, accusative, instrumental, or locative case forms, often in combination with prepositions,

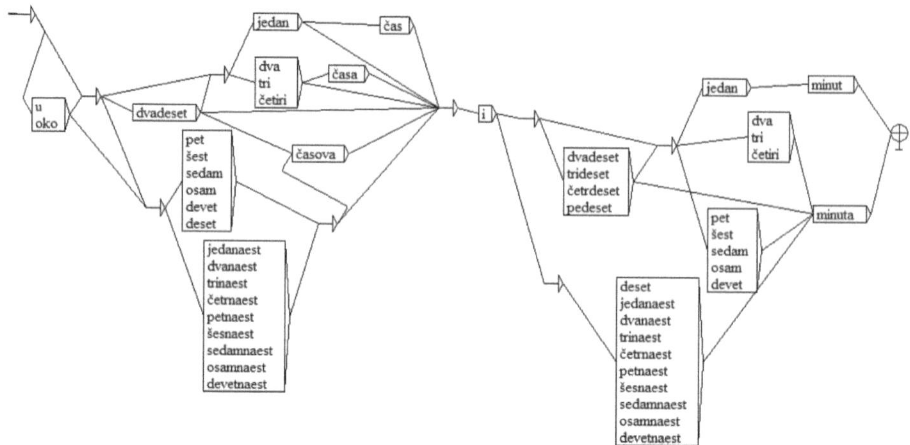

Fig. 2. A NooJ grammar of hours in Serbian.

for example *during* (in Serbian *током, за,* and in Ukrainian *протягом, упродовж, за*), as in Serbian *током недеље* and Ukrainian *протягом тижня* ('during the week').

Morphologically, duration phrases continue to exhibit numeral-dependent agreement patterns similar to those observed in date and time expressions, further emphasizing the importance of distinguishing the paucal form from the regular plural. Numerals from two to four take nominative plural forms in Ukrainian (e.g., *чотири дні,* 'four days'), whereas in Serbian they trigger paucal forms (*четири дана,* 'four days'), contrasting with the genitive plural forms used with numerals five and higher in both languages (*п'ять днів* in Ukrainian, *пет дана* in Serbian, 'five days').

Duration expressions can be further subcategorized according to whether they denote bounded or unbounded spans of time. Bounded duration (also referred to as an *interval* duration) indicates the amount of time required for the completion of an event, whereas unbounded duration refers to the temporal extent of an ongoing or habitual situation without implying its endpoint. This semantic distinction is often reflected in prepositional choice. The previous example with the preposition *during* followed by the genitive—Serbian *током недеље* and Ukrainian *протягом тижня* ('during the week')—illustrates a typical unbounded case. For a bounded counterpart, both Ukrainian and Serbian employ the preposition *за* followed by the accusative, which marks completion within a time limit, as in *за секунду* ('in a second, *i.e.,* within a period of one second). Although finer distinctions could be made, it is important to note that such constructions not only quantify temporal length but also interact with aspectual interpretation, marking whether an event is viewed as completed within a timeframe or as persisting throughout it.

RECURRENCE Expressions. The most straightforward type of recurrence expressions involves lexical adverbs of frequency, such as Serbian *често, понекад, свакодневно* and Ukrainian *часто, іноді, щодня* ('often', 'sometimes', 'daily'). Habitual or iterative actions can also be expressed through numeral–noun combinations (as in Ukrainian *двічі на тиждень* and Serbian *два пута недељно,* meaning 'twice a week'). Another productive strategy involves prepositional constructions with the genitive, which express iteration within a temporal frame, for example, in Serbian, *сваке недеље* and in Ukrainian *кожного тижня* ('every week'). A notable difference between the two languages lies in the fact that, in Ukrainian, many such expressions have become lexicalized adverbs formed with the prefix *що-* (*щосуботи, щороку, щомісяця,* etc.). Serbian lacks this particular prefixal mechanism, but uses a (partial) alternative strategy: the bare instrumental of days of the week to indicate regular recurrence, as in *суботом,* 'every Saturday'.

These strategies are reflected in the NooJ grammar of recurrence, an excerpt of which is shown in Fig. 3.

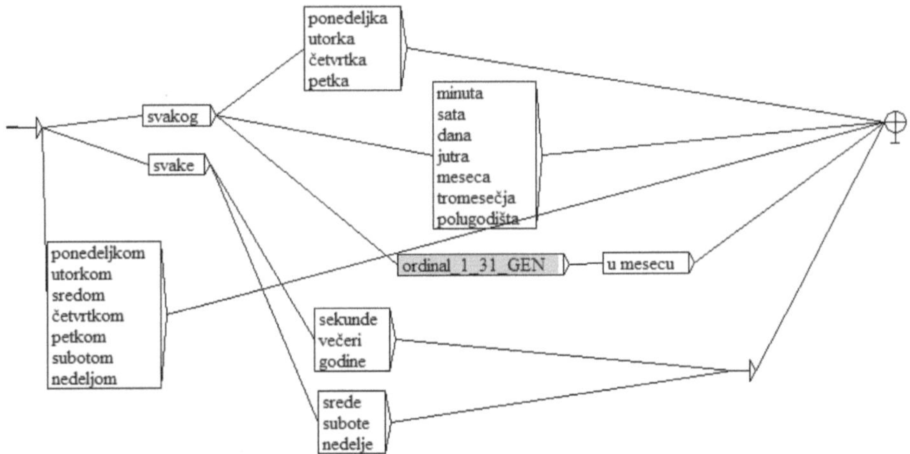

Fig. 3. Excerpt from a Serbian grammar of recurrence in NooJ.

In summary, from a methodological standpoint, NooJ offers a practical route for interpretable temporal tagging: rules are modular, auditable, and easy to extend as lexical coverage grows. Pedagogically and for digital humanities, such grammars enable transparent querying of texts by temporal functions, from very general (point vs. duration vs. recurrence) to various degrees of fine-grained, and provide reliable anchors for timeline construction and event sequencing in low-resource Slavic languages.

4 Conclusion

This paper presented the first step toward comparable NooJ grammars for temporal expressions in Ukrainian and Serbian. Grounded in a compact temporal vocabulary and four semantic modules (DATE, TIME, DURATION, RECURRENCE), our approach couples explicit morphosyntactic modelling (notably of paucal agreement and case selection) with portable local grammars that can be reused across categories. The contrastive design makes visible where the two languages converge (shared prepositional frames, numeral-driven plural/genitive alternations) and where they diverge in ways that are operationally relevant for NLP (ordinal vs. cardinal hours; lexicalized recurrence vs. instrumental habituals; interpretation of paucals; declension of numerals).

Future work will expand lexical coverage (including holidays, named periods, and prepositional phrases without an explicit temporal marker) and enrich range and coordination handling. We also plan a systematic intrinsic evaluation (precision/recall by category) and extrinsic tests in downstream tasks (e.g., event ordering), as well as hybridization with data-driven models that leverage our grammars as features or constraints. Finally, we intend to release the grammars alongside documentation and test suites, to support reproducible research and facilitate adaptation to other Slavic languages.

Acknowledgments. The authors gratefully acknowledge Olena Saint-Joanis for her guidance and expertise.

Disclosure of Interests. The authors have no competing interests to declare that are relevant to the content of this article.

References

1. Ahn, D., van Rantwijk, J., de Rijke, M.: A cascaded machine learning approach to interpreting temporal expressions. In: Proceedings of the Human Language Technologies 2007: The Conference of the North American Chapter of the Association for Computational Linguistics, pp. 420–427. Association for Computational Linguistics, Stroudsburg (2007)
2. Angeli, G., Manning, C.D., Jurafsky, D.: Parsing time: Learning to interpret time expressions. In: Proceedings of the 2012 Conference of the North American Chapter of the Association for Computational Linguistics: Human Language Technologies, pp. 446–455. ACL, Stroudsburg (2012)
3. Bethard, S., Styler, W.F., Sun, W., Uzuner, Ö.: SemEval-2022 Task 6: Temporal annotation in the clinical domain. In: Proceedings of the 16th International Workshop on Semantic Evaluation (SemEval-2022), pp. 700–712. ACL, Stroudsburg (2022)
4. Breu, W.: Paucal. In: Greenberg, M. L. (ed.) Encyclopedia of Slavic Languages and Linguistics Online. Brill, Leiden (2020)
5. Brucato, M., Ligozat, A.-L., Grau, B., Moriceau, V.: A rule-based approach to temporal expression tagging and normalization in French. In: Proceedings of the 10th International Conference on Recent Advances in Natural Language Processing, pp. 117–123. ACL, Stroudsburg (2013)
6. Devlin, J., Chang, M.-W., Lee, K., Toutanova, K.: BERT: pre-training of deep bidirectional transformers for language understanding. In: Proceedings of NAACL-HLT 2019, pp. 4171–4186. ACL, Stroudsburg (2019)
7. Filannino, M., Gkotsis, G., Groenwold, S., Karystianis, G., Velupillai, S., Ananiadou, S.: Temporal expression normalisation in clinical text. In: Proceedings of the 6th International Workshop on Health Text Mining and Information Analysis (Louhi), pp. 33–41. ACL, Stroudsburg (2013)
8. Grishman, R., Sundheim, B.: Message understanding conference-6: a brief history. In: Proceedings of the 16th Conference on Computational Linguistics, pp. 466–471. ACL, Stroudsburg (1996)
9. Lee, J., et al.: BioBERT: a pre-trained biomedical language representation model for biomedical text mining. Bioinformatics **36**(4), 1234–1240 (2020)

10. Pustejovsky, J., et al.: TimeML: robust specification of event and temporal expressions in text. In: New Directions in Question Answering, pp. 28–34. ACL, Stroudsburg (2003)
11. Saint-Joanis, O.: Formalisation de la langue ukrainienne avec NooJ: préparation du module ukrainien. PhD thesis, Université Bourgogne Franche-Comté (2024). https://theses.hal.science/tel-04690884/
12. Stankiewicz, E. The Slavic Languages: Unity in Diversity. Walter de Gruyter GmbH & Co KG, Berlin (1986)
13. Strötgen, J., Gertz, M.: HeidelTime: high quality rule-based extraction and normalization of temporal expressions. In: Proceedings of the 5th International Workshop on Semantic Evaluation (SemEval-2010), pp. 321–324. ACL, Stroudsburg (2010)
14. Uzuner, Ö., South, B.R., Shen, S., DuVall, S.L.: 2010 i2b2/VA challenge on concepts, assertions, and relations in clinical text. J. Am. Med. Inform. Assoc. **18**(5), 552–556 (2011)
15. Verhagen, M., Gaizauskas, R., Schilder, F., Hepple, M., Katz, G., Pustejovsky, J.: SemEval-2007 task 15: TempEval temporal relation identification. In: Proceedings of the 4th International Workshop on Semantic Evaluations (SemEval-2007), pp. 75–80. ACL, Stroudsburg (2007)
16. Verhagen, M., Saurí, R., Caselli, T., Pustejovsky, J.: SemEval-2010 Task 13: TempEval-2. In: Proceedings of the 5th International Workshop on Semantic Evaluation (SemEval-2010), pp. 57–62. ACL, Stroudsburg (2010)

Natural Language Processing Applications

Empirical and Linguistic Approaches to NLP: LLMs & NLP: Might Resistance Be Futile from Now on?

Christian Boitet[✉]

LIG/GETALP, Université Grenoble Alpes, 38400 Saint-Martin d'Hères, France
`christian.boitet@univ-grenoble-alpes.fr`

Abstract. Contrary to some popular views, the performance of general empirical approaches (statistical, neural) to many NLP tasks remains inferior to that of linguistic (expert) approaches, at least when specific sublanguages are concerned. This is demonstrated in the case of Machine Translation. But is that still true for LLMs? Is it true that expert, linguistics-based methods are, or might soon be, beaten by LLM-based tools, which would surpass the performance levels of expert humans in any task? Using as an example the title of a recent talk by Mathieu Lafourcade at EGS in Montpellier and the task of high-quality translation from French into three languages, we show that this is probably not the case. However, a synergy between LLMs and expert resources and tools (like NooJ-based dictionaries and grammars) might be used to "inflate" the data (corpora) fed to the LLM and improve performance.

Keywords: Empirical and linguistic approaches · NLP · MT · LLMs

1 Introduction

Three years ago, Max Silberztein asked me to write a foreword for the book "Linguistic Resources for Natural Language Processing: On the Necessity of Using Linguistic Methods to Develop NLP Software". In his preface, he developed his argumentation (already polished in publications and workshops, e.g., at COLING-2018 in Santa Fe) in favor of "linguistic" approaches, as opposed to "stochastic" (or "data-driven") approaches. The other chapters were about handling various languages using the NooJ platform. Almost all results compared favorably with available online resources (coverage & quality of the modelling) and running modules (precision, recall, F-measure, speed…).

Max called "data-driven" or "stochastic" the methods based exclusively on learning from "large enough" annotated corpora, and "linguistic" (as in the book title) those based exclusively on grammars and dictionaries. I prefer to call the first kind "empirical methods". Why? Because, in some cases, empirical methods are not based on frequencies and probabilistic or stochastic models. That is the case of example-based MT based on analogy of strings (Yves Lepage 2005, ATR [4]), which uses statistics on n-grams only marginally (to control contiguity). Also, analyzers based on large tree banks produce their

D. Petković et al. (Eds.): NooJ 2025, CCIS 2832, pp. 165–176, 2026.
https://doi.org/10.1007/978-3-032-17103-0_14

results by combining "treelets" that can be reformulated in dependency or constituent grammars, plus, these tree banks have been carefully edited by expert linguists. If not, the results are often wrong.

Symmetrically, expert methods are not always based exclusively on "carefully manually encoded linguistic knowledge". For instance, in machine translation (MT), corpora have been used since the very beginning of the field, both for development and testing. In 1961—67, the first CETA Russian-French system was developed using a large corpus of texts (400,000 wordforms, about 1,600 standard pages) on satellites and rocket engines, kindly given by the Rand Corporation. The morphological analyzer produced not lemmas and attributes but "lexical units" (LUs)—in fact, derivational families—and attributes, including morphosyntactic category (POS), number, case, person, tense, etc., plus LU and derivation code. Many lemmas found in the texts were not contained directly in the dictionary, but deduced from the LU and the (dictionary) potential derivations. As a derivation contains not only a morphological part, but a syntactic and a semantic part (e.g., verb → action noun), two advantages resulted: the size of the dictionary was smaller, and the information in the result was "multilevel".

In recent years, with the advent of LLM[1]-based systems ($\approx$2021), the "mainstream" attitude toward expert methods has become even more negative and pessimistic. At the Special Day of the EGC conference in Montpellier on 2/6/2025, Mathieu Lafourcade presented the incredible development of LLM-based applications since the last four years, entitling his presentation: « Grands modèles de langages et TALN: la résistance serait-elle futile désormais ?» ["LLMs and NLP: might resistance be futile from now on?"]. His final answer was: « pas encore, mais sûrement bientôt (dans 5 ans ? dans 10 ans ?)» ["not yet, but surely soon (in 5 years? in 10 years?)"].

I will develop several points. First, it is a common but, in many cases, false idea that empirical methods give better results, or even results "as good as those produced by human professionals". Simple example here: no online MT system or ChatGPT could correctly translate Mathieu's title in English. We got ["LLMs and NLP: is resistance futile from now on?"], where the important nuance carried by the conditional has disappeared, and "désormais" is badly translated by "now", instead of "from now on".[2]

Second, while results of systems based on very large multilingual LMs (up to 220 languages for Google's multilingual models, such as mT5 or LaMDA) are often baffling with usual language pairs, quality dwindles for "rare" languages and even more when it comes to sublanguages. Plus, problems such as lexical ambiguities are not signaled (e.g., plant → *plante/usine/espion*). That is true, but there are contrary arguments: (1) without these new empirical systems, there would be no comparable system at all, given the effort (expert time!) needed to build good linguistics-based systems (in NooJ or other). (2) Another argument seems to enforce M. Lafourcade's pessimistic conclusion: why worry about the quality of the intermediate (linguistic) representation of a text submitted to a classical "pipeline" approach if… the approach is "end-to-end", so that there is in effect no intermediate linguistic representation?

My third point is that, in many situations, in particular language study and language learning, intermediate annotations and graphical representations are needed. Perfection

---

[1] Large Language Models.

[2] See 3.2 below for a more detailed discussion.

is needed. If the automatic results are very good, users (teachers as well as learners) can interactively and incrementally improve them by "opportunistic post-editing". But if they are not good enough, no way!

The fourth point is the lack of explainability of LLM-based methods. Take the translation problem. With the end-to-end architecture, we have no direct way of improving the translation. An indirect way would be to build adequate prompts. A more radical way would be to augment the learning set and produce a new LLM, but that seems very costly and probably unfeasible.

Finally, a possible approach could be to try to "learn" how to build intermediate annotated representations from "good" I/O pairs produced by the LLM-based system. One would then learn elements of correspondence. That kind of learning has been developed at Microsoft Research between 1996 and 2001, when the researchers "learned" the transfer (lexical + structural) from L1 to L2 by aligning pairs of (source tree, target tree) and automatically produced a *"Mindnet"*.

2 Expert and Empirical Approaches to Machine Translation

2.1 Terminology and Evolution of Ideas

At the end of his preface, Max Silbersztein wrote: "this book aims at rehabilitating the linguistic approach to NLP". Is there a need for that rehabilitation, and if so, does the argumentation (in this book as in the NooJ-2024 and NooJ-2005 proceedings) successfully attain this goal? I would like to answer "yes" to the first question, with some added criticism to those who, in fact, ostracize proponents of methods based on linguistic knowledge, not only because it is totally unethical, but also because they often use what I consider to be patently false arguments.

Concerning the second question, I would like to answer "yes but not totally", at the same time stressing the intrinsic interest of all the articles in that book (and in recent NooJ proceedings), and the power and conspicuousness of NooJ, a descriptive and executable formalism usable in principle to describe all languages (as well as polylects), and in particular low-resource languages such as Quechua and Tango.

Now to the "ostracization" mentioned above. First, this is not the first time we have seen that kind of behavior in computational linguistics (CL) and Natural Language Processing (NLP). Remember the contempt of proponents of knowledge-based methods for automatic speech recognition (ASR), opposed to proponents of inherently stochastic HMM methods. But, at the end of the 1970–75 DARPA project on ASR, it appeared that the empirical HMM-based Harpy system (from CMU) clearly dominated the other competing systems, all knowledge-based (Hearsay-2 from CMU, HWIM from BBN, SUS from SRI). Then the "mainstream" swung to the opposite, so that papers on "expert" systems were rejected by reviewers of conferences and journals. It was the same for jobs. As a famous example, Jelinek at IBM wrote: "Every time I fire a linguist, the performance of my ASR system jumps up by 10%"!

2.2 Expert-Based MT of Sublanguages is Still Better Than SMT and NMT

In MT, this happened in the late 90s. There was a claim in the early 2000s that statistical MT (SMT), derived from the early (1980s) work of Jelinek, Brown & al. at IBM, was "beating" linguistics-based MT systems such as Systran, Reverso (Softissimo & ProMT), ATLAS-II (Fujitsu, Jp $\leftrightarrow$ En), AS-Transac (Toshiba), METAL (De $\rightarrow$ En, LRC & Siemens), or METEO [2].

Very often, the claim is based on an invalid evaluation method. Most SMT systems were and are "objectively" evaluated with a similarity measure (erroneously called "metrics"). Especially in technical domains, a far better measure is the time per page taken by humans for post-editing MT results. J. Slocum seems to have introduced it in 1984, for evaluating the Ge $\rightarrow$ En (German-English) METAL system on Siemens texts.[3] Using the same units (time per minute per standard page of 1,430 characters)[4], I proposed around 2005 to use what I called the *PEMT quality score* on a scale of 20 (used in French schools), given by the simple formula illustrated in Table 1. Each interpretation is a "fuzzy score".

Table 1. PEMT Quality Score[5] (mnPE = minutes of post-editing) PEMT quality = (20 – 2/5*mnPE/page)/20

mnPE/page	0	5	10	15	20	25	30
PEMT quality	20	18	16	14	12	10	8
Interpretation	Perfect	Excellent	Very good	Good	Fair	Average	Bad

It gives a good idea of MT results compared to human translation, where the first draft typically takes 1 h/page and the expert revision 20 mn/page. A reasonable goal of MT + PE is to automate the production of the first draft and to spend less than 20mn on post-editing. In Slocum's experiments, mnPE/page was on average 11.85 (=(10.9 + 12.8)/2), meaning better than just fair.

---

[3] Jonathan Slocum, Winfield S. Bennett, Lesley Whiffin, Edda Norcross (1985) *An evaluation of METAL: The LRC Machine Translation System.* Proc. Second Conference of the European Chapter of the Association for Computational Linguistics, Geneva, Switzerland [1].

[4] About 250 words in English, French, Spanish, etc., but in German there are many long compound words, so that the character count is more universal for languages using alphabets. For ideogram-based writing systems, a standard page (having approximately the same semantic content) is about 400–440 characters.

[5] PEMT is called TTE (Time To Edit) by experts of the (very large) Translated company. See https://translated.com/resources/translation-quality-metrics-time-to-edit-ai-measurement.

Let us also consider the case of METEO [2]. This system, specialized for translating weather bulletins, ran for nearly 20 years at Environnement Canada, on microcomputers, giving almost perfect outputs. PE time (by expert translators from the Bureau des Traductions) was about 1 mn/bulletin, or about 6 mnPE/page (a typical bulletin sentence is 7 tokens long). That gives a PEMT quality of nearly 18/20, that is, excellent.

In 2005, the RALI made experiments to test whether that quality could be approached or improved by reconstructing this system using empirical approaches, starting from a translation memory of 40M En → Fr sentence pairs produced (by MT + PE) over the last 2 years. In their article to EAMT-2005[6], they wrote:

We show how a combination of a sentence-based memory approach, a phrase-based statistical engine and a neural-network rescorer can give results comparable to those of the current system while offering a faster development cycle and arguably better customization possibilities.

We see here undue optimism, to say the least. First, what does "comparable" mean? The only measure mentioned in the paper is "70% of acceptability". If this means that a post-editor has to start from scratch for 30% of the sentences, so that PE time was more than 18 mn/page (60*0.3) for that part. Adding an optimistic 6 mn/page for the rest (70%), we get 24 mn/page, or a PEMT quality of less than average.

In reality, from a study by E. Macklovitch[7], we know that only 11% of the sampled sentences were different from the revised ones, which means that only 11% were post-edited by the senior translators, the rest being left as perfect. The authors then wrote:

Third, an informal evaluation on a random sample of translations that differed from the reference showed that 77% of these bad translations were found acceptable by humans.

But, in such a constrained situation, for a sentence to be accepted does *not* mean it is acceptable! Even if its meaning is quite exact, it must fit into the *sublanguage* at hand. That is so true that, when John Chandioux got a contract for adapting METEO-2 [3] (En → Fr) for the Atlanta Olympic Games, he not only had to introduce a lot of proper nouns (toponyms and patronyms), but he also had to modify the analyzer to take into account the American sublanguage of weather bulletins.

To continue with the false pretenses of quality that lead researchers and funders to ostracize proponents of expert approaches to NLP: in the case of MT, it has been widely said and written that neural MT produced outputs of the same or even higher quality than professional translators. The following excerpt demonstrates that these affirmations are quite false. Moreover, this METAL output dates back to February 1984, and is clearly much better than the DeepL output (in 2023). And no professional translator, even a very bad one, could produce (like GT did) «*The development of semiconductor*

---

[6] Philippe Langlais, Thomas Leplus, Simona Gandrabur and Guy Lapalme (2005) *From the Real World to Real Words: The METEO case.* Proc. EAMT-2005, Budapest. https://aclanthology. org/2005.eamt-1.23.pdf.

[7] Elliott Makclovitch (1985) *A linguistic performance evaluation of METEO-2.* Technical report, Canadian Translation Bureau, Aug. 1985.

technology, especially microprocessors, has in the opened up new prospects for EDP in recent years.» (Table 2).

Table 2. Comparison of outputs of MT systems on a technical German source text

Original German text	Ge→En by METAL (1984)	Ge→En by DeepL (2023)	Ge→Fr by Google (2023)
CSE Spracheingabe-Geraete Einfuehrungsschritt 1 Einleitung Die Entwicklung der Halbleitertechnik, insbesondere der Mikroprozessoren, hat in den vergangenen Jahren neue Perspektiven fuer die EDV eroeffnet. Im Bereich der Datenerfassung wurde mit der Spracheingabe in den Computer ein langgehegter Wunsch erfuellt.	CSE voice data entry devices Introduction 1 Introduction The development of semiconductor technology, in particular the microprocessors has opened ~~the~~ new prospects for EDV in the last years. In the range of data acquisition, a long-cherished wish was filled with voice data entry into the computer.	CSE Language Input Devices Introduction Step 1 Introduction The development of the semiconductor technology, in particular of the microprocessors, has opened new opened new perspectives for the EDP in the last years. In the field of data acquisition, a long-cherished wish has been fulfilled with the voice input into the computer.	Étape d'introduction des périphériques d'entrée vocale CSE 1. Introduction Le développement de la technologie des semi-conducteurs, en particulier des microprocesseurs, a dans le ouvert de nouvelles perspectives à l'informatique ces dernières années. Dans le domaine de l'acquisition de données, un vœu de longue date a été exaucé avec l'entrée vocale dans l'ordinateur.
Remarks	*EDV → EDP (electronic data processing)* *voice **data** entry: correct*	*voice input → voice data entry* *has opened new* *opened new: repetition!*	*le ouvert… : nonsense* *entrée vocale → saisie vocale* *informatique : not in source*

A similar discussion could be had about other applications, such as POS tagging. The performances in the 1970s were about 95%, with an apparent limit at 96%, for tag sets of 100~250 tags. Empirical systems don't do better. Often, claims are made that a performance of 90% or even 85% would be very good. Not so! Already, with 96% success, one gets 10 errors per page of 250 words (about 20 sentences), which means that further processing starts with about 50% of sentences containing a POS error. With 90% success, we get 25 errors per page, meaning that, on average, 100% sentences have at least 1 POS error.

2.3   How to Defend Expert Approaches to NLP or CL?

Max Silberztein is quite right in wanting to distinguish CL and NLP. The goal of CL is to improve our knowledge about languages, while NLP is about producing useful applications. In a sense, research in CL is the "fundamental research" of NLP. Two claims are possible at this point in defense of expert methods. First, one can observe that, in the history of sciences, fundamental research has often led, sometimes much later, to unexpected practical discoveries. Second, it is also true that experimental work has often led to the appearance of new insights at the fundamental level. There are well-known examples in physics. Another example: in CL, it has been claimed that empirical (here, stochastic) methods could not work for ASR (Automatic Speech Recognition) as well as knowledge-based methods. But we saw that the converse happened when Harpy beat the competing systems. Rather than deny the obvious, it is better to ask oneself *why* these systems could and did work better. Here is a new insight proposed by Yves Lepage after he worked from 1998 to 2006 on "analogical MT"[8],[9]: *«96% of analogies of form are also analogies of meaning»*.

Hence, it is often counterproductive to claim that some applications cannot be built without expert knowledge. Contradictors will answer that this is only because large and detailed enough corpora are not available. They may be right at first glance, but quite often—and we can see illustrations of that in the cited book—these corpora *would necessarily contain high-level expert knowledge that the application in view must deliver,* and producing them is simply unfeasible.

3   Do Expert Approaches to NLP Have a Future in the LLM Era?

3.1   Mathieu Lafourcade's Presentation at TextMine

Mathieu mentioned the incredible progression of LLM-based tasks on many tasks since 2022 and demonstrated it on 4 tasks: extraction of semantic relations, named entity recognition (NER), anaphoric resolution, and identification of figurative content. Let us quickly review these results before trying to answer his main question, formulated (in French): *LLMs and NLP: might resistance be futile from now on?*

Extraction of Semantic Relations. With ChatGPT and a prompt in NL, we get remarkable results, in several formats.

---

[8] Yves Lepage worked with the classical proportional analogies on written strings, of the form "**a: b :: c: d**" (**a** is to **b** what **c** is to **d**) and solved analogical equations to get translations (strings with the same meaning) between 2 languages, possibly not using the same writing system, like Japanese, English and French.

[9] Yves Lepage, Étienne Denoual (2006) *Purest ever example-based machine translation: Detailed presentation and assessment.* Machine Translation 19, pages 251–282 [4]. See also Proc. Workshop on example-based machine translation, Pukhet, 2005.

Prompt (short version):

Dans le cadre de la création d'une base de connaissances, une relation sémantique s'écrit A | R | B ; où A et B sont des termes et R un type de relation. La relation se finit par le caractère ;' Pour les types possibles, nous avons : r_est_un_type_de ; r_se_trouve dans (B est un lieu) ; r_a_comme_caracteristique (B est un adjectif) ; r_peut (B est un verbe à l'infinitif), r_a_comme_partie/element, r_fait_partie_de. Donne les relations sans faire de commentaire, sépare les relations avec la balise '<br>' sans les numéroter. Extrais environ 50 relations sémantiques (une par ligne) pertinentes en rapport avec le texte suivant : ...

Submitted text :

"Le professeur Marie Dubois de l'Université de Montpellier a publié une étude sur l'impact du changement climatique en collaboration avec l'équipe du Dr Jean Martin du CNRS. Cette recherche, financée par l'ANR, démontre une corrélation significative entre l'augmentation des températures et la migration des espèces méditerranéennes."

Output 1

```
{
  "entités": {
    "personnes": ["Marie Dubois (professeur)", "Jean Martin (Dr.)"],
    "organisations": ["Université de Montpellier", "CNRS", "ANR"],
    "concepts": ["changement climatique", "espèces méditerranéennes"]
  },
  "relations": [
    {"type": "AFFILIATION", "sujet": "Marie Dubois", "objet": "Université de Montpellier"},
    {"type": "COLLABORATION", "sujet": "Marie Dubois", "objet": "Jean Martin"},
    {"type": "FINANCEMENT", "sujet": "ANR", "objet": "recherche"},
    {"type": "IMPACT", "sujet": "températures", "objet": "migration espèces"},
    {"type": "DÉMONSTRATION", "sujet": "recherche", "objet": "corrélation"}
  ],
  "contexte": "Recherche environnementale collaborative inter-institutionnelle"
}
```

Output 2

*Marie Dubois **r_est_un_type_de** professeur*
*Marie Dubois **r_peut_se_trouver_dans** Université de Montpellier*
*recherche **r_a_pour_caracteristique** financée*
*recherche **r_a_pour_caracteristique** financée par l'ANR*
...
*augmentation **r_processus_agent** températures*
*migration **r_processus_agent** espèces méditerranéennes*
...

During the period 1/1–1/7/2023, precision was acceptable, but recall was limited. In *few-shot* scenarios, typical F1-scores were between 55% and 75%, depending on the complexity of relations. During the period 1/7–31/12/2023, long-distance relations were better captured, and more relations were extracted, with F1-scores ranging from 65% to 80% on benchmarks. During the period 1/1/24–1/6/25, there was a successful reduction of "hallucinations" and improved extraction in complex documents, as well as the integration of external knowledge via RAG, and the use of a very long context (10M tokens). The best models tested obtained F1 scores from 81% to 97% (97.8% with Gemini) on some complex datasets—that is, quasi-human performance.

On this task, it seems that, yes, progress has been dramatic, and LLM-based approaches cannot be surpassed. But keep in mind that these experiments were conducted on French documents, with the large size JeuDeMots database in the background (more than 1 G relations.[10]

Named Entity Recognition (NER). Here again, recent performance is so good that it seems unsurpassable.

Example of a prompt (rewritten) (Table 3):

> *Pour le texte fourni, veuillez **identifier toutes les entités nommées** et les **catégoriser précisément** parmi les types suivants : **Personne, Organisation, Lieu, Date, Événement, Produit**, ou **Œuvre d'art**. Si une entité ne correspond à aucune de ces catégories, proposez une catégorie appropriée.*

Submitted text (copied from Wikipedia)

> *Napoléon Ier lance des assauts contre le château d'Hougoumont et la ferme de La Haye-Sainte ; l'armée de Wellington résiste. C'est alors que l'armée prussienne intervient, attaquant le flanc droit de l'armée française. Le maréchal Grouchy, chargé de poursuivre les Prussiens après Ligny, a failli à sa tâche. La cavalerie française charge les lignes adverses à plusieurs reprises et menace de les briser. La Garde impériale avance et recule finalement. L'attaque générale des coalisés rend la défaite française inévitable.*

Result:

> ***Napoléon Ier*** *: Personne*
> ***château d'Hougoumont*** *: Lieu*
> ***ferme de La Haye-Sainte*** *: Lieu*
> ***Wellington*** *: Personne*
> ***Grouchy*** *: Personne*
> ***Ligny*** *: Lieu/Événement (bataille de Ligny)*
> ***Garde impériale*** *: Organisation militaire*

Table 3. F1-scores by entity types in NER

Entity type	spaCy	BERT-NER	GPT-4	Gemini / Grok
Person	92.1%	94.3%	95.7%	97.2%
Organization	85.4%	87.9%	92.3%	98.1%
Place	88.7%	90.2%	91.5%	97.3%
Date	93.2%	91.8%	94.9%	96.7%
Product	87.3%	85.6%	88.1%	95.9%
Event	72.8%	76.4%	82.2%	93.1%

---

[10] 1 017 174 936 relations and 15 509 700 terms on 9/9/2025 (see https://www.jeuxdemots.org/).

Those are very good results, but it is difficult to comment further as we don't know which NEs are already directly included in the large JdM knowledge base (more than 15M lexical nodes).

Anaphoric Resolution. Let us consider the example given by M. Lafourcade.

Text:

> *Le soleil tapait fort sur le vieux chêne. Ses branches étendaient une ombre généreuse, sous laquelle un jeune écureuil, nommé Noisette, s'abritait. **Il** cherchait désespérément une cachette pour **ses** dernières trouvailles. **Elles** étaient précieuses : quelques noisettes et une noix entière qu'**il** avait dénichées ce matin-là. Une pie, perchée plus haut, observait la scène. **Elle** attendait que l'écureuil soit parti pour tenter de s'emparer de son butin. Mais Noisette était vigilant.*

Result:

> *Il (sent. 2) : fait référence (refers to) à un jeune écureuil, nommé Noisette.*
> *ses (sent. 2) : [refers to] aux dernières trouvailles de l'écureuil Noisette.*
> *Elles (sent. 3) : [refers to] aux trouvailles, les quelques noisettes et une noix entière.*
> *il (sent. 3) : [refers to] Noisette (l'écureuil).*
> *Elle (sent. 4) : [refers to] "Une pie".*
> *...*

Here, the results are less convincing, in particular concerning non-pronominal anaphoras. For example, the first "ses" is not considered, and might refer to the sun or to the oak tree. "Elles" refers to "trouvailles", not to the appositive NP. Note also that the sentence numbering begins at 0, which is rather strange.

The best LLMs can reach F1 scores from 80% to 95% on standard benchmarks (CoNLL-2012). But the conclusion that they exhibit a "quasi-human competence (understanding) in numerous cases" is certainly exaggerated.

Identification of Figurative Content. For lack of space, we don't discuss this task, in detail and give only one example:

> *Après sa promotion, il **marchait sur des nuages** toute la journée. (After he was promoted, he **walked on cloud**s the whole day)*

Literal reformulation: *Après sa promotion, il était extrêmement heureux et euphorique toute la journée. (After he was promoted, he **was extremely happy and euphoric** for the whole day)*

This is a very interesting task from the point of view of language studies. Many dictionaries already contain collocations (or "multiword/multilexical expressions"), but often not enough. Figurative or not, most of the time they are non-compositional, which makes them quite difficult to understand.

3.2   A Fifth Task for LLMs: Very Precise HQ Translation into 3 Languages

What, then, might make expert methods necessary to "beat" LLMs? In NL understanding and consequently in translation, it might be the proper handling of modalities, of precise lexical meanings, and of scenarios.

Recall the question asked by Mathieu Lafourcade at TextMine (2/6/2025):

LLM & TAL: la résistance *serait*-elle futile *désormais* ?

$\approx$ LLMs & NLP: *might* resistance be futile *from now on*? [HT—human translation].

We did a small experiment on 14/6/2025, during NooJ-2025, in which we asked DeepL, Google Translate (GT), ChatGPT, and Gemini to translate this question from French into English, German, and Russian.

DeepL, GT, Copilot and ChatGPT translated it as:

LLMs & NLP: is resistance futile [vain] now? (same in English and German)

Only Gemini handled the conditional and the associated semantics/pragmatics:

LLMs & NLP: might resistance be futile now?

None translated "désormais" as "from now on".

As LLMs can explain and correct, we tried to induce them to learn better translations of "désormais". For example, we got the following answer from Copilot:[11]

Bonne remarque ! J'ai opté pour « now » en anglais, « jetzt » en allemand et « теперь » en russe, qui expriment une notion de présent, mais « désormais » peut aussi inclure une idée de changement permanent. Une traduction plus précise pourrait être :

Anglais *: LLM and NLP: Is resistance henceforth futile?*

Allemand *: LLM und NLP: Ist Widerstand von nun an zwecklos?*

Russe*: LLM и NLP: Отныне сопротивление бесполезно?*

But we did not succeed in getting the LLMs to learn to correctly translate the modality ("might") and the adjective "futile", which may mean "vain" but not "useless" (zwecklos / бесполезно). Note also that the explanation that "désormais" implies an idea of permanent change is not quite exact. Like "from now on", its exact synonym, it does not imply that something changes, but rather that a state or quality will remain as it is.

3.3 When Do We Need to Use the "CL" (Expert) Approach?

It is quite clear that a very precise translation is not obtainable fully automatically, unless the MT system, be it linguistics-based or LLM-based, is specialized to a sufficiently small sublanguage. A question rarely asked is "When do we need to produce very precise translations at all levels (lexicon, syntax, modality…)?".

Answer: of course, when studying languages, professional translation and interpretation, contrastive linguistics, etc., which rely on expert explicit linguistic models or aim at producing them. But such high quality is also needed when handling bilingual or multilingual discussions. In the case of dialogues, a very useful feature can be the addition of a reverse-translation component. Also, human post-editing can be used:

- when the goal is *human* understanding of language(s). For this, we need to access several levels of symbolic representations (morphosyntactic lattice, multiple concrete

---

[11] [Our translation] *Good remark! I opted for « now" in English, "jetzt" in German and "теперь" in Russian, that express a concept of time, but "désormais" can also include an idea of permanent change. A more precise translation could be: …*

and abstract linguistic trees, interlingual graphs like UNL or UMR, mapping into one or more ontologies).

- when we need to solve ambiguities for human understanding (for example, in Requirements Engineering (as in the UNseL project).
- when we want to build detailed knowledge. Information extraction can be faithful thanks to interaction, in a process of building, modifying, and using an ontology reflecting the consensus of experts about the "domain of discourse" at hand.
- when we need systems to provide explanations, hypotheses, and plausible scenarios.

4 Conclusion and Perspectives

Regarding M. Lafourcade's question (*"LLMs and NLP: Might resistance be futile from now on?"*), I would say *yes* "as is", but *no* if we replace resistance with cooperation/interplay. Some goals of the synergy might then be:

- to develop high-quality resources for resource-poor languages and sublanguages:

  - start from existing resources (corpora, dictionaries);
  - use LLMs to extract terms, collocations, Named Entities, patterns…;
  - "condense" that knowledge into LDKs (*Language Development Kits*) such as NooJ.[12]

- With those expert resources and tools, contribute to LLMs by inflating the corpus (or corpora), with associated annotations, using:

  - inflation by analogy;
  - inflation by paraphrasing/generation, monolingually/multilingually.

References

1. Slocum, J., Bennett, W.S., Whiffin, L., Norcross, E.: An evaluation of METAL: The LRC Machine Translation System. In: Proc. EACL-2, Geneva, Switzerland (1985)
2. Langlais, Ph., Leplus, T., Gandrabur, S., Lapalme, G.: From the Real World to Real Words: The METEO case. In: Proc. EAMT 2005, Budapest (2005). URL: https://aclanthology.org/2005.eamt-1.23.pdf
3. Macklovitch, E.: A linguistic performance evaluation of METEO-2. Technical Report, Canadian Translation Bureau (1985)
4. Lepage, Y., Denoual, É.: Purest ever example-based machine translation: Detailed presentation and assessment. Mach. Transl. **19**, 251–282 (2005)

---

[12] See article by Nicolas Boffo in the same proceedings (NooJ 2025).

Use of LLMs for Semantic Relation Extraction and Development of NooJ Lingware Applied to Drug Trafficking Language

Nicolas Boffo[1]([⊠])[iD], Mathieu Lafourcade[1][iD], and Christian Boitet[2]

[1] University of Montpellier, Montpellier, France
`{nicolas.boffo,mathieu.lafourcade}@lirmm.fr`
[2] University Grenoble Alpes, Grenoble, France
`christian.boitet@imag.fr`

Abstract. The operational treatment of sensitive textual data requires efficient natural language processing techniques running on local hardware. This paper investigates the possibility of using Large Language Models (LLMs) to extract semantic relations from specialized corpora, particularly drug trafficking language, not directly, but by generating Finite-State Transducers (FSTs) for the NooJ platform for local execution. In that hybrid approach, LLMs construct NooJ grammars and dictionaries, later compiled into deterministic NooJ automata, which run fast on normal PCs. Experiments on a corpus of 75 text files (164,000 tokens, 27,000 distinct words) highlight challenges in alias recognition and structured evaluation importance. Results show that while direct LLM extraction produces noisy outputs, to use an LLM to automatically produce a corresponding NooJ "grammar" (FST + dictionary), which can then be improved by human experts, is a distinct possibility for handling specialized sublanguages.

Keywords: Semantic relation extraction · Local processing · Large Language Models · NooJ Finite-State Transducers

1 Introduction

Our goal is to use AI and NLP tools to help investigators analyze drug trafficking encrypted messages by identifying persons, locations, times, and actions, and by proposing scenario hypotheses through semantic relations. This research contributes to AI applied to criminal analysis, building on Skipanes et al.'s work on NLP for crime investigation [1]. They developed a forward-looking framework for information analysis in criminal investigations with components for categorization, thematization, and exploration, leading to KriRAG, a Retrieval-Augmented Generation architecture for managing information overload. While their approach focuses on broader linguistic features, our research centers specifically on **semantic relation extraction**, crucial for attaining the three goals below.

D. Petković et al. (Eds.): NooJ 2025, CCIS 2832, pp. 177–188, 2026.
https://doi.org/10.1007/978-3-032-17103-0_15

- **Creation of Structured Knowledge Bases.** Unlike keyword spotting, semantic relation extraction transforms unstructured text into organized knowledge representations. Instead of identifying "pollen" and "sift," it establishes "pollen is_a_type_of sift." This builds knowledge graphs showing connections, actions, and locations.
- **Contextual Analysis and Inference.** Our method captures sentence context for deeper meaning extraction. It identifies relationships between persons and activities (`person | r_does | drug_trafficking`), directly relevant for investigation scenarios.
- **Operational Decision Support.** By transforming raw data into structured information, relation extraction provides investigators with actionable summaries, enabling quick visualization of complex connections without manually reading thousands of documents. KriRAG's ability to operate offline on limited hardware aligns with our objectives. Combining our hybrid LLM-FST approach with this framework could produce comprehensive law enforcement systems.

1.1   Goals

Large online LLMs excel at semantic relation extraction but cannot be used to process sensitive texts online due to confidentiality requirements. Local solutions must be used. Thus, our first goal was to determine if small local LLMs can be used on our relatively modest GPU servers (RTX4090) while achieving reasonable results. Our in-house specialists concluded that the computing time needed for processing large volumes of data would be too high for operational use. Also, the training time would be an even bigger obstacle. This led us to envisage to use locally trainable LLMs to generate NooJ-based equivalent extractors, compiled to Finite State Transducers for faster processing.

While LLMs are powerful but need GPU-equipped machines, FSTs can run locally on standard computers without GPUs, thus ensuring security and efficiency in operational contexts.

1.2   Experimental Design

First, we developed a specialized corpus by anonymizing existing sensitive data. Second, we defined prompts applied to input texts using LLMs, generating structured outputs of the form A | R | B (terms A, B with semantic relation R). Third, we developed NooJ-based systems producing equivalent outputs. We found in particular that spelling mistakes might block relation production while LLMs correct mistakes dynamically. Fourth, we tested local LLMs and conducted evaluations.

1.3   Evaluation Planning

System evaluation focuses on a representative corpus excerpt (drug sifting guide for cannabis, hashish), considering hallucinations, processing time, and extracted semantic relations counts. The evaluation methodology measures quantitative metrics (relation count, processing time) and semantic coherence through BERTScore against reference standards. Evaluating FST-based systems is not a unique challenge in itself; however, it becomes particularly difficult in specialized domains where no annotated ground truth is available, for example, in the context of drug trafficking language(s). In such cases, validation must rely on expert assessment rather than automated measures. This asymmetry between LLMs (which can be evaluated with standardized scores such as BERTScore) and FSTs (which require manual validation) complicates direct performance comparison.

2   Experiments

2.1   Corpus Development

We constructed a specialized corpus focused on cannabis cultivation techniques. A web scraping script extracted linguistic content from publicly accessible websites using HTTP requests through a Tor proxy[1], and the Requests library[2], Playwright fallback for dynamic rendering[3], and BeautifulSoup for HTML processing[4]. Extracted textual data was saved in timestamped plain-text files enabling reproducible analysis.

2.2   Language Model Prompting

The prompt extracts semantic relationships following structure A | R | B where A and B are 2 terms and R is a relation type (Figs. 1 and 2):

- `r_est_un_type_de` → "is a type of"
- `r_se_trouve_dans` → "is located in" (B is a place)
- `r_a_comme_caracteristique` → "has characteristic" (B is an adjective)
- `r_peut` → "can" (B is an infinitive verb)
- `r_a_comme_partie` → "has as part/element"
- `r_fait_partie_de` → "is part of"

---

[1] Tor Project. *Tor: Overview.* Available at: https://www.torproject.org/about/overview/.

[2] Kenneth Reitz et al. *Requests: HTTP for Humans^{TM}.* Official documentation. Available at: https://docs.python-requests.org/.

[3] Microsoft. *Playwright for Python.* Official documentation. Available at: https://playwright.dev/python/.

[4] Leonard Richardson. *Beautiful Soup Documentation.* Available at: https://www.crummy.com/software/BeautifulSoup/.

General prompt template: For attached text, semantic relations are written A | R | B where A and B are terms and R is a relation type, ending with ";". Possible types: r_est_un_type_de; r_se_trouve_dans (B is a place); r_a_comme_caractéristique (B is an adjective); r_peut (B is an infinitive verb), r_a_comme_partie, r_fait_partie_de. Provide only relations present in documents without comments, separated by the pipe "|" character.

Fig. 1. Prompt template used for semantic relation extraction.

2.3   Experimental Results and Analysis

The Streamlit-based system implements a modular architecture designed for reproducible LLM evaluation. The system accepts multiple input formats (TXT/PDF/DOCX/MD) and processes them through a standardized pipeline. The FileProcessor normalizes various document types into plain text, while the TextSplitter applies configurable chunking with overlap preservation. The PromptService manages template-based prompt generation, and the OllamaService handles local model communication with fallback mechanisms for format compliance. The LLME valuator performs post-processing, relation extraction, and BERTScore F1 computation against reference standards (Fig. 3).

Component Descriptions

Streamlit UI

It is a web user interface that collects user inputs (files, parameters, buttons) and displays results. It validates and normalizes client-side parameters, shows progress and status messages, and streams logs or errors. The UI triggers pipeline runs through AppController and supports asynchronous feedback. It also offers export options (CSV/JSON) and user-friendly error reporting.

App Controller

This central orchestrator accepts requests from the UI and coordinates the entire pipeline. It validates configurations, sequences steps (preprocessing, splitting, inference, evaluation), and manages task state and retries. It acts as a front-end to call FileProcessor, TextSplitter, OllamaService, and LLMEvaluator, enforcing timeouts and error handling. It returns structured status updates to the UI and writes operation logs.

File Processor

It handles loading and preprocessing of source files (plain text and common formats). It fixes encodings, strips unnecessary metadata, extracts raw text, and reports read errors.

It enforces size constraints and groups large inputs into coarse blocks suitable for splitting. It emits a uniform record structure (id, text, source, metadata) for downstream components.

Text Splitter

Splits documents into chunks optimized for LLM consumption while respecting token limits and configurable overlap. Uses heuristics (sentence/paragraph

---

Extraire toutes les relations sémantiques du texte.
FORMAT (une relation par ligne):
`ENTITÉ1 | TYPE_RELATION | ENTITÉ2 ;`
TYPES DE RELATION AUTORISÉS (6 uniquement):
`r_est_un_type_de | r_se_trouve_dans | r_a_comme_caracteristique | r_peut |`
`r_fait_partie_de | r_a_comme_partie`
EXEMPLES:
Dry Sift Hash | `r_est_un_type_de` | concentré ;
résine | `r_se_trouve_dans` | trichomes ;
tamis | `r_peut` | séparer ;
haschich | `r_a_comme_caracteristique` | pureté ;
trichomes | `r_fait_partie_de` | cannabis ;
Hash Shaker | `r_a_comme_partie` | tamis ;
CONSIGNES:
- Extrais TOUTES les relations que tu identifies
- Utilise les entités et concepts du texte
- Respecte le format exact ci-dessus
- Pas de commentaires, juste les relations
TEXTE:
{texte}[a]
RELATIONS:

---

[a] Here is the text used for our evaluation: `https://github.com/nicolirmm/`
`LLMs_NOOJ_SEMANTIC_EXTRACTION/blob/main/CORPUS/Result_webscrapping/`
`growbarato_net_20250531_134023.txt`.

Fig. 2. Optimized prompt used for semantic relation extraction evaluation. This balanced version maximizes recall while minimizing hallucinations through domain-specific examples and concise instructions.

boundaries and domain rules) to preserve semantic coherence across chunks. It produces position/index metadata for traceability and error reporting. Outputs batches ready for model inference and exposes tunable granularity parameters.

Ollama Service

It is a wrapper for communicating with Ollama that formats prompts and sends inference requests to the chosen model (local or remote). It manages inference parameters (model, temperature, max_tokens), normalizes raw responses, and implements retry/backoff and quota handling. Finally, it logs latencies and errors, and provides a testable interface (supports mocking). It returns structured responses for evaluation.

LLME valuator

It parses LLM outputs and applies extraction/evaluation rules (parsing, regexes, heuristics).

It computes confidence scores, flags contradictions and potential hallucinations, and normalizes extracted relations.

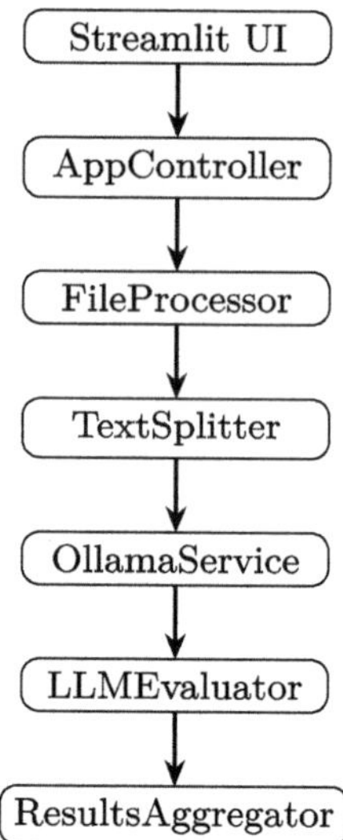

Fig. 3. System architecture for semantic relation extraction.

It enriches results with provenance (chunk id, position) and structured verdicts. It outputs evaluation metrics and verdicts for aggregation.

Results Aggregator

It merges per-chunk verdicts into a coherent document-level result and deduplicates extractions. It aggregates scores, computes overall metrics, and produces human-readable summaries of extracted relations.

It prepares final output formats (JSONL, CSV, reports) and includes traceability metadata for auditing. It exposes hooks for UI consumption, export, and persistence to logs or external storage.

2.4   LLM Semantic Relation Extraction

We evaluated a semantic relation extraction pipeline applied to our web-scraped corpus[5] using a representative text excerpt[6] containing **1,675 words (10,333 characters)**.

The text was segmented using adaptive chunking strategies optimized per model. Models with large context windows (8,192 tokens: mistral:latest, gemma3:4b-it-qat, deepseek-r1:7b) processed the entire text in a single chunk. Models with limited contexts (2,048–4,096 tokens: phi:latest, llama2:latest,

---

[5] https://github.com/nicolirmm/LLMs_NOOJ_SEMANTIC_EXTRACTION/ tree/main/CORPUS/Result_webscrapping.

[6] Our evaluation text is available at: https://github.com/nicolirmm/ LLMs_NOOJ_SEMANTIC_EXTRACTION/blob/main/CORPUS/ Result_webscrapping/growbarato_net_20250531_134023.txt.

gemma3:1b) used token-based chunking with 50-token overlap ($\approx$210 characters) to preserve semantic coherence across boundaries.

Table 1 presents the model-specific configurations used in our evaluation.
Temperature settings were optimized to balance creativity and determinism:
conservative values (0.1) for smaller models prone to hallucinations, moderate
values (0.15–0.2) for larger models to encourage comprehensive extraction.

Table 1. Model-specific configurations for semantic relation extraction

Model	Context (tokens)	Chunk (words)	Max Out (tokens)	Temp
phi:latest (1.6GB)	2048	1500	1200	0.10
mistral:latest (4.4GB)	8192	1675	2000	0.15
llama2:latest (3.8GB)	4096	1675	1800	0.20
gemma3:4b-it-qat (4.0GB)	8192	1675	2000	0.15
gemma3:1b (815MB)	4096	1675	1500	0.10
deepseek-r1:7b (4.7GB)	8192	1675	2000	0.15

All models used additional inference parameters: top_p = 0.95 for nucleus
sampling, repeat_penalty = 1.1 to reduce repetitions, and stop sequences
(`<think>`, `</think>`, \n\n\n) to prevent verbose outputs. GPU acceleration
was enabled (num_gpu=-1) for all models during Phase 1 extraction.

Post-processing employed a two-stage validation approach. First, lines containing $\geq$2 vertical bars were extracted as candidate relations. Second, intelligent
filtering rejected malformed outputs: placeholder patterns (`[ENTITY1]`), all-caps
templates (e.g., `TERM A | RELATION | TERM B`), and entities with insufficient
semantic content (<2 significant characters). Legitimate acronyms (e.g., BHO
for Butane Hash Oil) were preserved through exception rules.

When models produced narrative text instead of structured relations, a fallback mechanism re-prompted them to reformat the output. This two-pass approach significantly improved format compliance for models like llama2:latest.

Semantic evaluation was performed using BERTScore F1[7] with the
`bert-base-multilingual-cased` model. Extracted relations[8] were compared
against reference triplets[9] generated by online AI and validated by human
experts. The evaluation employed a two-phase architecture: Phase 1 performed

---

[7] BERTScore calculation methodology: https://github.com/nicolirmm/LLMs_
NOOJ_SEMANTIC_EXTRACTION/blob/main/EVALUATION/bert_f1_
calculation.md.

[8] Complete extracted relations: https://github.com/nicolirmm/LLMs_NOOJ_
SEMANTIC_EXTRACTION/blob/main/EVALUATION/relations_extracted.
md.

[9] Gold-standard references (36 relations): https://github.com/nicolirmm/LLMs_
NOOJ_SEMANTIC_EXTRACTION/tree/main/EVALUATION/relations_ref.

GPU-accelerated extraction via Ollama, followed by a 2 s pause to release GPU memory; Phase 2 computed BERTScore metrics on GPU, ensuring optimal resource utilization without conflicts (Table 2).

Table 2. Comparative evaluation of local language models for semantic relation extraction

Local LLM (SLM)	Words	Time	Rel(N)	Rel-U(N_u)	Prec.	Recall	F1
gemma3:4b-it-qat (4.0GB)	1675	74.86	344	41	0.86	0.77	0.81
llama2:latest (3.8GB)	1675	8.72	6	6	0.85	0.76	0.80
mistral:latest (4.4GB)	1675	4.62	13	13	0.85	0.68	0.76
gemma3:1b (815MB)	1675	3.64	6	6	0.87	0.60	0.71
deepseek-r1:7b (4.7GB)	1675	12.88	6	6	0.84	0.59	0.69
phi:latest (1.6GB)[†]	1675	4.17	0	0	0.00	0.00	0.00

[†] Negative control: 16 configurations tested without success. Illustrates the minimum capacity threshold required for structured extraction tasks.

Note: Times are in seconds. Three performance groups emerge: high-performance (F1 > 0.75), moderate-performance (0.65 < F1 < 0.75), and structural failure (F1 = 0.00). The complete failure of phi:latest contrasts with the success of gemma3:1b despite comparable sizes, suggesting that raw capacity is not the sole determining factor for structured extraction capability.

3   NooJ-Based System Design

We experimented with 3 LLMs (ChatGPT, Claude AI, Gemini) to analyze NooJ functioning and to design prompts producing automata (NooJ FST) description. These prompts, applied to linguistic corpora, generated automata including thematic dictionaries and complex structures representing sentence sets as regular expressions Fig. 4.

This NooJ FST (Fig. 5) cannot properly handle context and inferences/coreferences, as shown by the results that cause problems, particularly with term A:

1. *en utilisant des techniques de tamisage à sec*/**en r_utilise techniques de tamisage à sec**
2. *nous utiliserons une pile de*/**nous r_utilise pile de**
3. *en utilisant quelques petits morceaux de ruban pour maintenir le papier tendu autour du périmetre du rouleau de peinture*/**en r_utilise petits morceaux de ruban pour** maintenir le papier tendu autour du périmètre du rouleau de peinture
4. *nous utilisons la technique de cardage pour tamiser le hash vers l*/**nous r_utilise technique de cardage pour tamiser le hash vers l**

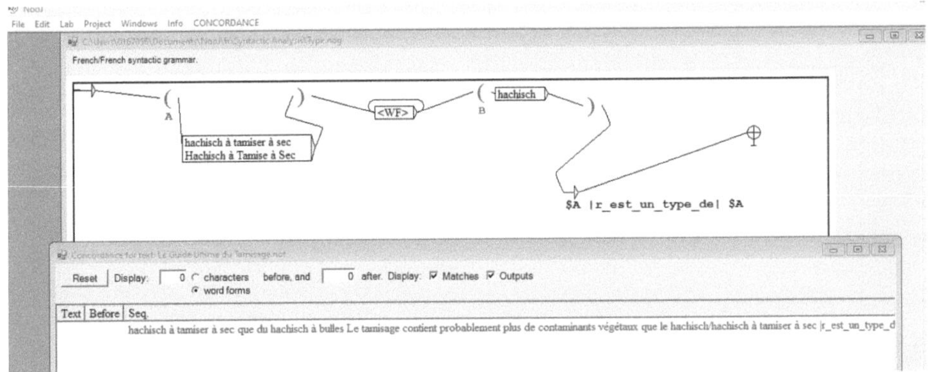

Fig. 4. NooJ Finite-State Transducer for extraction of orthographic variation of the relation "hashisch à tamiser à sec | **r_est_un_type_de** | Hashisch".

5. *En utilisant la même technique avec un outil de dab propre et froid/***En r_utilise même technique avec un outil de dab propre et froid**
6. *en utilisant la Technique du Rollo de Peinture/***en r_utilise Technique du Rollo de Peinture**
7. *en utilisant la méthode /* **d/en r_utilise méthode d**

For a simple ARB relation, a NooJ finite-state automaton processes the entire 4487-word corpus in approximately 0.2 s. Furthermore, for a large-scale extraction task, it can process approximately 300 simple relations in 1 min. While NooJ FSTs are highly efficient for straightforward syntactic patterns, they face significant challenges with inference and long-distance dependencies between terms A and B.

However, while some of these automata could be parsed by the NooJ compiler, they frequently required revision. This necessity arose either from the presence of small bugs introduced during their generation by the LLM, or from some features of the syntax used to describe NooJ automata, such as constraints on node numbering or on coding outgoing arcs, which tends to complicate their automatic generation by LLMs.

As highlighted in the literature on weighted finite-state transducers, adopting a simpler formalism like that of OpenFst [4] or of grammar compilers such as Thrax [5] may help overcome these limitations. Moreover, recent research on prompt engineering shows how linguistic properties of prompts significantly affect the quality of structured outputs from LLMs.

3.1 Prompt Engineering for NooJ Automata Generation

The generation of high-quality NooJ automata directly from a Large Language Model (LLM) requires a carefully structured prompt to guide the LLM. Our prompt was specifically designed to strive for exhaustive extraction and to pro-

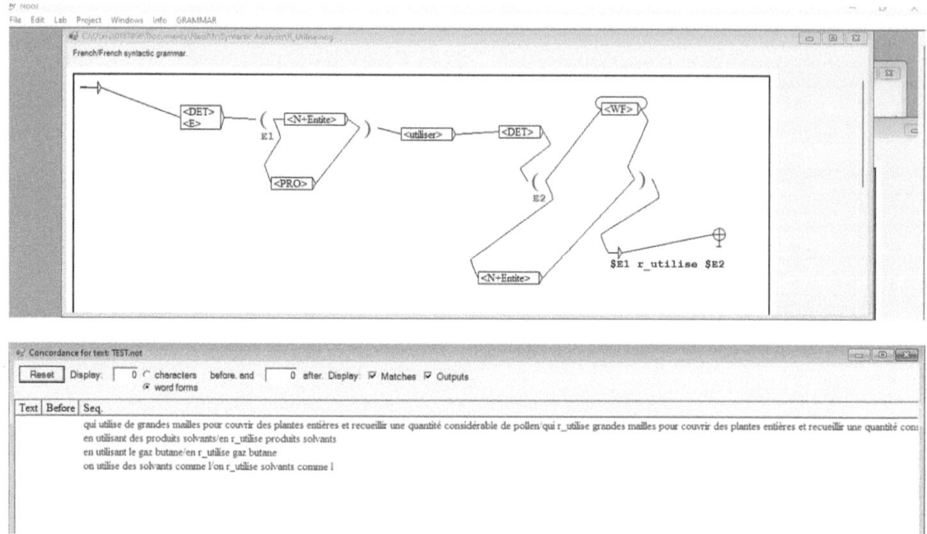

Fig. 5. The first screenshot shows the NooJ Finite-State Transducer for extraction of the **r_utilise** relation. The second screenshot shows the results.

duce an optimized, rigorously formatted output, immediately usable within the NooJ platform.

In our methodology, we rely on online LLMs to generate Finite State Transducers (FSTs) for NooJ. These automata can be associated with dictionaries, when lexical resources are needed to support morphological or lexical analysis, or without dictionaries, when they are intended to capture purely formal patterns. The accessibility of advanced LLMs available online makes it possible to rapidly test multiple approaches and compare the resulting automata (Figs. 6 and 7)

The following LLM platforms have been used in our experiments: Chat-GPT[10], Claude[11], Gemini[12], and Perplexity[13], etc.

4   Conclusion and Perspectives

Our hybrid approach adapts to various operational needs including processing power, deployment time, and data sensitivity. Local LLMs show significant variability in semantic relation extraction capability, with BERTScore F1 ranging from 0.00 to 0.81. Three distinct performance groups emerged from our evaluation: high-performance models (F1 > 0.75: gemma3:4b-it-qat, llama2:latest,

---

[10] https://chat.openai.com.

[11] https://claude.ai.

[12] https://gemini.google.com.

[13] https://www.perplexity.ai.

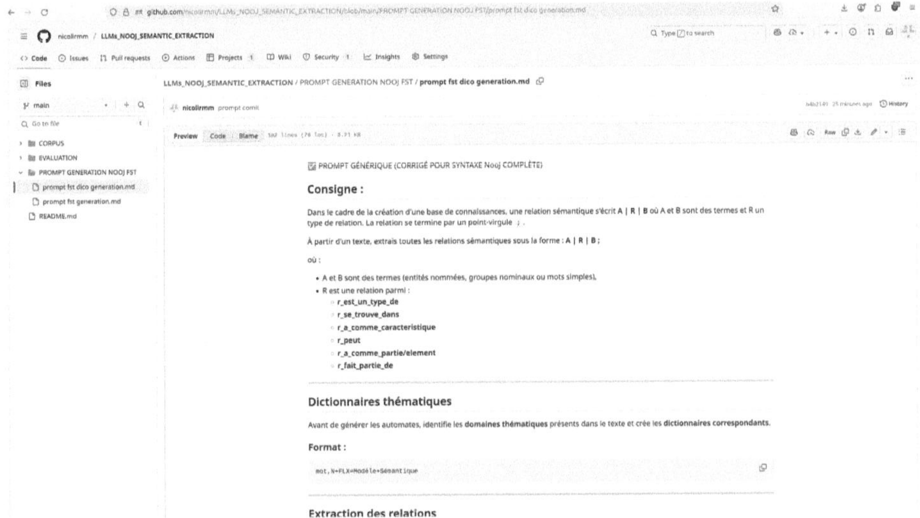

Fig. 6. Prompt for FST generation in NooJ with thematic dictionaries. (https://
github.com/nicolirmm/LLMs_NOOJ_SEMANTIC_EXTRACTION/tree/main/
PROMPT_GENERATION_NOOJ_FST).

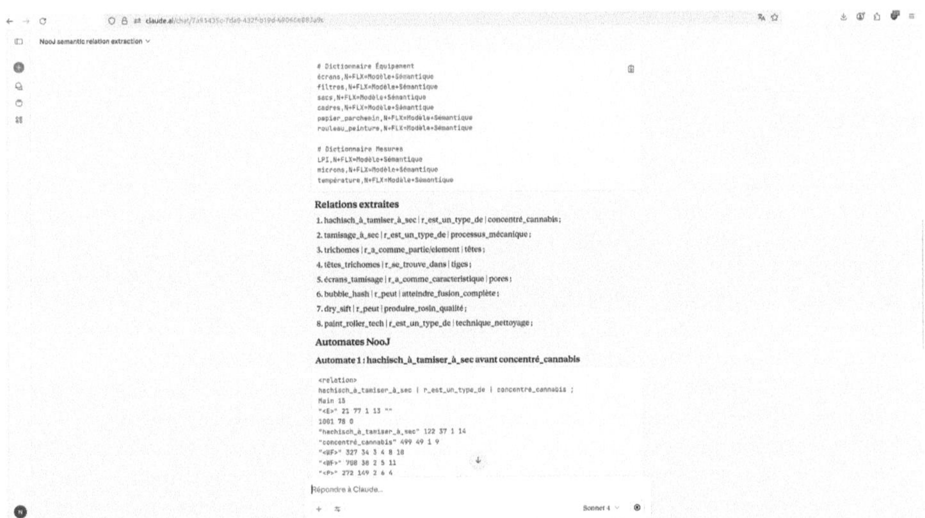

Fig. 7. Response (result) from the Claude.ai online LLM generating a NooJ
dictionary and a NooJ FST. (https://github.com/nicolirmm/LLMs_NOOJ_
SEMANTIC_EXTRACTION/blob/main/GENERATION%20FST%20FROM
%20ONLINE%20LLM/Claude%20AI%20GEN%20FST.md).

mistral:latest), moderate-performance models ($0.65 < F1 < 0.75$: gemma3:1b, deepseek-r1:7b), and structural failure ($F1 = 0.00$: phi:latest).

The complete failure of phi:latest (1.6 GB) despite 16 tested configurations contrasts sharply with the success of gemma3:1b (815 MB, F1=0.71), demonstrating that raw model capacity is not the sole determining factor for structured extraction capability. This finding validates the importance of including negative controls in comparative LLM evaluations and establishes a minimum capacity threshold for viable structured extraction in specialized domains.

NooJ FSTs provide deterministic, fast processing for small, well-defined patterns and are particularly suitable when used like regular expressions, but require substantial effort to create resources equivalent to LLMs. They struggle to handle orthographic and syntactic variations, making it cumbersome to anticipate all possible cases (results from Fig. 5). We will continue our evaluation of NooJ as soon as we have sufficient resources to carry out the full assessment. The results will be published online at: https://github.com/nicolirmm/LLMs_NOOJ_SEMANTIC_EXTRACTION/tree/main.

In contrast, LLMs perform particularly well on heterogeneous corpora, leveraging context and inference with relatively low development cost if adequate GPU resources are available. Our results suggest a complementary use: rely on LLMs for extraction in diverse and complex corpora, while FSTs remain valuable for precise, regex-like patterns in controlled environments.

Future work will explore hybrid architectures combining LLM-generated FSTs with runtime LLM validation, potentially offering the best of both approaches: FST speed and determinism with LLM flexibility and context awareness [2,3].

References

1. Skipanes, M., et al.: Linguistic analysis for crime investigation: a case study of online radicalization. In: Proceedings of the Language Resources and Evaluation Conference (LREC), Marseille, France (2022)
2. Silberztein, M., Donabédian, A., Khurshudian, V.: Formalising Natural Languages with NooJ. Cambridge Scholars Publishing (2013)
3. Barone, L., Monteleone, M., Silberztein, M. (eds.): NooJ 2016. CCIS, vol. 667. Springer, Cham (2016). https://doi.org/10.1007/978-3-319-55002-2
4. Allauzen, C., Riley, M., Schalkwyk, J., Skut, W., Mohri, M.: OpenFst: a general and efficient weighted finite-state transducer library. In: Holub, J., Žd'árek, J. (eds.) Implementation and Application of Automata, CIAA 2007. LNCS, vol. 4783, pp. 11–23. Springer, Heidelberg (2007). https://doi.org/10.1007/978-3-540-76336-9_3
5. Tai, T., Sproat, R., Skut, W.: Thrax: an open source grammar compiler built on OpenFst. In: 2011 IEEE Automatic Speech Recognition and Understanding Workshop (ASRU), pp. 397–402. IEEE (2011). https://doi.org/10.1109/ASRU.2011.6163933

Personalizing Learning Paths: Analyzing Student Interactions on Moodle Using the NooJ Platform

Amira Abbes[1(✉)], Héla Fehri[1], Leila Ghorbel[1], Corinne Amel Zayani[1], and Ronan Champagnat[2]

[1] MIRACL LABORATORY, University of Sfax,
Pôle Technologique de Sfax: Route de Tunis, Km 10 B.P. 242, 3021 Sfax, Tunisia
amyyraa29@gmail.com, hela.fehri@yahoo.fr,
corinne.zayani@fss.usf.tn
[2] L3i Laboratory, La Rochelle University, Avenue Michel Crépeau, 17042 La Rochelle, France
ronan.champagnat@univ-lr.fr

Abstract. The evolution of educational technologies has encouraged the development of adaptive systems that can personalize learning paths. In this context, this paper proposes a method for classifying learning paths on Moodle using syntactic transducers built with the NooJ platform. The proposed method consists of three main steps: (1) Data Extraction from Moodle event logs, (2) Data Classification through NooJ grammars that model activity sequences, and (3) Interactive Dashboard Development to visualize student progress and provide personalized recommendations. To evaluate and validate the method, we applied it to a Moodle course titled "Semantic technology". The obtained results were highly satisfactory and demonstrate the method's effectiveness in analyzing learning behaviors and supporting personalized education.

Keywords: LMS · transducer · recommendation systems · learning analytics

1 Introduction

For more than two centuries, education has undergone continuous evolution. In the 19th century, industrialization created an urgent demand for a skilled workforce, which encouraged the establishment of public education systems in many parts of the world. In the 20th century, teaching methods changed: education became more learner-centered, with approaches that encouraged active participation and critical thinking. In the 21st century, the digital revolution introduced online and blended learning, offering more flexibility and accessibility [1].

This digital transformation has also highlighted the diversity of learner profiles. Each student learns in a different way and at their own pace. To better respond to this diversity, adaptive learning systems have emerged [2]. These systems use data from student behavior, such as results, preferences, or interactions, to automatically adjust

© The Author(s), under exclusive license to Springer Nature Switzerland AG 2026
D. Petković et al. (Eds.): NooJ 2025, CCIS 2832, pp. 189–200, 2026.
https://doi.org/10.1007/978-3-032-17103-0_16

content and learning paths to individual needs. In doing so, they help to improve learner engagement and performance [3, 4].

In this context, personalized recommendation now plays a central role in online education. The main objective is to provide each learner with a customized learning path that is adapted to their rhythm, needs, and preferences [5, 6]. Recent studies confirm that such personalization not only increases motivation but also supports long-term retention of knowledge [7].

To achieve such personalization, researchers often rely on Learning Management Systems (LMS), which record detailed traces of student activity. These platforms provide rich interaction data that can be analyzed to classify learning behaviors and generate adaptive recommendations [8]. Moodle, one of the most widely used LMSs, offers a variety of activities such as quizzes, assignments, and discussion forums. Each interaction is stored in event logs, creating valuable data for analyzing how students progress in their learning journey [9].

Among the challenges in personalization, two aspects have attracted particular attention. The first is the classification of learning paths, which helps to group students according to their activity sequences and performance levels [10]. The second is the development of interactive dashboards, which transform raw data and classification results into visual feedback. Dashboards provide learners with personalized recommendations and teachers with insights into student engagement and performance [11, 12].

The aim of this paper is to propose a method for classifying learning paths on Moodle using syntactic transducers created with the NooJ platform. The proposed method is based on three main steps: (1) extracting event logs from Moodle, (2) classifying sequences of activities using NooJ grammars, and (3) developing an interactive dashboard that allows students to visualize their progress and receive personalized recommendations.

The remainder of this paper is organized as follows: Sect. 2 reviews several pertinent studies related to our work. Section 3 outlines the various phases of our proposed method. Section 4 discusses the experimentation and evaluation conducted on a Moodle course titled "Semantic technology". Lastly, Sect. 5 concludes the paper and suggests directions for future research.

2 Related Work

Research in technology-enhanced learning has increasingly focused on understanding and supporting learners through the analysis of their digital traces. With the widespread adoption of Learning Management Systems (LMS) such as Moodle, vast amounts of interaction data are available for mining and analysis.

In this study, we divided the related works into two groups:

Research on learner classification based on Moodle logs,
Research on dashboards and recommendations.

2.1 Research on Learner Classification Based on Moodle Logs

A large number of studies have focused on predicting or classifying student performance from Moodle log data.

For example, [13] applied several data mining techniques to Moodle log data with the objective of predicting students' academic performance. Their work focused on identifying how different algorithms could support early detection of at-risk students. Similarly, [14] analyzed more than 54,000 Moodle log entries to predict student outcomes based on course activities. Their study emphasized how classification models can be used not only to anticipate final exam results but also to provide timely predictions earlier in the semester, allowing for more effective pedagogical interventions. More recent work has explored advanced modeling techniques. For example, [15] combined Moodle data with in-class activity, forum contributions, and exam results, showing that data fusion improves prediction quality by capturing multiple aspects of learning behavior.

Similarly, [16] introduced an ontology-based framework to model student actions, which allowed classification models to transfer effectively between different courses without losing accuracy.

These findings confirm that Moodle event logs, when processed carefully, can provide reliable features for learner classification and dropout prediction. While these works mainly rely on machine learning or data mining algorithms, our method differs by adopting a linguistic perspective using a NooJ syntactic transducer.

2.2 Research on Dashboards and Recommendations

A second line of research focuses on providing feedback to students and teachers through dashboards and recommendation systems.

The research by [17] presented an adaptive support system that recommends review materials based on students' past quiz errors. Their experiments showed that students who used the system performed better on later quizzes, and more than half of the participants rated the dashboard as useful.

More recently, learning dashboards have been studied as tools for self-regulation. For example, [18] designed a student dashboard that supported self-regulation by providing progress tracking and goal-setting functions. Their evaluation demonstrated that students using the dashboard showed significantly higher engagement levels.

Other works, such as those proposed by [19], studied the effect of dashboard framing on motivation, showing that presenting data as progress rather than as a ranking increased participation in online discussions.

The authors of [20] proposed an explainable AI-enhanced dashboard for academic writing support. Although task performance was not significantly improved, students who used the explainable version showed a better understanding of writing principles.

These studies demonstrate that they can increase engagement, support reflection, and provide targeted learning support, especially when combined with adaptive or explainable features.

Departing from this state of the art, we notice that, to date, no study has specifically addressed the classification of learning paths extracted from Moodle using a linguistic approach based on transducers built with the NooJ platform, combined with interactive dashboards that deliver personalized recommendations. Our proposed method aims to fill precisely this gap.

3 Proposed Method: Classification of Learning Paths on Moodle Using the NooJ Platform and Dashboard Development

Our main objective in this work is to classify learning paths on Moodle using syntactic transducers created with the NooJ platform, and to complement this analysis with an interactive dashboard that delivers personalized recommendations. The ultimate goal is to increase student engagement and provide effective learning support.

As illustrated in Fig. 1, the proposed method is divided into three main phases: "Data Extraction", "Data Classification", and "Dashboard Development".

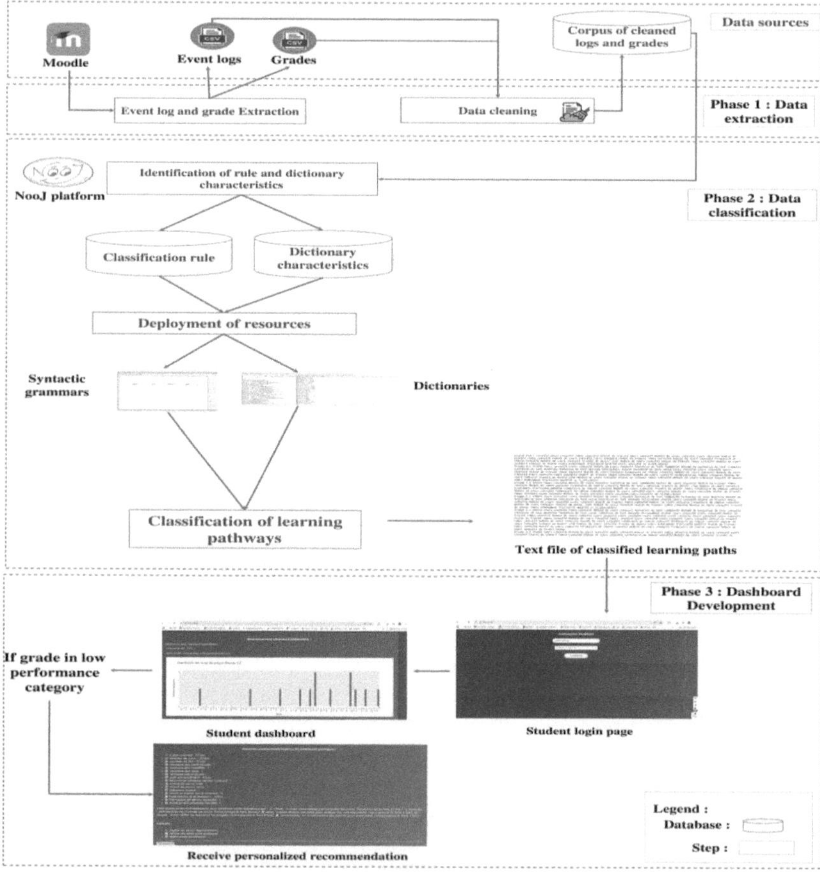

Fig. 1. Overview of the proposed method.

The first phase, "Data Extraction", focuses on collecting raw data from the Moodle platform. Event logs that record student interactions and files containing academic grades are merged into a single structured dataset.

The second phase, "Data Classification with NooJ", is dedicated to processing this dataset using the NooJ platform. A custom dictionary of activities and syntactic transducers is applied to classify learning paths into different performance categories.

In the final phase, "Dashboard Development", we design an interactive dashboard that displays student results. It provides visualizations of grades and group statistics and generates personalized recommendations based on successful learning paths.

In the following subsections, we present and explain each phase of the method in detail.

3.1 Data Extraction

In this step, we collected raw data from the Moodle platform, including detailed event logs that recorded every interaction made by students, as well as separate files containing their grades. The dataset used in this study was drawn from the second semester of the academic year and focused on second-year computer science students enrolled in the course "Compiler Techniques" at the Faculty of Science of Sfax.

To make the collected data usable for analysis, we developed a preprocessing script that merged the two CSV files, one containing the event traces and the other containing grades, into a single, well-structured dataset.

This preprocessing stage involved several critical steps. First, we cleaned the data by removing unnecessary or irrelevant information, such as incomplete entries or duplicate records, which could otherwise interfere with accurate analysis. Next, we organized the data into key attributes that are essential for understanding student learning behavior. These attributes included student identifiers, ordered sequences of learning activities, group assignments, and final grades.

As shown in Fig. 2, this phase produced a final CSV file ready for classification.

	A	B	C	D
1	Id	concept:name	Note	groupe
2	351639	['Cours consulté', 'Module de cours consulté', 'Cours consulté', 'Cours consulté', 'Module de cours consulté', 'Tentati		13 Groupe 2.2
3	353230	['Cours consulté', 'Cours consulté', 'Module de cours consulté', 'Tentative de test commencée', 'Résumé de tentative		12 Groupe 2.2
4	390247	['Cours consulté', 'Module de cours consulté', 'Tentative de test commencée', 'Module de cours consulté', 'Statut du t		10 Groupe 2.2
5	390264	['Cours consulté', 'Cours consulté', 'Module de cours consulté', 'Tentative de test commencée', 'Tentative de test mo		15 Groupe 1.2
6	390274	['Cours consulté', 'Cours consulté', 'Module de cours consulté', 'Tentative de test commencée', 'Résumé de tentative		15 Groupe 1.2
7	390291	['Cours consulté', 'Module de cours consulté', 'Cours consulté', 'Statut du travail remis consulté', 'Module de cours cc		2 Groupe 2.2
8	390298	['Cours consulté', 'Module de cours consulté', 'Cours consulté', 'Cours consulté', 'Cours consulté', 'Cours consulté', 'l		17 Groupe 2.2
9	390307	['Cours consulté', 'Module de cours consulté', 'Cours consulté', 'Module de cours consulté', 'Cours consulté', 'Cours c		13,5 Groupe 2.2
10	390308	['Cours consulté', 'Cours consulté', 'Module de cours consulté', 'Tentative de test commencée', 'Résumé de tentative		18 Groupe 1.2
11	390313	['Cours consulté', 'Cours consulté', 'Module de cours consulté', 'Tentative de test commencée', 'Résumé de tentative		17 Groupe 1.2
12	390347	['Cours consulté', 'Module de cours consulté', 'Cours consulté', 'Module de cours consulté', 'Tentative de test comme		17,5 Groupe 2.2
13	390351	['Cours consulté', 'Cours consulté', 'Module de cours consulté', 'Tentative de test commencée', 'Résumé de tentative		19 Groupe 1.2
14	390354	['Cours consulté', 'Module de cours consulté', 'Cours consulté', 'Module de cours consulté', 'Tentative de test comme		17 Groupe 2.2
15	390363	['Cours consulté', 'Module de cours consulté', 'Cours consulté', 'Module de cours consulté', 'Cours consulté', 'Module		19,75 Groupe 2.2
16	390366	['Cours consulté', 'Cours consulté', 'Module de cours consulté', 'Tentative de test commencée', 'Résumé de tentative		15 Groupe 1.2
17	390519	['Cours consulté', 'Module de cours consulté', 'Module de cours consulté', 'Module de cours consulté', 'Module de co		13,5 Groupe 2.2
18	390548	['Cours consulté', 'Cours consulté', 'Module de cours consulté', 'Module de cours consulté', 'Tentative de test comme		17 Groupe 1.2
19	392969	['Cours consulté', 'Cours consulté', 'Module de cours consulté', 'Tentative de test commencée', 'Résumé de tentative		15 Groupe 1.2
20	392971	['Cours consulté', 'Module de cours consulté', 'Cours consulté', 'Cours consulté', 'Cours consulté', 'Cours consulté', 'l		17 Groupe 1.2
21	392972	['Cours consulté', 'Module de cours consulté', 'Cours consulté', 'Module de cours consulté', 'Tentati		16 Groupe 1.2
22	393050	['Cours consulté', 'Cours consulté', 'Module de cours consulté', 'Tentative de test commencée', 'Résumé de tentative		18,5 Groupe 2.2
23	395611	['Cours consulté', 'Module de cours consulté', 'Cours consulté', 'Cours consulté', 'Module de cours consulté', 'Tentati		15 Groupe 2.2
24	396110	['Cours consulté', 'Statut du travail remis consulté', 'Module de cours consulté', 'Statut du travail remis consulté', 'Mo		7 Groupe 2.2

Fig. 2. Event logs.

3.2 Data Classification

Using the linguistic platform NooJ, we moved on to the second step of our method, "Data Classification". From the cleaned log file obtained in the previous "Data Extraction" step, we constructed a corpus specifically adapted for linguistic analysis. While the cleaned log represents the raw event data after preprocessing (removal of duplicates, missing values, etc.), the corpus organizes this information into structured learning paths that can be directly processed in NooJ. Each entry in this corpus includes: the group number to which the student belongs, the student identifier, the ordered sequence of activities performed within Moodle, and the corresponding grade.

Identification of the Rule. From the corpus of student learning paths, we designed a single classification rule that encodes the structure of each learning path. This rule begins with the group label (e.g., groupe 1), followed by the student identifier, then the ordered sequence of activities performed in Moodle by the student. To account for repeated behaviors, a loop is included to capture multiple occurrences of the same activity. The rule ends with the final grade, which determines the performance category: not good (0–9), good (10–15), very good (16–18), or excellent (19–20).

$$< Rule >:= < Group > < Student\_ID > \left[< Activity > + \right] < Grade >$$

Identification of Dictionary Characteristics. An important part of this classification phase involved working with dictionaries within NooJ. For our study, we used two main dictionaries. The first was the "dm" dictionary, which is the default French language dictionary provided by NooJ [21]. This dictionary helped the system recognize standard French words and grammatical forms, ensuring that any textual elements associated with student interactions could be properly interpreted.

In addition to the default dictionary, we created our own dictionary named "activities", specifically tailored to capture all the actions performed by students on Moodle.

This dictionary included a comprehensive list of possible activities, such as "view resource", "attempt quiz", "view course", and other actions that students typically perform while engaging with the platform. Figure 3 illustrates the "activities" dictionary.

```
Dictionary contains 13 entries

# NooJ V7
# Dictionary
#
# Language is: fr
#
# Alphabetical order is not required.
#
# Use inflectional & derivational paradigms' description files (.nof), e.g.:
# Special Command: #use paradigms.nof
#
# Special Features: +NW (non-word) +FXC (frozen expression component) +UNAMB (unambiguous lexica
#                   +FLX= (inflectional paradigm) +DRV= (derivational paradigm)
#
# Special Characters: '\' '"' ' ' ',' '+' '-' '#'
#use _dm.nof

Cours consulté,N+activité=activity
Module cours consulté,N+activité=activity
Tentative de test commencée,N+activité=activity
Tentative de test modifiée,N+activité=activity
Tentative de test envoyée,N+activité=activity
Tentative de test relue,N+activité=activity
Résumé de tentative de test consulté,N+activité=activity
Travail de devoir créé,N+activité=activity
Travail de devoir remis,N+activité=activity
Utilisateur évalué,N+activité=activity
Statut du travail remis consulté,N+activité=activity
Formulaire de remise consulté,N+activité=activity
Achèvement d'activité modifié,N+activité=activity
```

Fig. 3. Dictionary of student activities used in NooJ.

By combining the "_dm" dictionary with the "activities" dictionary, we provided NooJ with both linguistic and domain-specific resources. This combination allowed the system to effectively identify, interpret, and classify the sequences of activities for each student.

Identification of Transducers. The identification of the syntactic transducers consists of classifying students' learning paths based on their activities and final grades. Each transducer is defined by a start node and an end node, and it processes the sequence of actions from left to right.

The deployment of resources involves using the identified rules and prepared dictionaries to design a transducer tailored for our classification purposes. Specifically, the transducer was structured to begin with the group label, such as "groupe 1" or "amphi 2.1", which allowed us to distinguish between different class groups. Immediately following the group label, the transducer identified the student ID, ensuring that each sequence of actions could be linked to the corresponding learner.

The core of the transducer consists of the ordered sequence of activities performed by the student on Moodle. To handle cases where students repeated certain actions multiple times, we incorporated a loop structure within the transducer. This feature enabled the system to accurately capture repeated behaviors without losing information or breaking the sequence.

Finally, the transducer assigned a performance category to each student based on their final grade. Grades were mapped into four distinct performance levels: "not good" (0–9), "good" (10–15), "very good" (16–18), and "excellent" (19–20). This categorization allowed us to link patterns of activity with performance outcomes, providing a clearer understanding of how different sequences of learning behaviors relate to student success. Figure 4 illustrates the NooJ transducer used for this classification process.

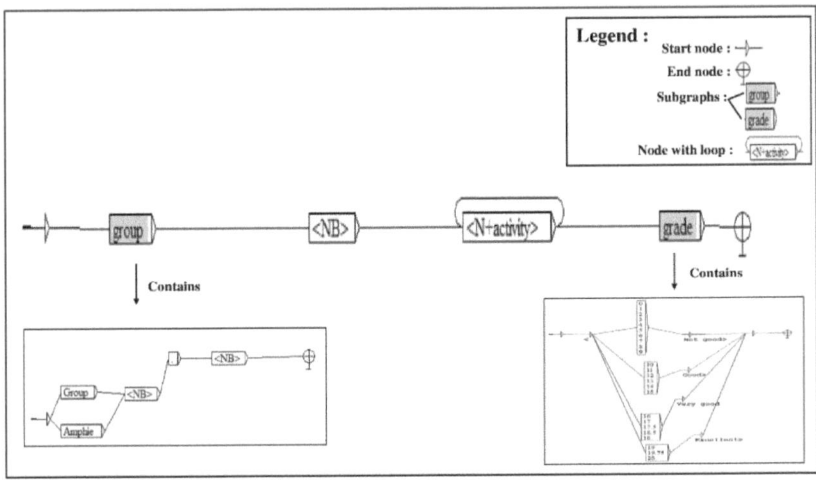

Fig. 4. NooJ transducer for classifying student learning paths.

As an example, one student's path begins with the label "groupe 1" followed by the student ID, then a sequence of activities including quiz attempts and forum posts, and ends with a grade of 18. According to our classification rules, this student is placed in the "Very good" category.

After executing the transducer with the *noojapply* command, we obtained a text file containing all the classified student paths, as shown in Fig. 5. Each entry in this file corresponds to a student and includes the structured sequence of activities along with the assigned performance category. From this output, we focused specifically on extracting the most successful learning paths, those labeled as "excellent." These high-performing sequences provide insight into effective learning behaviors and strategies. By analyzing them, we can identify patterns and approaches that contribute to better outcomes.

```
Groupe 2.2 351639 Cours consulté Module de cours consulté Cours consulté Cours consulté Module de cours consulté Tentative de test
commencée Résumé de tentative de test consulté Tentative de test modifiée Tentative de test relue Tentative de test envoyée Utilisateur
évalué Cours consulté Cours consulté Cours consulté Statut du travail remis consulté Module de cours consulté Cours consulté Statut du
travail remis consulté Module de cours consulté Cours consulté Statut du travail remis consulté Module de cours consulté Formulaire de
remise consulté Module de cours consulté Travail de devoir créé Module de cours consulté Statut du travail remis consulté Module de cours
consulté Travail de devoir remis Achèvement d'activité modifié Cours consulté 13 0,755,<Good>
Groupe 2.2 353230 Cours consulté Cours consulté Module de cours consulté Tentative de test commencée Résumé de tentative de test consulté
Tentative de test modifiée Tentative de test envoyée Utilisateur évalué Tentative de test relue Cours consulté Cours consulté Cours
consulté Statut du travail remis consulté Module de cours consulté Formulaire de remise consulté Module de cours consulté Module de cours
consulté Cours consulté Cours consulté Statut du travail remis consulté Module de cours consulté Formulaire de remise consulté Module de
cours consulté Travail de devoir créé Module de cours consulté Statut du travail remis consulté Module de cours consulté Travail de devoir
remis Achèvement d'activité modifié 12 7,729,<Good>
Groupe 2.2 390247 Cours consulté Module de cours consulté Tentative de test commencée Module de cours consulté Statut du travail remis
consulté Module de cours consulté Formulaire de remise consulté Module de cours consulté Travail de devoir créé Module de cours consulté
Achèvement d'activité modifié Formulaire de remise consulté Module de cours consulté Travail de devoir remis Formulaire de remise consulté
Module de cours consulté Formulaire de remise consulté Module de cours consulté Cours consulté Module de cours consulté Statut du travail
remis consulté Cours consulté Module de cours consulté Cours consulté Cours consulté 10 14,650,<Good>
Groupe 1.2 390264 Cours consulté Cours consulté Module de cours consulté Tentative de test commencée Tentative de test modifiée Résumé de
tentative de test consulté Tentative de test relue Tentative de test envoyée Utilisateur évalué Cours consulté Statut du travail remis
consulté Module de cours consulté Cours consulté Statut du travail remis consulté Module de cours consulté Formulaire de remise consulté
Module de cours consulté Travail de devoir créé Module de cours consulté Statut du travail remis consulté Module de cours consulté Travail
de devoir remis Achèvement d'activité modifié 15 21,618,<Good>
```

Fig. 5. Excerpt of the classified student paths file.

Importantly, these sequences can be used as a reference or recommendation for students who achieved lower grades, particularly those below 14. By following the strategies observed in the "excellent" paths, these students may be able to improve their engagement and performance in the course.

In this way, the classification not only organizes and interprets student data but also provides actionable insights that can guide personalized learning interventions.

3.3 Dashboard Development

The final step of our method focuses on dashboard development, which serves as the interface through which students can access and interpret the classified learning paths. Once the learning paths were processed and categorized, the next challenge was to present this information in a way that was both clear and useful for students. To address this challenge, we designed an interactive dashboard that allows learners to visualize their progress and performance in a user-friendly manner.

To use the dashboard, students first enter their identifier and group information. The system then retrieves the corresponding data and displays their grade, which is derived from the NooJ classification, along with a personalized feedback message tailored to their performance. This message provides guidance and encouragement based on the student's classification category, helping them understand their current standing and areas for improvement.

Additionally, the dashboard includes a visual chart representing the grade distribution within the student's group. This feature allows students to contextualize their performance relative to their peers, offering insights into both individual and collective achievement patterns.

Figure 6 presents this interface, showing the grade, feedback, and group distribution for a student in the "excellent" category.

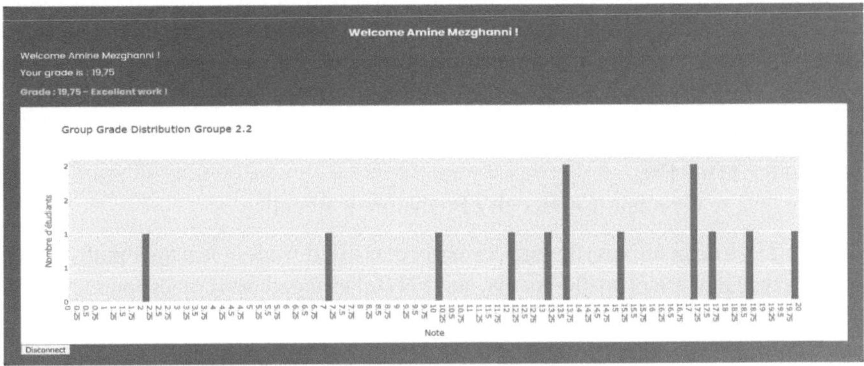

Fig. 6. Interactive dashboard for student feedback and recommendations.

Beyond visualization, the dashboard also delivers targeted recommendations. Students in higher performance categories see their feedback and group distribution, while those in lower performance categories additionally receive personalized suggestions. Figure 7 illustrates the recommendation feature, highlighting the suggestions generated from the NooJ-produced file that correspond to the most successful learning paths identified during the classification phase.

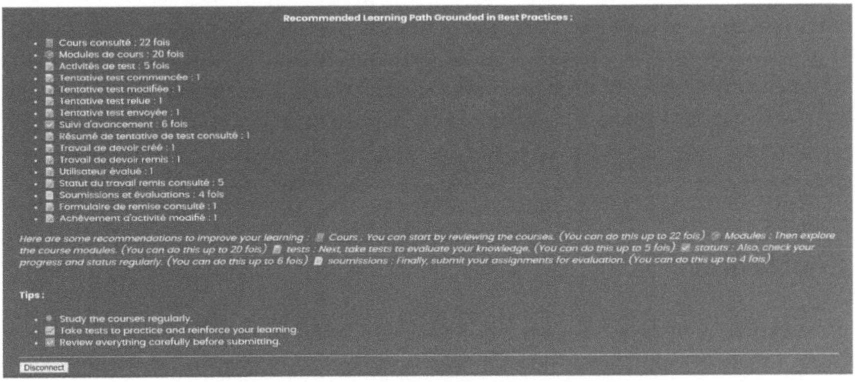

Fig. 7. Personalized learning recommendations.

This final step ensures that the methodology not only analyzes student behavior but also delivers tangible benefits for learners in the form of enhanced guidance and support.

4 Experimentation and Evaluation

Evaluating our work is essential to determine the effectiveness of our proposed method. To assess the Data Classification phase, we conducted experiments using a Moodle course titled "Semantic Technology". In this evaluation, we followed the same methodology as described previously, including the extraction of event logs, preprocessing of the data, classification of learning paths using NooJ transducers, and the identification of successful sequences for recommendation purposes. For evaluation, we used standard metrics including precision, recall, and F-measure defined as follows:

Precision = TP / TP + FP,
Recall = TP / TP + FN,
F-measure = 2 × (Precision × Recall / Precision + Recall)

Where TP (true positives) denote correctly classified student learning paths, FP (false positives) represent misclassified paths, and FN (false negatives) correspond to paths that were not detected by the system. Table 1 below presents the values obtained.

Table 1. Interpretation of the result obtained.

Precision	92%
Recall	90%
F-measure	91%

By examining the results, we see that, even though the performance is high, some problems remain. These problems are mainly caused by the limits of the rule in the NooJ transducer. For example, a student with a grade of 12 was placed in the category of students with grades above 15, which is wrong. Sometimes, students with grades like 19.12 are not detected because their grades are not included in the transducer category.

Another problem is that some activities are missing from the dictionary, so the system cannot detect them. For example, if a student performs an activity like "submit_asignment" and this activity is not included in the dictionary, the transducer will fail to recognize it.

5 Conclusion

In this work, we have proposed a method for classifying student learning paths on Moodle using the NooJ platform. This method was designed to provide a comprehensive understanding of student behaviors and support personalized learning. It began with the extraction of event logs from the Moodle platform, which record detailed information about student interactions with educational resources. These logs served as the foundation for building structured datasets representing each student's learning journey.

Next, we employed syntactic transducers in NooJ to classify learning pathways based on the sequences of actions captured in the event logs. The transducers allowed us to organize student activities into meaningful sequences and map them to performance categories, facilitating the identification of effective learning paths. Finally, we developed an interactive dashboard that enables students to visualize their performance, compare their progress with peers, and receive personalized recommendations aimed at optimizing their learning journey. By integrating data analysis, classification, and visualization, our method provides actionable insights that can guide students toward more effective learning practices.

In terms of future perspectives, we plan to focus on several key improvements to enhance our approach. First, we aim to deploy the dashboard online by hosting it on a web server, making it accessible to both students and teachers, and facilitating its use in real educational environments. Next, we intend to integrate new behavioral indicators such as login frequency, forum participation, and learning styles into our analysis to improve the accuracy of learning pathway classification. Additionally, we plan to enrich and generalize the activities dictionary used in NooJ so that it captures a broader range of student behaviors, beyond just specific activity types. Finally, we aim to conduct an experimental study in which students receive system-generated recommendations, allowing us to assess the practical impact and effectiveness of our approach on their learning outcomes.

References

1. Bates, A.W.: Teaching in a digital age: guidelines for designing teaching and learning. BCcampus, Vancouver (2015)
2. Brusilovsky, P., Millán, E.: User models for adaptive hypermedia and adaptive educational systems. In: Brusilovsky, P., Kobsa, A., Nejdl, W. (eds.) The Adaptive Web, pp. 3–53. Springer, Berlin (2007)
3. Ifenthaler, D., Yau, J.Y-K.: Utilising learning analytics to support study success in higher education: a systematic review. Educ. Technol. Res. Dev. **68**(4), 1965–1990 (2020)
4. du Plooy, E., Casteleijn, D., Franzsen, D.: Personalized adaptive learning in higher education: a scoping review of key characteristics and impact on academic performance and engagement. Heliyon **10**(21), e39630 (2024)
5. Shemshack, A., Spector, J.M.: A systematic literature review of personalized learning terms. Smart Learn. Environ. **7**, 33 (2020)
6. Romero, C., Ventura, S.: Educational data mining and learning analytics: an updated survey. Wiley Interdisc. Rev. Data Min. Knowl. Disc. **14**(2), e1355 (2024)
7. Halkiopoulos, C., Gkintoni, E.: Leveraging AI in e-learning: personalized learning and adaptive assessment through cognitive neuropsychology a systematic analysis. Electronics **13**(18), 3762 (2024)
8. Hildebrandt, T., Mehnen, L.: Cross-course process mining of student click-stream data – aggregation and group comparison. arXiv preprint arXiv:2409.14244 (2024)
9. Hachicha, W., Ghorbel, L., Champagnat, R., Zayani, C.A., Amous, I.: Using process mining for learning resource recommendation: A Moodle case study. In: KES International Conference on Knowledge-Based and Intelligent Information & Engineering Systems (KES 2021), pp. 853–862. Elsevier, Amsterdam (2021)
10. Huang, Y., et al.: Adaptive learning path navigation via reinforcement learning and knowledge tracing. arXiv preprint arXiv:2305.04475 (2023)
11. Ruesch, A., et al.: Multimodal learning analytics dashboards: Integrating biometric and behavioral data in MOOCs. arXiv preprint arXiv:2305.12561 (2023)

12. de Vreugd, R., Kalz, M., Scheffel, M.: Supporting students' self-regulation through a learning analytics dashboard: design and evaluation. Educ. Inf. Technol. **29**, 12401 (2024)

13. Shawareb, N., Ewais, A., Yaseen, Q.S.: Utilizing data mining techniques to predict students performance using data log from MOODLE. KSII Trans. Internet Inf. Syst. **18**(9) (2024)

14. Kaensar, C., Wongnin, P.: Analysis and prediction of student performance based on Moodle log data using machine learning techniques. Int. J. Emerg. Technol. Learn. (iJET) **18**(9), 133–152 (2023)

15. Chango, L., Cerezo, R., Romero, C.: Using multimodal data fusion to improve student performance prediction. arXiv preprint arXiv:2403.05552 (2024)

16. Zambrano, D., Romero, C., Ventura, S.: Toward ontology-based student modeling for transferable predictive models in MOOCs and LMS. arXiv preprint arXiv:2410.07358 (2024)

17. Okubo, F., Shiino, T., Minematsu, T., Taniguchi, Y., Shimada, A.: Adaptive learning support system based on automatic recommendation of personalized review materials. IEEE Trans. Learn. Technol. **16**(1), 92–105 (2023)

18. de Vreugd, R., Kalz, M., Scheffel, M.: Supporting students' self-regulation through a learning analytics dashboard: design and evaluation. J. Learn. Anal. **11**(1), 1–16 (2024)

19. Hatala, M., Nazeri, N.: The effect of dashboard framing on student motivation and contribution in online discussions. J. Learn. Anal. **11**(2), 45–63 (2024)

20. Chen, Y.: Explainable AI-enhanced dashboard in academic writing: effects on student learning. arXiv preprint arXiv:2506.16312 (2025)

21. Trouilleux, F.: Le DM, a French dictionary for NooJ. In: Automatic Processing of Various Levels of Linguistic Phenomena: Selected Papers from the NooJ 2011 International Conference, pp. 16–28. Cambridge Scholars Publishing, Newcastle (2012)

The Annotation of Indonesian Clitics by Nooj and Other Computational Tools

Prihantoro[(✉)] [iD]

Faculty of Humanities, Universitas Diponegoro, Semarang, Indonesia
`prihantoro@live.undip.ac.id`

Abstract. Scholars have discussed Indonesian clitics theoretically from various perspectives. Regardless, their application in the corpus annotation field remains challenging and understudied. In this paper, I will qualitatively compare three corpus annotation tools that can be used to analyse Indonesian clitics: MorphInd, TreeTagger and NooJ. I find that these three computational tools have a number of fundamental differences. TreeTagger requires a separate tool to delineate a clitic from its host, before annotation. Conversely, NooJ and MorphInd integrate the clitic delineation and clitic annotation process, as shown in SANTI-POS. In terms of resources, MorphInd resource development seems to be restricted to its developers. Unlike MorphInd, TreeTagger and NooJ resources can easily be developed as they are available to the public. A survey confirms that NooJ is preferred due to its user-friendly installation and visual and transparent analysis. Going beyond annotation, I demonstrate how NooJ allows users to identify a clitic's surface form, as well as its free form, in the Task Annotation Structure (TAS).

Keywords: Indonesian · Clitic · Annotation · Tokenisation · Corpus

1 Indonesian Clitics

Clitics are widely known to be free linguistic items, but are bound [1, 2] phonologically or orthographically in writing. One of the languages where clitics are present is Indonesian, the national and official language of Indonesia [3]. It is one of the modern standardised varieties of Malay, a language family whose standard or colloquial varieties are widely used in Southeast Asia.

Indonesian clitics have been widely discussed by a number of scholars in linguistic papers and Indonesian reference grammar books [4–6]. While the realisation of clitics may vary in other languages, in Indonesian, the type of linguistic item that may be cliticised is pronouns, to be more specific personal pronouns, and restricted to certain pronouns, namely *aku* (1st person singular pronoun, standard), whose clitic form is = *ku*; *kamu* (2nd person singular, standard), whose clitic form is = *mu*; *dia* (3rd person singular pronoun, no difference between standard and honorific) whose clitic form is = *nya*. Clitic = *nya* can also be used to refer to a definite pronoun, *itu*, which can ambiguously be used as a demonstrative (distant) pronoun. A generic illustration comparing the pronoun (1) and its free form (2) is shown below.

© The Author(s), under exclusive license to Springer Nature Switzerland AG 2026
D. Petković et al. (Eds.): NooJ 2025, CCIS 2832, pp. 201–210, 2026.
https://doi.org/10.1007/978-3-032-17103-0_17

(1) *Kuambil bantal besar* (1st person pronoun, singular, clitic form)
    ku=ambil bantal besar[1]
    1.SG=take pillow big
    'I took a big pillow'

(2) *aku ambil bantal besar* (1st person pronoun, singular, free form)
    1.SG=take pillow big
    'I took a big pillow'

In example (1), *aku* (1st person singular pronoun) is cliticised as = *ku,* while in example (2) its free form is used. Note that among the aforementioned three pronouns, only *aku* may serve as both proclitic (attached before the host – shown earlier in examples (1) and (2)) and enclitic (attached after the host). *Kamu* and *dia* can only be cliticised after their host (enclitic). In addition, a clitic can also be used in a possessive construction. When the free form of a pronoun is used in Indonesian, it does not undergo any change, as in English (cf. I have a dream vs. my dream).

The above glossing examples illustrate three essential tasks: clitic delineation from its hosts, identification of free form, and annotation. These have been widely discussed in the theoretical literature on Indonesian grammar, but understudied in the Natural Language Processing (NLP) and computational fields. Only Larasati et al. (2012) specifically discuss clitic handling. In other works [7, 8], it is not discussed in detail. Regardless, they focus on very specific systems without relative comparisons. This study aims to 1) compare how NooJ and other computational tools handle Indonesian clitics and 2) survey users' preferences.

2   Methods

In this paper, I review three computational tools that can be used to analyse Indonesian clitics: MorphInd [9], TreeTagger [8], and NooJ. One of my considerations for my choice of these three computational tools is that all this software is open to the public. Note that while NooJ and TreeTagger are available in both Windows and Linux, MorphInd can only be used in Linux.[2] I will first explain how the three systems handle clitics, with a focus on NooJ, before moving on to TreeTagger and MorphInd.

The analysis focuses on the computational resources present in the three programs. Then, I discuss how they are used to perform two tasks: delineation of clitics from their host as part of tokenisation and annotation of clitics. This helps to achieve the first aim. To achieve the second aim, a small survey was conducted. Twenty-five students were randomly recruited from an Indonesian university. These students had passed the Introduction to Corpus Linguistics class.

The survey procedure is as follows. First, they are tasked with downloading each program independently without any tutorial. Thus, they should rely completely on the tool's documentation. I review how many are successful. For those who fail to download

---

[1] This example is obtained from LCC Indonesian 2023 CQPweb version (concon-cordance output link:https://cqpweb.lancs.ac.uk/lccindonesianv3/concordance.php?qdata=kua mbil&qmode=sq_nocase&pp=50&qstrategy=0&t =, accessed 27-July-2025).

[2] But Windows users can use Ubuntu as a sub-system.

the software, a human tutorial is provided, and if they still fail, they have it installed. Next, they are tasked with analyzing a text with Indonesian clitics by relying on any documentation/ manual/ user guide available from the website. Similarly, successful users are calculated. Eventually, a human tutorial is provided for those who fail to analyse. Then, finally, I survey these students' preferences. They can choose more than one program. They are also tasked with writing a note reflecting their experience from installation to analysis.

3   Analysis

3.1   Clitic handling by NooJ

A NooJ morphological grammar is used in both SANTI-POS (POS tagger) and SANTI-morf (morpheme tagger) [7] to annotate an Indonesian clitic; then, suppose the Indonesian language module is downloaded correctly, either automatically via Preferences or manually by copying and pasting the folder from the NooJ resources repository. In that case, users will see two.noj configuration files (as shown in Fig. 1, one of which they can load, depending on whether they want to use a POS tagger or a Morpheme tagger for the Indonesian corpus they wish to annotate). Clitic grammars handle clitics in resources. In Fig. 2, the clitic morphological grammar clitic.nom in SANTI-POS handles clitic annotation.

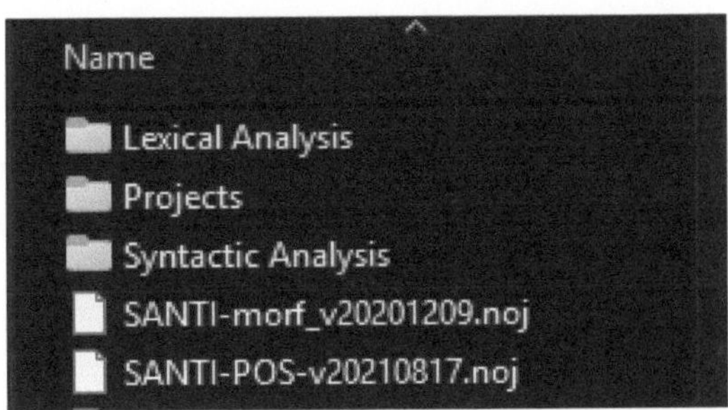

Fig. 1. NooJ SANTI-morf and SANTI-POS.noj configuration files.

In general, a clitic grammar performs two main tasks. First, it delineates a clitic from its host (also known as tokenisation). Therefore, letters agglutinated as one string are analysed as two different Atomic Linguistic Units (ALUs) or tokens. Consider examples 3 and 4, below.

(3) *kuambil*
  1.SG=take
  'I took'
(4) <kuambil> → <ku> <ambil>

In example (3), we observe a standard three-liner glossing to illustrate how a first-person singular pronoun ku = attaches to its host. Example (4) illustrates an application

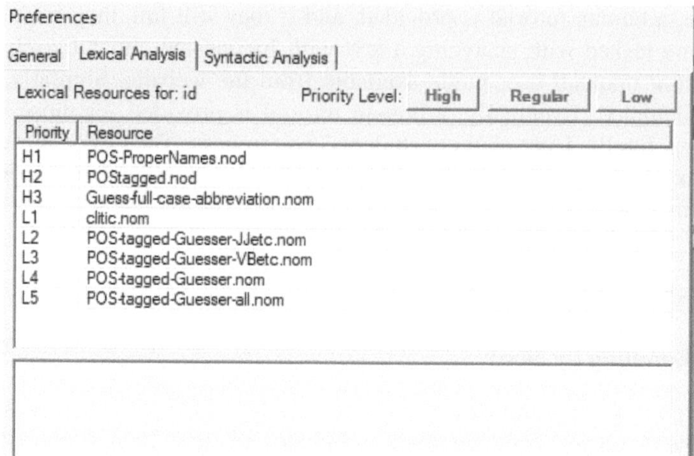

Fig. 2. SANTI-pos resources and their priority levels in NooJ's.

in NooJ that separates them automatically. If such a resource is absent, there are two options. If there are no other resources (e.g., NooJ grammar for guessing), the string is left unanalysed. NooJ will skip this string and move on to the following string. If a resource for guessing is available, that resource is used. However, it is essential to ascribe to the guessing grammar a lower priority. Otherwise, it will result in unnecessary ambiguity, which will be hard to resolve.

In addition to delineating a clitic from its host, a NooJ morphological grammar that handles clitics also delineates a clitic from its host, assigns a category label, and shows its free form. I will begin by illustrating how clitics are handled in SANTI-morf (See Fig. 3).

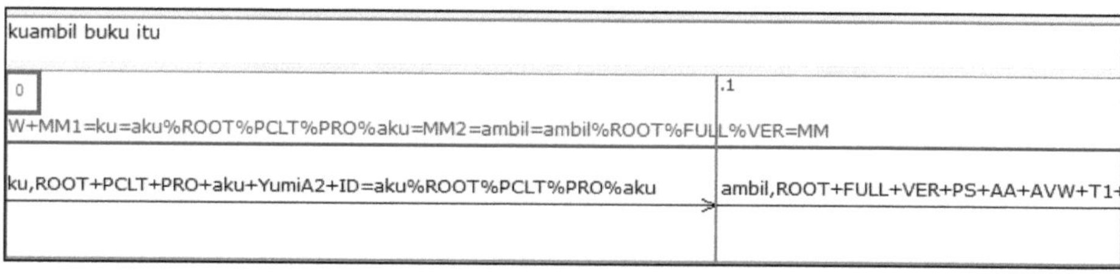

Fig. 3. The annotation of ku = 'I' by SANTI-morf.

In Fig. 3, we observe that in addition to delineating *ku* = from its host *ambil,* NooJ assigns annotation labels to these two ALUs. For <ku>, the annotation labels are <ROOT+PCLT+PRO+aku>. These labels can be read as follows. The ALU <ku> is a root morpheme (ROOT), whose surface form is a proclitic (PCLT). Its POS category is a pronoun, and its free form is 'aku'. These category labels are obtained from a NooJ grammar. Note that the subsequent label for the root morpheme *ambil* is obtained from a NooJ morphological grammar. This can be observed in Fig. 4. The main graph shows the possible structure of cliticisation, where a host may be preceded or followed by clitics (sub graphs:PCLT and:ECLT). The sub-graph:WORD is a placeholder for the host word.

```
Main =  (:PCLT | <E>)  :WORD (:ECLT1 | <E>) ( :ECLT2 |<E> );

#proclitic morpheme list (only one)
PCLT = ku/<ku,ROOT+PCLT+PRO+aku+YumiA2+ID=aku%ROOT%PCLT%PRO%aku>;
```

Fig. 4. Annotation labels for <ku> as a proclitic in EN-v4-YumiA2.nom.

As shown in Fig. 4, we observe the whole sequence of annotation labels. Note that other than <ROOT+PCLT+PRO+aku>, the remaining labels are for debugging and output generation purposes, not analytic, as shown in Prihantoro [7]. As for the root morpheme *ambil,* its annotation labels are obtained from a NooJ dictionary. If we observe Fig. 4, we see:WORD as a sub-graph. Within this sub-graph, there are other sub-graphs, one of which is:VERBA rule number 11 (see Fig. 5).

```
#RULES 11: VERB
VERBA = :VERBA_A | :VERBA_B | :VERBA_C | :VERBA_
### i am not sure what's wrong with rules within verba
### and they work! rule is exactly the same!


VERBA_A = :VER | :VER_beR- | :VER_beR-_ber-ke-an |
#======11.1====11.2============11.3========

VERBA_B = :VER_beR-kan |  :VER_di- | :VER_di-i| :VER
#========11.10=======11.11=======11.12====1
===
VERBA_C = :VER_meN- | :VER_meN-i | :VER_meN-kan
#=========11.22=======11.23==========11.24=


VERBA_D = :VER_N- | :VER_N-_-i | :VER_N-_-kan  | :V
#=========11.29====11.30=======11.31======1

# rule 11.1
# monomorphemic
VER= :varX <E>/<$X=:ROOT+DykaA1+VER> :out1 ;
```

Fig. 5. Matching a monomorphemic verb root in the grammar with a constraint variable.

Within the VERBA subgraph, we observe VER (one of 62 sub-graphs accounting for all morphological word formation rules – compounding, affixation – excluding clitics), which accounts for monomorphemic words (words without any affix, or non-compounding words). The host *ambil* 'to take' falls within this category. We see a constraint variable <$X =:ROOT+DykaA1+VER>, which restricts the root to be a verb. Here, X, the variable, is expressed in the other sub-graph in the same NooJ morphological grammar file. Variable X, as shown in Fig. 6, is declared under:varX sub-graph. The output generated by the morphological grammar is expressed in:out1 sub-graph.

As for SANTI-POS (POS tagger), the principle remains the same. Figure 7 shows a sentence in which *kuambil* has been delineated into two ALUs, <ku> and <ambil>. In

```
# varX: any string within under variable X
varX= $(X <L>* $) ;

#out1 : for root in the first position (that is vari
out1= <E>/<$1L,$1C$1S$1F>;


#for root in the first position, output all codes f
# for example rule 060407X
out1L= <E>/<$1L,$1C+Lost$1S$1F> ;
```

Fig. 6. Subgraph to a variable and its output.

addition, each ALU has also been annotated. Note that the annotation is much simpler for POS tagging as compared to morpheme tagging, due to the absence of output generation labels.

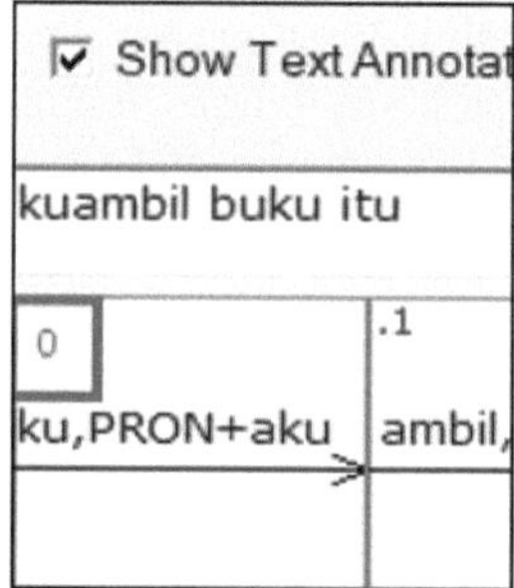

Fig. 7. The annotation of *ku =* by SANTI-POS.

As we can see, the grammar is much simpler for a few reasons. First, it is unnecessary to further decompose words into morphemes in SANTI-POS instead of SANTI-morf. Second, no constraints regulate clitic-host combinations. The variable only requires that the host is any word listed in the dictionary (:ALU). The system will use guessing resources if the host word is not present in the dictionary (Fig. 8).

```
Main = :kuambil| |:bukumu| :rumahku | :mejanya1| :mejanya2;
bukumu = $(X <L>* $) <E>/<$X=:ALU> mu <E>/<$1E,$1C$1S$1F><mu,PRON+kamu
rumahku = $(X <L>* $) <E>/<$X=:ALU> ku <E>/<$1E,$1C$1S$1F><ku,PRON+aku>
mejanya1 = $(X <L>* $) <E>/<$X=:ALU> nya <E>/<$1E,$1C$1S$1F><nya,PRON+d
mejanya2 = $(X <L>* $) <E>/<$X=:ALU> nya <E>/<$1E,$1C$1S$1F><nya,PRON+it
kuambil = ku $(X <L>* $) <E>/<$X=:ALU> <E>/<ku,PRON+aku><$1E,$1C$1S$1F> ;
```

Fig. 8. SANTI-POS grammar to handle Indonesian clitics.

3.2 Clitic handling by TreeTagger and MorphInd

In this section, we discuss how TreeTagger handles clitics. It will explain how the clitic separator script for Indonesian is built by following the principles of clitic delineation implemented in SANTI-morf and SANTI-POS.

TreeTagger cannot directly analyse Indonesian clitics, even though an Indonesian parameter file for tagging is available. Unlike NooJ, where tokenisers and annotators are present within the same system, a preprocessing script is required in TreeTagger. As shown in Fig. 9, we can see two tokeniser scripts (tokenize.pl and utf8-tokenize.perl).

token.txt	10/2/2023 7:39 PM	Text Document	0 KB
novel.token	10/2/2023 7:38 PM	TOKEN File	0 KB
novel.txt	10/2/2023 7:37 PM	Text Document	1,105 KB
filter-chunker-output.perl	3/26/2023 9:18 AM	PERL File	3 KB
filter-chunker-output-french.perl	3/26/2023 9:18 AM	PERL File	6 KB
filter-chunker-output-german.perl	3/26/2023 9:18 AM	PERL File	3 KB
mwl-lookup.perl	3/26/2023 9:18 AM	PERL File	3 KB
mwl-lookup-greek.perl	3/26/2023 9:18 AM	PERL File	2 KB
tokenize.pl	3/26/2023 9:18 AM	Perl program file	5 KB
utf8-tokenize.perl	3/26/2023 9:18 AM	PERL File	6 KB

Fig. 9. Some of the TreeTagger resources.

Inside the script (see Fig. 10), we can see an option to choose a language, which can be further incorporated into the command line. When one of these options is selected, the script will choose pre-written rules corresponding to the language to tokenise the text in the format of one word per line. It will omit punctuation, parentheses and contracted forms, among other things. However, an option to process Indonesian language text is not yet available.

```
Options:
-e : English text
-f : French text
-i : Italian text
-a <file>: <file> contains a list of words which are either abbreviations or
           words which should not be further split.
```

Fig. 10. Language option in tokenize.pl.

I then decided to write a clitic separator script following the logic implemented in SANTI-morf and SANTI-POS. The separator must rely not only on rules but also on a dictionary or, in TreeTagger, a 'lexicon'. If a word is found, check if it begins with characters identical to those used in a clitic (words beginning with *ku*, ending with *mu*, among others). Next, the script separates the suspected clitic from its host. Subsequently, it matches the host with words present in the lexicon.

If a match is found, a delineation is established. However, if there is no match, the two units will be merged again and considered a single token. This means no clitic is detected in the strings. Figure 11 shows a text before a clitic separator script was applied.

```
1. Aku Ingin
Aku ingin mencintaimu dengan sederhana
dengan kata yang tak sempat diucapkan
kayu kepada api yang menjadikannya abu

Aku ingin mencintaimu dengan sederhana
dengan isyarat yang tak sempat disampaikan
awan kepada hujan yang menjadikannya tiada
```

Fig. 11. A raw text (clitic unmodified).

In Fig. 11, line 2, we can see the word *mencintaimu* 'to love you', in which a singular second-person pronoun *kamu* 'you' is encliticised as = *mu* 'you' after *mencintai* 'to love'. In Fig. 12, in line 2, we can observe that this clitic has now been separated. Note that this clitic separator is not now part of the resources in Prihantoro [10]. After this, the tokenisation script is applied and the Indonesian parameter file can be applied to tag -mu as a pronoun (PRP) and its host as a verb (VB), as shown in Fig. 13.

```
1. Aku Ingin
Aku ingin mencintai -mu   dengan sederhana
dengan kata yang tak sempat diucapkan
kayu kepada api yang menjadikan -nya   abu

Aku ingin mencintai -mu   dengan sederhana
dengan isyarat yang tak sempat disampaikan
awan kepada hujan yang menjadikan -nya   tiada
```

Fig. 12. Clitic separated text.

```
1.          RP        @ord@
Aku         VB        aku
Ingin       RB        ingin
Aku         VB        aku
ingin       RB        ingin
mencintai             VB        cinta
-mu         PRP       -mu
dengan  IN            dengan
sederhana             JJ        sederhana
```

Fig. 13. Word, POS, and base form.

The procedure for MorphInd is much simpler. Like NooJ, it does everything in one pass. Users do not need to write a script to separate a clitic from its host, tokenise, and tag each item. Instead, a simple command line generates output (see (6), the output of (5) – presented with interlinear glossing).

(5) *kumengirimkannya*
      ku=meng-kirim-kan=nya
      SG=ACV-send-CAUS=3.SG
      'I sent him'
(4) aku<p>_PS1+meN+kirim<v>+kan_VSA+dia<p>_PS3

We can see that the 1st person singular proclitic *ku* = 'I' in the output is presented as its free form *aku* 'I'. The third-person singular enclitic = *mu* 'him/her' is presented as its corresponding free form *dia* 'him/her'. Both are tagged with a shallow tag <p> meaning pronoun, and fine-grained tag PS1 (first person singular) and PS3 (third person singular), respectively.

3.3 Users' Perspectives

As shown in the methodology, 25 students in an introduction to corpus linguistics class were the respondents in this research. Regarding the installation, Table 1 shows that all students successfully installed NooJ. For TreeTagger, no installation was required as the files are executable. But only one person could install MorphInd. This aligns with students' responses in the interview session, i.e., that NooJ was very easy to install. After all programs were installed, NooJ again outperformed the other two groups in terms of usage, as all 25 students could use it. While for TreeTagger, only five people could use it. For MorphInd, the number of students who could use it is the same as TreeTagger. Note that these are the same five students. Among the 25 students, these five have some technical skills (i.e., coding, executing command lines). This means that NooJ is a program that may be used with little to no programming knowledge.

Table 1. Comparison of installation success, usability, and preference among three NLP tools.

System	Can install	Can use	Preference
NooJ	25	25	25
TreeTagger	–	5	10
MorphInd	1	5	5

The preference of all of these students was NooJ (25). Ten students also chose TreeTagger. Based on their answers, TreeTagger has a tabular output that is easier to read, as compared to MorphInd. MorphInd's output does indeed use some characters for delineating morphemes and words, but it felt challenging for them. As for NooJ, the output is visualised in the task annotation structure, and thus easier to read.

4 Conclusion

In this study, I have compared three computational tools that can handle Indonesian clitics: NooJ, MorphInd, and TreeTagger. The tasks were to delineate a clitic from its host, annotate it, and recover its free form. These three tools can accomplish the goals set. Regarding the processing steps, NooJ and MorphInd are simpler as they can implement all steps in one pass. In terms of usage, NooJ can outperform the two other tools (assuming that users have no or minimal technical knowledge). As for output transparency, NooJ's output presented in the TAS proved to be helpful to users for identifying clitics, their free form, and their annotation labels. Of the three pieces of software, only NooJ has a visual graphical user interface (GUI), which users argue is their preference.

References

1. Dixon, R.M.W.: Clitics. In: A New Grammar of Dyirbal, 1st edn., pp. 384–397. Oxford University Press, Oxford (2022). https://doi.org/10.1093/oso/9780192859907.003.0017
2. Klavans, J.L.: The independence of syntax and phonology in cliticization. Language **61**(1), 95–120 (1985). https://doi.org/10.2307/413422
3. Eberhard, D.M., Simons, G.F., Fennig, C.D. (eds.): Ethnologue®: Languages of Asia, 25th edn. SIL International, Dallas (2022). https://www.ethnologue.com/. Accessed 27 May 2024
4. Alwi, H., Lapoliwa, H., Moelyono, A.: Tata Bahasa Baku Bahasa Indonesia. Badan Pengembangan dan Pembinaan Bahasa, Jakarta (1998)
5. Larasati, S.D.: Handling Indonesian clitics: a dataset comparison for an Indonesian-English statistical machine translation system. In: Proceedings of the Pacific Asia Conference on Language, Information and Computation, pp. 146–152 (2012)
6. Sneddon, J.N., Adelaar, K.A., Djenar, D., Ewing, M.: Indonesian: A Comprehensive Grammar, 2nd edn. Routledge, London (2012). https://doi.org/10.4324/9780203720882
7. Prihantoro: SANTI-morf dictionaries. Lexicography **9**(2), 123–139 (2022). https://doi.org/10.1558/lexi.23569
8. Schmid, H.: Improvements in part-of-speech tagging with an application to German. In: Armstrong, S., Church, K., Isabelle, P., Manzi, S., Tzoukermann, E., Yarowsky, D. (eds.) Natural Language Processing Using Very Large Corpora, Text, Speech and Language Technology, vol. 11, pp. 13–25. Springer, Dordrecht (1999). https://doi.org/10.1007/978-94-017-2390-9_2
9. Larasati, S.D., Kuboň, V., Zeman, D.: Indonesian morphology tool (MorphInd): towards an Indonesian Corpus. In: Mahlow, C., Piotrowski, M. (eds.) Systems and Frameworks for Computational Morphology. CCIS, vol. 100, pp. 119–129. Springer, Heidelberg (2011). https://doi.org/10.1007/978-3-642-23138-4_8
10. Prihantoro: The creation of the Indonesian TreeTagger for use in LancsBox and CQPweb. RICL J. **13**(2) (2025). https://doi.org/10.32714/ricl.13.01.11. Article no. 2

Author Index

A
Abbes, Amira   189

B
Bartulović, Anita   77
Boffo, Nicolas   177
Boitet, Christian   165, 177
Brnjaković, Anja   137

C
Champagnat, Ronan   189
Colussi, Celina   112

D
Duran, Maximiliano   89

F
Fehri, Héla   189

G
Ghorbel, Leila   189
González, Carmen   112
González, Mariana   101

H
Hetsevich, Yuras   53

K
Kocijan, Kristina   27, 137
Koza, Walter   39

L
Lafourcade, Mathieu   177

Landsman Vinković, Mirela   137

M
Meroni, Fabio   3
Mijić, Linda   77

O
Oliva, Iván   112

P
Petković, Divna   150
Prihantoro,   201

R
Rabiet, Victor   150
Reyes, Silvia Susana   101
Rodrigo, Andrea Fernanda   101

S
Saint-Joanis, Olena   16
Schmidt, Sol   39
Silberztein, Max   65
Suprunchuk, Mikita   53
Šojat, Krešimir   27

V
Varanovich, Valery   53

W
Watabe, Masako   124

Z
Zayani, Corinne Amel   189